# OUT OF THE
# SHADOWS

# OUT OF THE
# SHADOWS

book

two

## ASHLEE BIRK

Cover and Interior Design: Kathryn Campbell
"The Moments We Stand" logo and cover background by Hannah Craner

The Moments We Stand: Silence Breaks
Print Edition ISBN: 978-0-9904810-3-4
MOBI Edition ISBN: 978-0-9904810-5-8
EPUB Edition ISBN: 978-0-9904810-4-1

Library of Congress Control Number: 2015901420

Printed in the United States of America by CreateSpace

# DEDICATION

**THIS BOOK IS DEDICATED TO THE LITTLE** moments—the bright rays of hope that have pulled my family through so much darkness. I pray that I will be able to look for them each day I live. I hope I will be able to always remember the tender mercies of the past and the grace that has given me each one. My life is a gift—the people in it are my treasures—but the lessons that have strengthened my family make up our foundation. Our faith in the grace of God is what truly has pulled us out of the shadows—and into the light.

These are those moments…the moments we learned to stand.

PREFACE

# *Every little moment*

**I NEVER KNEW THAT LIFE WAS GOING** to be filled with moments: moments of darkness, moments of sorrow, and moments when I would fail to see the purpose of who I am. So much darkness had surrounded me, and I almost could not breathe as I fought my way out of it.

Some of those moments caused me to doubt my very existence—and yet there was always something light trying to pull me through it. I had been blessed with thousands of Heavenly reminders that I was being carried out of the pain of the past—but I continued to fall.

Each day was like a roadblock preventing me from the life I wanted to live. I spent endless hours rustling through boxes and paperwork to try to find the answers to my past. I longed for the man who had given me the memories in my dreams—but I cursed his name when I remembered it was him who had left me here alone.

My children still needed me and longed for me to see them. My mind still wanted to connect the broken pieces that were scattered around in it; and my heart wanted to fill its holes … but walls surrounded me—walls of fear and hate; walls of the shadows that hid themselves deep in my soul. I started to learn there were more to the silent pleadings and deep-rooted fears that portrayed themselves as anger and panic.

I began to face realities that I had never planned. I was a single woman with five young children. My husband had been killed for sleeping with another man's wife. I still had a murder trial to attend, and a future to find.

All the heart I had put into my life felt broken—I had a new ending that still needed to be written. Some days the stark, bleak road that lay ahead of my children and me was overwhelming and daunting—the "ending" to our story felt as if it had already come.

The joys that had once come easily began to be impossible. The simple role of parenthood—that used to come with little thought—was heavy and daunting. It was a constant battle between my feelings of inadequacy and my desire to be the best mom I knew how.

Each day was a battle—and boy did I fight! I fought every moment to find myself. I prayed every hour not to hate. I cried every night for the answers I still yearned to hear. Then more and more, I also prayed for the ability to laugh. I yearned for the power to smile. I fought for the desire that once came naturally—to love. I begged God for the sparkle I used to have in my eyes to one day shine brighter than it ever had before. I begged every night that I would some day feel whole again.

But through all of these trying days—there were little glimpses of *light*. The sun started to shine and the little miracles that were all around began to carry me. I started to learn that I was not born to fall—I was created for greatness ... and I was not going to give up as I searched for it.

Then step by step, I started to see the moments that were being sent to help me heal. I began to feel the darkness fade away. I started searching not only for a feeling of being whole but the little patches of hope that were all around me. I began taking leaps out of the midst of the fog ... catching glimpses of the rays of light trying to shine through.

It was like a dance—a constant battle— between the heavy gloom of the past and the brightness of the future. There were many days of darkness but they were always followed by the moments when we found ourselves being pulled out of the shadows—testimonies of the truth that we were never alone.

# CONTENTS

# Love where you stand

**A FEW MONTHS AFTER EMMETT DIED I** met an old man who had his own story of pain. He had no family. His wife had passed away years before and his kids were all gone. He was absolutely alone. He was so lonely you could see it in his eyes. He didn't have much life left in his soul. He didn't have a lot to say, but he did say in all of his years of raising kids and being a husband—he wished he just stopped and enjoyed the little moments. He yearned to take back the years he missed life while working late hours and stressing about his career. This man spoke about all the time he lost with his wife ... moments that slipped by. And he didn't realize he was missing them—until she was gone.

I believe we are all a little like this man. Every one of us, at times, sees what we have as a burden in one way or another. We find fault with our spouse; we are totally annoyed by our children. We think our boss is just a jerk; our wife always nags us. Our roommates eat all of our food and leave their hair all over the bathtub.

We forget that the blessings that are strung about in those strands of hair—and spilled cereal bowls—are waiting to be seen too.

We forget to see all the clothes put away because we are still looking at the socks thrown in a pile at the foot of the bed. We don't look at all the macaroni that actually made it into the baby's mouth because all we can see are the 19 pieces that are now all over her new outfit. We don't appreciate the half an hour our husband sits and listens to us vent about the PTA, because we are too worried about the singing performance he missed at the preschool today.

We spend our whole lives wishing we had just a little bit more—a little bit better. And yet, once something is ripped from our lives … we spend the rest of the years wishing we could have all the imperfection back.

Right where you stand at this very moment can be amazing. You can find joy. You can see beauty. You can find goodness … because it is all around you.

We must realize that our husband who throws his underwear on the floor and has the worst gas we have ever smelled—is still the man we fell in love with only now he is so comfortable with us that he has let his guard down. That doesn't mean he needs to be told to change. He still needs to know we love him, that we want him and need him just the way he is.

It is then that he wants to be a better man for the wife that makes him feel like a real one. He still wants to be your super hero. He still wants to make you laugh. He still craves to hear you tell him how amazing his body is and how handsome he looks in his new suit.

Our wife that hangs her bras on the door handles, and burns the crap out of our toast—she is still the beautiful young woman who caught our eye at the swimming pool all those years ago. She is still craving you to idolize her and tell her she is beautiful. She still wishes you told her that her outfit looked amazing and you thought about her all day. She still yearns for your tender kisses and your gentle encouragement when she "invents" a new recipe that makes everyone want to hurl.

The moments in life we are missing aren't just the soccer games and first days of school. The moments that really matter are in every second of every day. The times when we love where we stand. Whether that is the mother of 8 little kids who spends her day covered in spaghetti sauce and stinks of baby spit up, or a CEO of a major company in charge of thousands of people, or a ballet teacher working hard each day for pennies to teach her students the dance she once found a passion for in herself, or a

NBA star who gets millions of dollars for playing a game.

Wherever we stand—we can make a difference...if we let love guide us.

Anytime we feel love or have the ability to give love—it is a gift from God. The darkness in this world is not of Him, but everything light comes from our Heavenly Father. Therefore, even when we do the mundane tasks around our house or office—we are serving Him.

Sometimes we forget that all we have is only possible because of Him. Our very existence is only possible because of Him. So why is it so hard to include Him in it? He has given us everything we have—and all He asks is that we seek for His help to do it right. I love that feeling—if He is part of our every day lives, each one can be good. He is always there waiting to offer His hand. He stands at the door, and we are the one who has to decide if we let Him in. He loves us regardless if we remember Him or not—but He can only enter our lives when we ask.

So let us remember Him. Let us live our lives for Him. Let us climb the little hills and giant mountains with Him in the lead. He will never lead us astray; He will always be there. And when life gets so hard that we don't know if we can take another step—He will pick us up and carry us through.

Maybe you have never lost anything to know how bad you will miss it when it is gone. Let's take it from this sweet old man—time is short. Life is only going to happen once. If it passes us by, it is not coming back. Wherever you stand, today and always, remember to cherish the little moments. Speak more tenderly and love a little deeper for all of the tiny blessings that are right before your eyes.

Sometimes your dreams have already been reached as you are striving for them. Don't aim too high—you might not ever see you were there all along.

The dream isn't about how far we can go—it's about how deep we can love.

CHAPTER ONE

# Watching Me

**ONE DAY I TOOK THE KIDS TO** the park. It was a nice day; the sun
felt amazing on our bodies that had been hibernating inside for so long. The
park was empty. Well technically, I had driven around in search of a park
where no one was playing. The kids and I were enjoying ourselves; I was
engrossed in their laughter. We ran up and down slides, hid under ladders,
and reached our toes up to the sky on the swings. Everyone was happy.

Tytus, who had been sleeping in his car seat by the bench, began to
stir. I ran over and got him out of his chair. His grin was as bright as the
sun; reaching from ear to ear. He looked like a little man. His wide eyes
looked like they were about to pop out of his head. He loved being outside and looking around at all the colors.

I knew he had to be starving, so I grabbed his bottle out of my bag and
began to feed it to him. As he was drinking his milk, a car pulled up and a
father with his two kids began walking toward the playground. I was sad
that our solitude had been compromised, but I was also excited because
the little girl walking over to the playground looked about the same age
as Kaleeya.

The new kids and mine all began to play together. All I could hear was
laughter; all I could see was light. I whispered quiet messages to Tytus
as he continued to suck with all of his might. Soon, Kaleeya was walking
towards me. She seemed a little frazzled. She plunked down on the seat,
almost on top of me, and latched onto my arm.

I looked down at her tiny hand. It was so small, but her grip on my arm was very tight. I moved my gaze up to her eyes, "Monkey, hey! Are you having fun? Isn't this a perfect day in the sun?" She looked out over the playground silently, then back up at me. "Mom, I don't have a dad anymore."

The lump in my throat found its usual spot. I looked out at the father who was now pushing his son on the swing. I squeezed her hand a few times, still contemplating exactly what to say. "Baby, I can't imagine how badly that hurts." A tear formed in her eye and began its journey down her cheek. "Mom, I miss him, does he miss us? Did he want to leave?"

Questions I had asked myself, all of the sudden had a voice in a wise little girl. "Kaleeya, I am sure he misses us more than we will ever know. He didn't want to leave YOU. He didn't deserve to be taken from YOU. I am sorry it is so hard— it is not fair. I am here for you. I love you. I am right here watching you."

Her little lips reached up and kissed mine. "You are right here, Mommy, and you are watching me!"

She had nothing more to say about it. I thought she might talk about the little girl who had a dad there watching her. She didn't. It seemed our conversation was going to go on, but that was all she said. She didn't even take another minute to wallow in her pain the way my heart wanted to. After my kiss, she was off playing again.

I didn't take my eyes off of her. I loved seeing her walk on her tiptoes, like she always had since the moment she took her first step. It was like she was born to be a dancer. Her calves were so buff. I loved seeing the little dimples in her cheeks every time she spoke. She had a natural beauty that captivated me. Her stunning beauty on the outside was rare, but the sincere sweetness inside of her was one in a million.

That night, as I was tucking each child in their beds, I asked them what their favorite part of the day was. When I got to Kaleeya's room, her answer was as tender as the sweet kiss she had given me at the park, "My favorite part of the day was ... watching you ... watching me!"

She didn't care about the slides; she didn't talk about the ice cream cone that we bought on the way home from the park…all she remembered was that…I was watching.

We only have this one chance; they will only be tiny for a blink of an eye. They are waiting for us to see them; they are pleading for us to notice. Their needs can be daunting and sometimes overwhelming. At times they cling; they are always underfoot. They ask a million questions, or repeat the same thing over and over.

Is it annoying…or is it because all they care about is for us to see them?

I wish that every day I did everything right; I wish I had never yelled or lost my temper with my children. Looking back it is easy to see how simple my problems seem; but in the moment, those problems feel so overwhelmingly powerful. I hate that I have gotten frustrated when my child has wet the bed, or mad when they spill their cereal all over themselves and the floor. Are they really doing these things to bug me? Do they spit up all over my new shoes to make me mad?

If it is not intentional maybe I can use these moments to make a difference in their lives. Cleaning up pee in a bed, though it is not a fun job at three a.m. , can be a perfect opportunity for me to remind my sleepy child how much they mean to me and how thankful I am to have them in my life. Wiping up milk from all over the floor, takes a bit of effort and scrubbing, but is it really the end of the world? These seemingly daunting, momentary jobs that are so hard and frustrating…maybe they aren't moments for us to teach our kids how to be more responsible and independent… maybe they are meant to be little reminders for us to slow down and pay attention. What if these little mishaps our children have endlessly, are really just our test to see if we can stay spiritually and emotionally centered on what is really important? Maybe God sends us children, not only to bless us, but to test us and give us opportunities to show Him that we can sacrifice for these stewardships He has blessed us to be over.

When things get hard, or days get long, it is easy to look for anything to be frustrated with. Fingerprints all over my freshly cleaned windows; footprints in the carpet; boogers all over my clean clothes as I am walking out the door; toothpaste squeezed in the bathroom sink; whining; complaining; demanding; and poop all over the floor. Laundry is never complete and dishes are not always done.

As parents we do a lot of dirty work, and it gets easy to forget the simpleness of childhood. On those days when it feels like all you have done is paid bills, folded laundry, and cleaned more food off of the floor than actually made it into their mouths…don't forget to watch. Maybe we should stop watching for the messes and crankiness that overwhelms… and more for the simple love they have for life.

Milk is going to spill; beds are going to get wet; vases are going to get shattered by footballs; and crayons are going to be in pockets in the washing machine. Why can't we just expect it, and show our kids that they are what really matters? Laundry can be rewashed, and windows can be replaced. There still must be consequences for actions, but can't we teach them their consequence with love?

It would do us good to watch…and do. Jesus taught that we need to become as a little child: submissive, humble, patient, and full of love. It is easy to miss the subtle perfections that are sent our way. Hearts can be heavy; our thoughts can weigh us down. Watch for the little eyes that are searching for yours ... and don't let your heavy mind talk you into missing the perfect smiles that are waiting for your reassuring kisses.

They are miraculous. Cherish the children in your life. Emulate their childlike attributes that allow them to be carefree and enjoy every minute ... even when it is hard. The park is not always going to be empty, the sun is not always going to shine, the children are not always going to laugh ... but when those perfect moments come ... watch.

CHAPTER TWO

# *Weak*

**I REMEMBER WALKING INTO A GROCERY STORE** for the first
time by myself after Emmett's death. I felt like I was in a dark cloud; I was
filled with anxiety. I couldn't understand why my body seemed to lock up
when it came to the day-to-day tasks. Things that seemed so simple, just
months before, now were almost impossible for me to do. I started out on
the cereal isle, hoping that my love for that food group would help ease
my apprehensions about grocery shopping.

The moment I went to reach for my favorite box of cereal, my heart
stopped. The box fell out of my hands and onto the floor. I looked
around— luckily I was alone on the aisle. I fell down to the ground and
began to sob. What the heck was wrong with me? I felt weak, like thinking
about preparing food was a sedative for my soul. It didn't make sense—I
had always loved planning meals and cooking for my family.

Once I finally picked myself off the floor, and caught my breath, I stumbled my way out of the front doors of the store and got back into my car. It
was too much. I had no idea why, but something about shopping for food
and preparing for my families' meals was too much for my heart to take.

Another day as I anticipated making a meal, I felt the same uneasy feeling. I walked into my pantry and glared at the boxes of food. They looked
like mountains, and I had no idea where to begin to climb. I became very
overwhelmed and tears started to swell in my eyes. I walked into the pantry and slammed the door behind me. The light automatically turned off

when the door was shut, so now it was just me alone in the dark.

Again, I fell to the ground, but this time in the darkness. I said a silent prayer, "Heavenly Father...why can't I do this? Why am I so scared of cooking, and cleaning? The thought of preparing a meal sends me into a full-on anxiety attack. I want to be a good mom; I want to be able to do the things I have always done. I am SCARED! I am broken. Why is this such a struggle for me? Will it ever go away? When am I going to be normal again?"

I closed my eyes, even though it was dark, and the tears continued to fall. I had no idea where I was going to go to get help with an illness that seemed to be plaguing my mind.

In a brainspotting therapy session, a few weeks later, everything began to make more sense. During my session L. Jay asked me to close my eyes and through a series of techniques he employed, the path to my fear became very clear.

My mind took me back to the night Emmett died. I had spent hours that day trying to make everything just perfect; I had put all the energy I had left into making his favorite food. In my mind's eye, I saw him walking in the door. He didn't even look at his dinner. He never took one bite; he never said how grateful he was for my sacrifices in the kitchen that day. I pictured every pot I stirred, and every crumb I put into serving bowls. I could see his face as he sat there with his arms folded and his cell phone in his hand. I could almost hear the phone ring and I watched him go answer it in our bedroom. I saw the look in his eye as he told me he was going to Walgreens. I could hear the words that the detectives spoke. Dead. Affair. Alone. Kandi. Rob. Gun. It was like I was living the whole night again.

As my tears burned my cheeks, I began to understand why I had developed a fear of cooking for my family: cooking had become a trigger of the emotions that had consumed me that day...and a purposed catalyst, in my head, for the chaos that followed. It began to make sense. The thought of preparing food was overwhelming because somewhere inside me it was directly linked to the tragedy that followed.

Cooking was a battle that I felt I would never win; it was a reminder of every pain that had become a part of me. I hadn't lost my desire to feed my family because I didn't love them anymore, but I couldn't bare the pain, or face the heartbreak my mind told me might follow.

I longed to step back in time to the days when our favorite meals had brought us so much joy. All food, in some way, reminded me of a memory. I can remember we spent an entire day during the law school years—before Kaleeya was born—making Kalua Pork for our entire ward party. Emmett had the whole thing down to a science. We had many ovens going all day long. I did exactly what he told me to, and by the end of the party the whole barn-full of people were fed and happy.

Every night of our marriage Emmett would laugh at me as I crunched down a bowl of cereal before bed. It was an on-going ritual that was a constant in my routine. I couldn't go to sleep without a full belly. He always joked that I was like a newborn baby with my need for constant snacks and midnight meals.

Every New Years we always made prime rib; it was delicious, juicy, and perfect every time. Anyone who ever took a bite, could taste the passion for its flavor that Emmett craved. He sold his favorite foods to any ear that would listen; everyone within the sound of his voice would be talked into eating it. He could have sold a red popsicle to a lady in a wedding dress. If he liked it, he wanted to share its perfection with everyone he knew. He would talk about my cooking to strangers…like it was a masterpiece. There was a time in our marriage when he bragged to co-workers about his lunches, and took them my goodies to enjoy. He wrote down my recipes for people at the grocery store; and begged me to make his favorites for Christmas presents. His excitement for the creations that came out of my kitchen gave me a silent drive to keep inventing.

We had so many memories that were centered around our favorite foods, and all of the sudden these positive meals and yummy snacks were blaring in my face the fact that Emmett would never enjoy them with me again, but also that these foods—which had once meant so much to our marriage—had failed me.

Most of the time as I drove to the grocery store, or sat in my pantry, I longed to get the memories back. The fear of the pain that would follow stopped me in my tracks every time I went to turn on a stove burner or open the fridge. I didn't want the reminder that he was gone, and I certainly didn't want to open the floodgates for my fears to come true again. Somewhere inside my head, cooking food and creating my concoctions, would ultimately lead me back to the hurt that still baked inside of me.

One day, after I had just about lost my mind with my anxieties about cooking, I went to see my bishop, the ecclesiastical leader of my church. I told him about my troubles and the strain they were having on me as a mother. He sat quietly and listened to me sob; I could tell he was baffled as to how to help my broken despair. Finally he looked at me and said, "I want you to read a scripture tonight. It is Ether 12:27. Read it as often as you need to. I think it will be a great reminder for you on the days when you feel so weak."

He wrote down the reference and then offered to give me a blessing. When the blessing was over I headed home. That night, after my kids were in bed, I read its words over and over:

> [27] And if men come unto me I will show unto them their
> weakness. I give unto men weakness that they may be humble;
> and my grace is sufficient for all men that humble themselves
> before me; for if they humble themselves before me, and have faith
> in me, then will I make weak things become strong unto them.

I hadn't spent any time on the thought that this weakness could one day be made strong. I thought maybe I had given it all I had, and my chance to overcome it had passed. I had not realized that this weakness, which seemed to consume me daily, could one day become my strength.

The next morning I woke up to the sound of Bostyn gleefully cheering from her room. She came running down the stairs with a dollar bill in her hand. She squeeled, "Mom...check it out...the toothfairy came and brought me a dollar for my tooth!" My heart sank. *Toothfairy?* I had forgotten. I stared at her excitement as my jaw fell to the floor. Behind her Bailey came walking towards me. As she got closer she whispered, "I thought you might forget...so I took care of it!" With that she gave me a little wink and walked away.

My weaknesses were so transparent...my oldest daughter came prepared to pick up my slack? It was clear I needed to remember how to find my strengths again—but first I had to figure out how.

On our first date, Emmett and I spent a lot of our evening talking about our pasts. He told me about his mission, and all he had learned while he was in Brazil. I could tell he had been an amazing missionary; he had worked his butt off for the people with whom he came in contact with. I loved hearing stories about the people; I enjoyed hearing about the special spirits he had baptized.

One thing I will never forget from that night was when he told me about the day his mission was over. He had a long release meeting with his mission president talking about all the accomplishments of his two years. He said the final counsel his president gave him was that he should spend his life living the standards he had learned. He reminded him that Satan would work hard on him and try to minimize the importance of fighting for the light every day. Emmett's mission president asked him to work hard to continue on the mission he had begun there in Brazil, and to never remove the spiritual armor he had worn those last two years.

That counsel, in my young twenty-year-old mind, was exactly what I wanted my future husband to be doing: fighting every day, alongside me, to win the battles that seemed to make us weak.

Emmett's mission president is right. We cannot think that because we sacrificed, for a time, that all the hard parts have come to an end. Just because you work hard for years to become an amazing missionary, doesn't mean that the rest of your life will come easily, or even naturally. The mission might have taught you much and helped you learn about sacrifice…but it was just the first step to the faith that you will have to fight for every day.

Life is full of moments we think we have reached the height of our mountains, and the glide downhill is all we have left to steer.

When I was finally coming close to delivering Tytus I knew exactly how my birthing experience would go. I would fight nurses all day to let me do everything naturally. They would beg me to get an epidural, after hours of no progression, and I would finally give in. My body always seemed to be the same; the desires inside my head to have a natural birth would always make way for the fact that I wouldn't dilate past a "3" and would need an epidural to continue on.

Walking into my birthing room that day I decided I would put aside my bull-headedness and just let them know up front that I would have to get an epidural. I asked them to let me buy a little time by administering some pain meds in my IV. They did so, and the next thing I remember was waking up with an urge to push. The IV meds had knocked me out; I had been sleeping for a long time. I looked over to Emmett, who was sitting next to me, and said, "Babe, I think it is time. Did they give me an epirdural yet?"

They had not; but within minutes I found myself surrounded by medical staff and I was pushing our baby into the world. My intense desire to have a natural childbirth had finally come, but not as a fight…as a surprise! After three other labors ending in a forced epidural, I was excited to have the chance to get my wish. I looked over at Emmett. He looked a little nervous, which scared me. For all the other births he had been the cool cucumber who calmed my doubts. The look in his eyes made me begin to doubt my ability to handle the pain. I kept looking to him for reassurance that I could do this. He tried hard to engage, but I could see in his eyes that his mind was somewhere else. I tried hard to ignore his glances to his phone; I purposefully looked away when I felt like I should ask him where his heart was. The man who usually seemed so proud and present, looked like he was a hundred miles away.

When the pushing got intense, I began to question why anyone in their right mind would do this without the drugs that had been forced on me all those times before. I was in so much pain, it was like a hot piece of metal was trying to make its way out of me. I tried hard to focus on my breathing and ignore the pain. I am not sure which was worse: the pain of giving birth, or the pain that the man standing by my side was nowhere to be found.

As the baby's head and shoulders came all the way out, the doctor handed ME his arms and let me pull him the rest of the way toward me. Emmett had always been the one to do that in the past; he never missed an opportunity to be the one to deliver the baby, so I had never been the first to hold one of our babies. It was amazing to grab onto my little infant and pull him onto my lap.

I didn't realize then how symbolic this experience would become for me. Emmett didn't hold Tytus as he took his first breath, and he wouldn't get to see many more of the breaths our baby boy would take. Tytus was a light for me. He was my breath of life in many ways. That moment I held him on my chest and watched him take his first breathe will forever be imprinted in my mind. He needed me in every way; without me he wouldn't have a life, and yet... he was the one that, just six weeks later, would become the reminder for me to breath and keep living.

That night, that moment of pure pain, felt like an unimaginable hurdle that seemed too high to jump. I had never experienced the excruciating pain of childbirth as I did that day. It felt like one of the weakest and yet strongest moments of my life. I doubted my ability to persevere and continue on. Then when I held that little boy in my arms, I knew without a doubt that all the pain I had endured was worth the fight.

My mission to bring Tytus into the world was just the first step of many hard things I would be asked to do as his mother. It would have been easy to think that all the pain and hardships of being a parent had passed. I had, after all, endured excruciating pain for him. It was hard, and it took great sacrifice to go through for him, but my selflessness was not over. It was not the pinnacle of the pain I would overcome as a parent, but just an initiation for becoming his mom.

We will have rights of passages: becoming a spouse, becoming a parent, becoming a professional, serving a two-year mission. But those things are just that…the first steps to a long journey of hard work. Tytus' birth was not the end of the pain it would take to be his mom, but it was the obstacle I overcame to prove to God I would do whatever it takes to be the best mom I could be for him, no matter how hard it hurt.

Our relationships, our lives, our moments…they have been hard. They have brought us to our knees. In one way or another, we are all weak, we are alone, and we are afraid. We try to overcome the death of our loved ones; we struggle to deal with rejection from someone who no longer loves us. We fight to see where our paths of pain will lead us. We try to understand why our weaknesses seem to hold us down.

For those of you who have served a mission for your church, or had a calling or an assignment at work that put you through years of strain… your mission, your assignment, was not the end of the work you must do. The hard times when you struggled to do your best—no matter who you were doing them for—are not over. Your mission to fight for the next journey has not come to an end … and neither was my mission of doing hard things as the mother of this household. I had to work every single day to put my life in His hands and become the tool I was capable of being. Tytus' birth, when I didn't get the epidural, was damn hard…but the work and pain I was asked to bear wasn't over when he was out and my body's pains were done. That was just the first step of my journey as his parent. Life is not over when we stand at our crossroads. It has only begun. Before

Emmett died, I truly thought the hardest days in my life had come. They had not. Make every day a little more meaningful than the last. Read a little more faithfully, be a little more patient. Laugh. Smile. Hug. And live the life you always wanted by fighting the things that will tear you down. The hard parts aren't over, but each battle you win, is a hurdle you jump as you show God the gracefulness at which you fall down at His feet.

Keep up the good fight. It isn't over until it's over, and until then… may God be with you, and always inspire you to keep your armor on. We win battles against evil by fighting them every day. Keep on the armor of God. Never let go of the shield that blocks out the world. Even when your arm gets tired… keep holding it up. Even if you feel your days to hold your armor up seem like they have passed. Don't take it off, for anyone or for anything.

Yesterday might have been hard, but today still needs you to fight, love and learn for tomorrow.

We are weak. As humans, we have learned that there have been many before us who have been willing to fall for anything. Complete nations have fallen for power; kingdoms have been overturned because of selfishness. Many have fallen fighting, and others have fallen because of their weaknesses. When one falls, another is born and takes his place. Some see it as the circle of life, that we all have to be born, and we all have to die. It is true that we will all pass on, and someday death will end at our last breath… but we don't have to fall. You have had times of strength, and you have been burdened with times of weakness. Let those weaknesses be a reminder of the strength for which you are still fighting. They will try to hold you down, but use them to lift you higher.

You may feel overwhelmed, that this weakness will never end; that it will always rob you of the carefree days that you crave. There is a way out of the tired soul that is pulling at your ankles and wrapping its dreary burdens on your shoulders. Christ died to help you make the weak things that torment you, one day become the strengths that carry you.

He gave me this weakness of fearing my kitchen as an opportunity for me to turn to Him and make it one of my strengths again.

The events that shaped the days of my past had created memories that held me hostage from living my future. Just like the pain of childbirth tried to get me to doubt my abilities as a mother for my son, my past tried to sprout doubts for my future.

We are not just as good as our pasts; we have the strength to overcome them. The years may have left a hole in your heart...but the future can bring the strength that will repair it.

"I give unto men weakness that they may see my good works and glorify their Father who is in Heaven." Glorify Him. Humbly ask of Him to see His good works; they are all around you. Look for the light that is there, even in your darkest days. As you see Him, and ask with a sincere heart, and with real intent, He will show you where your weaknesses can become your strengths.

I testify that this promise made to us by our loving Father in Heaven is real. I have seen it in my own life. I have fasted and I have prayed that my weaknesses and my fears would be calmed. I have been given strength inside of myself to overcome the trials I have been presented, and when my own was not enough...I have felt his strength pulling me over the hurdle that tried to knock me on my back.

Sometimes my strength has come in the form of humility, in getting professional help for my struggles. Other times, it has merely been an "aha moment" on my knees in my closet.

Humility and aha moments come in many forms. Even in parenting, what is inspiration for one mom is different from the next. Some moms get to show their love for their babies raising them all their lives. Other moms have died trying to prove their love through childbirth. Then there is a group of woman who get to show the love for their babies by letting them go. Not one of these ways of love is weak; raising a baby takes strength...but so does letting one go. Coming to terms with the fact that you cannot be the parent that baby deserves, can be a life-changing self-less act that a mother does out of love.

Selflessness is not weak; selflessness is a strength. Weakness is selfish-ness; weakness is breaking others to make yourself feel better. But some-times our weaknesses are out of our control. Some might read of my fight in the grocery store and in my pantry as a weak, selfish act that I could have snapped out of easily. I can, with every cell of my body, tell you... my weakness had all the power in those moments. I had no idea of *how* to snap out of the state of panic I was in.

Next time you stand in line at the pool for the high diving board, and the little teenage girl in front of you has almost dropped to her knees in panic... try to remember that there may be more to her fear than just a selfish desire to piss you off. Maybe her anxiety to take that leap runs deeper than any pain you have ever encountered in your life. Somewhere inside her little mind, that leap may mean a remembrance of a hurt that buried itself inside of her long ago... which hasn't been set free.

We all walk around with smiles, but a lot of the time, inside we are weak. We want to know that we are safe, and sometimes we don't even know what that looks like.

When you feel like your weakness is eating you alive, turn to the one source who knows exactly how you feel. Maybe the people in line behind you—as you cry for help on that high dive—have no idea what pain your screams hold... but Christ does. He hears the hidden messages in every fear you face and in every moment that has found you paralyzed in your pain.

Remember the counsel of Emmett's mission president. It is not over. Your time to fight Satan will never end. Keep on the armor that protects you and never let him find your Achilles heel. He waits patiently for those weaknesses to win, so he can step in and rip you to shreds.

I know that if Emmett had a voice today he would testify to anyone within the sound of his words—just like he did all those times about his favorite foods—"Fight the darkness. Live the life and be the person you want to die as. Your chance to search for light is right now, your time to see the goodness you have … is lying in front of you. Please take it. Don't wait for tomorrow to let go of the weakness that will make you fall for anything. Turn to Christ for strength when Satan finds your vice. He will use it to destroy you. You do not have to be weak. You do not have to fall. Fall to your knees and let a power greater than darkness make you strong."

Turn to Him when *you* are the weak thing that needs strength; He will make YOU strong.

CHAPTER THREE

# Single

**A FEW DAYS AFTER EMMETT'S FUNERAL, I** had a doctor's appointment. I sat in the office waiting for someone to come in and speak with me. As the door opened, I was expecting to see my usual nurse, but instead, in walked a woman I had never seen before. She looked so casual and calm and asked, "What is it that you are here for today?"

"Well," I said. "I would like to have my IUD removed." She glanced quickly through my chart. "It looks like you just barely had it put in ... like a week ago. Is there a reason you don't like it?"

I took a deep breath, and let it out slowly. "Well, actually, a few days after I came in here to have it put in, my husband died ... so ... I just will not be needing it."

She glanced up from my chart, and asked "Then what are you going to be using?"

I looked into her eyes with an inquisitive glare. "Um ... well, I am not going to be using anything."

This conversation must have been a new one for this poor nurse. "I am just worried that you might not want to take it out," she said. "Have you thought about keeping it in as your form of birth control? Should we discuss the other forms of protection we offer here before you make your decision?"

Again, I tried to make my point clear. "Well ... like I said, my husband passed away, and I am no longer in need of birth control, so that is why I am here…to take OUT my IUD."

The baffled look on her face made it clear she was doubtful of what I had just said. "Are you ready to get pregnant already…looks like you just had a baby about two months ago?"

This time she *had* to understand. "So…I am a single mother now, my baby is not quite two months old. I have four other children all under the age of six…I am no longer married…and I will not be having sex, because I am…not married…I…am… I am single."

As the words slipped out of my lips, I got a pit in my stomach. Single. I was now a single woman, a place I never thought I would be again. I had not even considered my recent step into widowhood as a catapult throwing me back into the realms of single life. Just seven years earlier, I had pictured my wedding day as the moment I overcame the obstacle of being a single woman, but here I was again…and this time, the odds of ending another period of being single were even less in my favor.

Sitting in that doctor's office, and fighting the nurse about birth control, was an eye-opener for me. I had some work to do. The morals I held as a single adult—before my marriage to Emmett—were still just as important to me now, as they were back then. I was a single woman again, but this time…I was dragging behind me five beautiful additions.

As I drove home from my appointment, I pictured walking into a singles' ward at church carrying Tytus in his car seat on one arm, Kaleeya on my hip, and my other three children waddling behind me. I chuckled to myself as I pictured all the eyes that would turn their gaze toward me… not as an inappropriate "check-out"…but to watch my circus entering the building. Yes, a singles' ward sounded like it would be a lot of entertainment…but it probably wasn't the crowd I was looking for. I might have become a single woman again, but the single life I once knew was far from where I was now.

One night, a few weeks later, I got a crazy idea that I should go looking around in Emmett's e-mail account. It seemed like it would be a nice break from going through his box of crap in the garage. Since receiving his e-mail and password for Facebook, I figured it would be easy to get into his g-mail account and see what it contained.

My heart was racing. I felt like I was a high school girl again…driving by a cute boy's house. I slowly typed in the username and password. It worked! I looked around me to make sure no one was watching, as if I were doing something sneaky. The list of recent e-mails pulled up. Many of them were messages he had received on his Facebook account after his death. Some of them I had read, and others were new.

I kept scrolling down…searching for any juicy e-mails from the days before he died. I just knew the e-mails I was searching for had to have some new information for me. I kept scrolling, and scanning the names from whom the e-mails were sent.

KANDI! And there it was. The first of any saved e-mails I had seen from Kandi. I opened it. It was a picture of her, in what looked like her daughter's high school prom dress. That wasn't what I was looking for. I wanted the meat of the case. I wanted to see hate mail from Rob and love letters from Kandi. I craved to see the ugly facts with my own eyes, so my heart could shut the book that was permanently waiting on its shelf to be read. I needed real closure.

I kept scrolling. His account was strewn with singles' websites. Singles? Dating? It hadn't crossed my mind that there could have been more women than her. I had secretly hoped her spell was the only thing that had made his eye wander.

That night, I came to know even more about the man I had loved, who was now gone. He didn't have just one stupid affair with a woman he thought could help him progress in his career. No, he had been out searching for more women!

This time, my detective work did not bring me the peace for which I was hoping. It stirred up new emotions within me.

Single life…was that really the path he was seeking?

I was sitting alone at a computer... still trying to do the impossible—save a marriage that no longer existed. And while Emmett had had all that I still craved... he was looking for something else. Something less! It didn't make sense to me. What part of this lonely life of being single did he find so appealing?

Before I met Emmett, I had a lot of experience with being single. It was a title I can't say I would ever search for again. I had some great times as a single adult, but there was nothing about it that appealed to me as an alternative to the safety I felt in being committed in marriage.

Now, I found myself forced back into the single life, which before my marriage, I had spent so much time ... trying to "overcome."

In my young single years, I can remember many dates I had with lots of different types of men. A few times, I even thought I had found "the one." The minute I felt like "I could see myself with this guy," I would plan out our life in my mind. I threw my heart in before the guy even asked for it.

I would put so much thought into the idea of being with him, that I no longer held the power over my own happiness. I would sit by my phone... and its silence would shatter my night... or my month, for that matter. At that time, my ultimate feeling of self-worth could come from a phone call... or could be destroyed by the lack thereof.

In the end, a few of "the one"s never did call again. It wouldn't just break my heart, it would cause me to doubt myself and my worth. I spent many weekends in a state of depression because of the lack of a promised call. Why? In that moment, when my feelings of self-worth were at an all-time low, I truly believed I had lost my chance at love. If that boy didn't call back after the first date, somehow I was no longer beautiful or lovable. Somehow, I would never be enough.

Then with the ones who did call back. . . I would find reasons why they weren't good enough for me, and I would push them away. Sometimes it would be as stupid as hating the shoes he wore, or I couldn't stand that his mother still did his laundry for him. I didn't like the fact that he spent more time on his hair than I did, or that he was too quiet...or too loud. The list of stupid reasons for which I would push guys away was longer than the number of first dates who never called again.

Unfortunately, between those two types of dating experiences, I found myself allowing my view of myself to come from my experiences with men. I didn't have enough self-worth to keep from allowing the missed phone calls, or the stupid shoes, from determining if I was happy or not. I believed my happiness was based on the perfection others found in me. I needed *them* to tell me I was worth their time, before I allowed *myself* to be worth my own time.

Some of us, as singles, spend our days walking around looking for Mr. Right. Instead of becoming "right" ourselves, we look for him on the outside and hope he can generate a belief of our worth, which we can't seem to find in ourselves. Until Emmett came into my life, I walked around secretly hoping I was on the right sidewalk at school to lead me to my Mr. Perfect. Every morning, I got ready just in case I ran into him. I went to the grocery store to buy healthy foods so I would be perfect for him. I went to the gym so I would have the type of body he was looking for. Most of my decisions were not made for me, but for the imaginary dream boy for whom I was searching.

And when I found him, it WAS perfect. He believed in me, he told me I was special, and he adored everything I did. My worth was safe, and my fears of rejection seemed to be in the past.

The night Emmett died, it was much more than just automatically getting thrown back into singlehood. Once again, I had to face all those fears that Emmett had calmed. I didn't want to be single. I didn't know how to find worth in myself because I had used him as my gauge if ever I wondered if I was a good person, a good mom, or a good wife. And up until about three months before he died...it had worked! He believed in me. He encouraged me, and he lifted my feelings of self-worth higher and higher.

Being single again was daunting. Sitting at that computer reading notes from a singles' website changed something inside of me. He had been searching for others to fill the void in *his* view of *his* worth. That was crazy to me, especially as his wife who had done my very best to let him know of his worth. And yet, hadn't I been searching and waiting for him to fill the void I had within myself? Wasn't that just as crazy? Did he really need other women to give him his sense of worth? Did I really need a husband to let me know that I was a wonderful person?

Now was my chance to search, but not for another single person to tell me that I was enough. It was my turn to search for myself. Who was Ashlee? What does Ashlee want, and who is Ashlee supposed to become? Questions raged inside me, helping me look past the loneliness of singlehood and fueling the desire to know who I really was. Being married could not be what defined who Ashlee was anymore. I had to remember—for the first time in my life—who God had sent me to earth to be, and who I really was.

It wasn't Emmett that had made me great. It was ME. His words, though they were encouraging, were not what I needed anymore. He was gone. I was single, and I wanted to become okay with the single life that had come back upon me. I vowed to myself that I would never again let another person determine my happiness. I knew I had a long road ahead of me. I knew that one day, I would have to do the things I had done in my past as a single person. It didn't have to be scary; it didn't have to be lonely...because this time around, I wasn't going to look for anyone to tell me something I didn't already know on my own.

Being single offered a new view for me. I didn't need to let my happiness be determined by a phone call or a date. I was going to be happy being single. I figured it would be years before I decided to head down the road of commitment again, but until that time, I was going to make the most of my life. In the past, my desire for marriage had always driven my choices. Where to live and who to be was driven by the hope of finding "the one." Even a walk to school could become an imagined heavenly intervention for me to find Mr. Right. Don't get me wrong, I know Heavenly Father helps our paths cross with those who can bring us joy, but constantly seeking it, is not a way to live. What I wish I had known then as a young single adult, which I know now, is to just live. Find happiness in yourself and not in a phone call that does or does not come. Happiness is inside of you. It's not a gift that comes in the form of another person. Yes they can increase the happiness we have, but it cannot be another person that creates it.

Search for the man who is compatible with you, as you are right now. Search for a girl who can sacrifice and forgive and work hard. Find a partner who can complete you. Quit waiting for an imaginary perfect being, because even if you find him or her, what will he or she see in you? I know we want what we want, but we must seek what the Lord wants for us. He knows the qualities that will bring you lasting happiness…and they aren't usually measured by the world's standards. Find the standard that the Lord has set.

Your future doesn't have to hold riches for it to be wonderful. You might be blessed with an amazing person who adores and cherishes you, who is merely just "an apple picker." Happiness is not promised; it is achieved through hard work. If that apple picker puts God above him or herself, and can sacrifice and encourage and be kind, then those are the things that will really matter in the end.

Looks can be shattered in a moment. Cars will crash, houses can burn, diseases can cripple, and bullets can fire. Money can be spent, investments can go bad, and cars can be taken away. What really matters is what is inside a person. Look deeper than the surface.

They may not be the star basketball player your mom always told you to find; they may not have ever been invited to step onto a runway…but these imperfect single people who are right where you are…maybe all they need is for you to let them in. Maybe then, you will see how amazing they are.

It is true, you have to be attracted to a person. What attractions are holding you back from meeting the right one? What standards have you set for the person you seek that will never be realized? If you are a single adult, now is your time to put both feet in. Be you … maybe that won't be enough for everyone … but let it be enough for yourself.

Until you realize that the true kind of love will only come when you are true to yourself, you will push them away. Be you, and if they walk away, at least it is *you* they are leaving and not a pretend person you were trying to be. If they let you go when you are yourself, at least they leave you standing. If it is the other person holding you up, you will fall. Standing tall as yourself is a lot easier than being crushed into a million pieces and gluing the broken bits back together.

You may find that even after you have found yourself, people still leave. That's okay, because if they don't see you now, they never will. Before you commit to your dream spouse, become the person you always dreamed you would be. But if you have found someone who truly sees *you*, even when you can't see yourself… it's okay to let him in too. He might see the part of you you're trying to hide, and still not walk away.

What if we get rejected? What if we aren't enough? I can promise you, that at some point in our lives, we will all face rejection. Maybe not today, and maybe not tomorrow, but someday you might not measure up for someone you care about. So what? Who cares? You are still the same person you started as. It doesn't mean you turn on yourself as well.

Rejection, and suffering losses don't just come to those of us who have been married. A loss can be as simple as that phone call that never comes. Rejection can be interpreted as being anytime our desires are not met. Feelings of serious loss, betrayal, and confusion can cloud your mind. The stages of grief can come from the loss of a love you once thought was going to be yours, even if it was just one date.

As single adults—single, divorced, or widowed—there are many lonely nights and many depressing days. We cannot let them define who we think we are. Those nights when you feel you are suffering alone, seek peace from a God who is always there. He knows you are suffering alone, let Him join you and remind you of the worth He sees in you.

Spend less time worrying about your checklist for others and more time figuring out what qualities on the list *you* want to develop. So he doesn't ever call you back, or friend you on Facebook? What matters is that you are true to the 'you' God made you to be. It would be easy to pretend to be someone you are not, but in the end, you will forget who you really are. Be you, and let it be enough. It is only you that can find the mission you were sent to this earth to fulfill.

Single life before Emmett, was just a search for the "one" to help me progress. Once he was gone and I realized I must still find a way to move forward, my eyes became open to a new view of being a single adult. I was not the little girl who was searching for reassurance; I was an adult searching for myself. I knew being single would be a different experience this time around, but I was determined to just have faith. I couldn't wait around for someone to hold me up. All I had was myself, my family, and God. I was a single mom who was not going to fall. I had to stand.

Being single can suck. Love can be hard. But love for yourself and for another is what life is all about. Don't let anyone break you. Don't let another person determine if you smile. That phone call wasn't meant to be. Let it go. Cling to the things you *can* control, and let the others go. Ready or not, love might come your way, but you must remember who you are.

Being single is not a punishment or a sentence. It is a time in our lives when we get to put our needs first. It is a time to reflect upon the person we want to be; and a chance for us to realize that who we are is enough for Him.

We hear stories about rejection and loss, and it almost furthers our cause to just remain single forever. Mine is one of those stories. Emmett's choices and Rob's anger put me in a state of raw rejection and serious loss: the loss of a life I loved, the loss of the life I thought I had, the loss of the love I had shared so deeply, and the loss of any sign of true commitment. A perfect storm for a recipe of a life of forever being single... Right?

Before March 11, 2011, if you were to tell me that I would have to tread through a pain so immeasurable... I would have run away. I had heard simple version of stories like mine, and sworn that there was no way I would still be breathing. I didn't know I could do hard things... until they were done.

As I stand today, I can see that even through those hell storms... I am still the same person I was before, but with even more strength and belief in myself.

You might get rejected, you might even lose at love... but what do you really have to lose, if you don't have it right now?

I lost everything in love, but here I am. Yes, it still hurts sometimes. It still brings me to my knees every single day. I still cry, I still have doubts... but I am still me. If changing my past meant not having my five children and the relationship I've developed with my Heavenly Father as He sent Angels to lift me up, I wouldn't change anything. My past embodies the fears of all the singles who are afraid of commitment. Don't let your fears of losing, stop you from loving. The love that surrounds me today is stronger than any I have ever known, even though the losses I have endured have hurt more deeply than any I could have imagined.

Set standards for yourself, and don't waver. Set expectations for your future lover, but don't get so set on who they are supposed to be... that you cannot see them. If you are too busy staring at your list, you will miss seeing the qualities that are uniquely theirs. Strive to be the best you, and hope for the best them... and then when you find each other, and you both seem to fall short... Let God fill in the gaps. He believes in marriage. He believes in love. He cries when we do; and He hurts when we hurt. Marriage is hard; love can hurt... but so can being alone.

Maybe you have never had a second date in your life. So what if you have never had the passionate embrace of a first kiss? Maybe your dream boy has always been in your view, but has never asked you out. Maybe your perfect girl has been your best friend all along, but you have been too busy watching all the other girls who walk by her.

Where ever you are, if you are not in a serious relationship...you are single. You may feel alone, but you are not. There are so many of us who have sat home alone, single, wishing for a life that we righteously desired. Don't give up on love...but even more importantly...please don't give up on yourself. God believes in marriage, and he created love...but he also created us. Even if you have never loved, or never do...He believes in you.

CHAPTER FOUR

# Buried Deep

**ONE MORNING TYTUS WOKE ME UP REALLY** early. I grabbed him out of his bed and began to feed him in my chair. His big blue eyes stared up into mine. I loved rocking him and enjoying every smile he gave me out the side of his mouth.

Within minutes, his smiles ran out, and he was fast asleep in my arms. I didn't want to move. He looked so peaceful, and I loved every second of watching him sleep. It didn't happen very often. For a while, I just stared at his perfect little face. He was an angel, that was for sure, but I don't think that even at the moment, I could fully comprehend what a great blessing he was for my life.

After some time, I began to look around my empty bedroom. Not much had changed within its walls. The bedspread was still the same as when Emmett was there. I had moved the furniture around a bit, but that was nothing new for me. Almost everything in that room, at that very minute, felt completely the same. It felt as if at any second, Emmett would come walking into the room to tell me about his day. I could almost smell his body wash steaming out from the shower. If I closed my eyes and ignored the pain in my heart, I could step back in time before he died and pretend I was there. Maybe it had all been a dream!

The clock read five a.m. I knew that time well. Emmett always woke up that early to leave for the gym. On many mornings, I would get up with him to make him some eggs before he headed out the door. I never thought twice about how early it was. I was excited to get up and show him how much I cared. I would sit on the counter and watch him scarf down every bite.

Eggs. I craved to lay Tytus down and go out into the empty kitchen to make Emmett some eggs. I wanted to show him one last time that I didn't even look at it as a sacrifice. I wanted nothing more than to be there for him, no matter what time the clock said.

It had been months since I had been wakened by the sound of his voice, asking me for a quick pre-workout snack. I could almost hear his deep voice, "Hey babe, do you mind making me some eggs before I go?" It hurt how badly I wished he would wrap his arms around me, and whisper in my ear.

I snapped out of my daydream as the clock turned to 5:10. It was still hours away from the moment when tiny feet would come running into my room, but I couldn't sleep. Somewhere buried deep inside of me, a pain was raging. It was so heavy that I could almost see it in my empty bedroom. There was no sign of any change, but deep inside my soul, a storm was brewing. In that moment, the room might have looked the same, but I knew everything was different.

My bitterness chimed in with a stark reminder of all the pain Emmett's obsession with his body had brought me. The gym. Every morning, I had dragged my exhausted body out of bed so he would have the energy to go prance around half-naked with a bunch of other people! Regret for every egg I had ever cooked him simmered deep inside me. All of the positive memories of waking up to make him breakfast turned black. Why had I been there at his beck and call? Why had I put everything into him, when he had not returned the favor for me?

A deep-rooted anger seemed to be pulling me further and further into despair. By the time morning came, the house was all abuzz with excitement because the twins were graduating from kindergarten that morning. Their joy was apparent, but my heart still felt black.

I showed up at the school just in time to find a seat. Kindergarten graduation, though very exciting for the twins, was just one more thing for me to do alone. The anger and bitterness that had churned inside of me all morning about the eggs seemed to be bubbling up into my throat. I felt like everyone was watching me, just waiting for the pain to explode out of me. The eyes in the room felt heavy as I slid past a few parents to an empty seat.

The twins looked beautiful. Their eyes were fixed on me. They sang a song called *Big Dreams*. It started out, "Big, big dreams, lots of big dreams, things I want to be someday..." I choked up as I tried hard to keep my feelings buried inside. Dreams. Big dreams. My twins were standing up on a big set of risers singing at the top of their lungs about all the dreams they had for themselves someday. Tears streamed down my face as I pictured the semblance of the normal life I had once enjoyed being wiped away, like my tears, never to be experienced again. Once more, I tried

hard to push my fears and emotions back inside of me.

By the end of the performance, I was ready to run out of the room. I didn't want to talk to any of the teachers, or parents ... or children for that matter. I wanted to run away, and hope that no one had caught a glimpse of the tears that had forced their way out of me. I had to be strong, I had to bury the pain, I couldn't let anyone see how truly broken I was.

The mother of one of my daughter's friends came over to say hello. She asked how I was doing—a question for which I had no answer. That particular question had been asked so many times that I actually stressed out about how to answer it every single time it was asked. I assumed she wanted me to answer honestly. Maybe she had been reading my thoughts, and wanted me to tell her about the eggs I was fretting about all morning? Maybe she wanted me to break down and cry, and remind her of all the legal hell I was climbing through? I almost saw her as a threat—an enemy who wanted me to unveil the unbearable pain I had been masking all day.

Instead of answering her, I started making jokes about Kandi and Em-mett. I didn't look her in the eye, just rattled off joke after joke about all the crap Emmett had pulled, and all the horrible thoughts I still carried around about Kandi. My friend stood there silently as I made fun of every possible angle of the story, and rattled off all of the degrading and inap-propriate slang terms I could think of to describe Emmett and Kandi's decisions.

She gave me a little side hug and said, "Hang in there friend." Then she walked away. *HA! She hadn't won. She hadn't seen my pain. I had fooled her for sure. She had no idea of the secrets I was concealing, right? If all eyes were off of me, that meant no one could see my pain.* But even if they couldn't see it, it was there, and there was no way I could let it go because it had become a part of me ... and I almost needed it to survive.

That pain, the pain I thought would go away as I directed my friend's thoughts off of me and onto Kandi and Emmett ... it didn't leave. It didn't even feel better; it actually felt completely worse. My plan seemed to work for a few seconds. I didn't have to share any of the things I was struggling with, I didn't have to open up about my breakdown over eggs that morning… but the words I *did* use spoke more about my insecurities than a detailed description of them would have. I didn't have to describe my pain because it came straight out of me in the form of hate!

That moment of hate would not be my last. In fact, it became my companion. Anytime I didn't want to look someone in the eye—for fear they would rat out my buried anguish—I would make them laugh by telling jokes. I would make light of the horrific story I had learned to call my life. I would mock and tease and try hard to get any ear to hear about how "well" I was doing. I truly believed they thought my humor was a sign that I was doing "better," that I had overcome my grief.

They could *laugh* with me, but I never let them *cry* with me. No, that was something I continued to do alone in my closet or while driving in the car.

One of Emmett's friends came over that night to help Teage with some soccer moves. He ended up staying until way past the children's bedtime. When the kids were all in bed, we found ourselves watching TV. He sure was a cute guy. He had never been married, and the thought crossed my mind that maybe he was there for more than to just help Teage. I kind of enjoyed having a man in the house again, and sitting on the couch talking with him reminded me of having Emmett. They had a lot in common, and I could see why they had been friends.

He had come over a few times to play with Teage since Emmett had died, but he'd never before stayed until the kids were tucked in bed. I had only met him a few times before Emmett's funeral, but I remember having seen him at the viewing. He had been very emotional, and I remembered feeling so badly for all the single guys who had looked up to Emmett so much. It was as if they had all looked to Emmett as an example of the men they wanted to become and the lives they longed to have. Now they were all in the difficult situation of trying to figure out where he had gone wrong, so they could make certain they didn't follow the same path.

I figured he was at my house to find more answers about why Emmett had failed, so he could know where to look for a new hero. We talked for a few hours about "Emmett stuff," and after some time, he grabbed my hand. My heart began to race. All the emotions and fears that had been bottled up all day began to try to find their way out. What if he could feel them through my hand?...What was I doing letting a man hold my hand in Emmett's house? I was panicking inside...and every feeling I had buried deep down was trying to make its way through my hand and into his.

I was afraid that by getting that close to me, he would be able to know how broken I was. He held my hand the rest of night, but I never relaxed. He probably felt like he was holding onto a zombie's cold, unattached lifeless fingers. I shared no emotion through my touch. I didn't want to tell him to let go, but I held onto the fear that was trying to let him in. I wasn't about to share it with anyone. It was mine, and there was no way a cute smile was going to talk me into allowing it to leave.

I never let him come over again. He called and texted a few times after that, but there was no way I was going to let myself be vulnerable again and risk exposing all of the broken pieces I held inside, by having him too close. I had buried those feelings, and nobody was going to be able to crack me open to let them free. I wasn't ready to have a man hold my hand; I hadn't let go of the hand for which I still longed. But even worse, although I wished Emmett were there to hold me...I hated him at the same time. That was one toxic relationship I would have to overcome before I let anyone hold my hand ever again.

Feelings buried inside feel safe. When we are the ones suppressing them, we truly believe that no one can see them. Our fear of them being revealed keeps us from letting anyone in. The moment others' love and concern for us causes us to believe they are after our buried treasure... we want to run.

There is no freedom from our pain when we are running from it. It doesn't get left behind when it is hidden inside of us.

So many of us have been hurt. We long to find peace, and yet we refuse to let go of our hurt. We bottle it up as if it were a prized possession. There is no good in storing our pain, there is no place for it to reside inside our heart. Its power is darkness, and its message is deceiving. Somehow, it causes us to believe that we need it to survive. It creates a bond inside us that causes us to feel that it must stay there.

The darkness of the world has left many of us stuck. We have buried its secrets within us, and we are afraid to let them free.

Abuse, neglect, and anger have allowed others to define who we are. We have all fallen victim to the cruel and evil secrets of our past, and the pain that has followed has settled in comfortably inside our hearts.

But, we don't have to keep it in! Just like a buried treasure in the sand, we can find the riches of digging it up and letting it free. If you have scars from your past holding you down...let them go. If someone in your past has wronged you...let them know. If you have a secret eating you alive... today is your day to set it free.

You are not alone. Every one of us has something buried deep inside—a secret from our past...or a deception causing pain. Satan will try to get us to believe that its home is permanent; that its power to hold us back will never leave.

I can testify that Christ knows the truth about our pain. He knows of the fears that eat us up inside. He has heard every prayer and seen every tear we cry. Even if those tears have been shed alone in our closets...He has counted every single one of them.

When you are alone looking in the mirror, do you hate yourself? Do you purposefully draw attention away from yourself and onto others? Do you spend your days trying to point to everyone else so you can continue to hide?

Pretending my pain didn't exist...didn't take it away. It didn't even hide it, because my screams about Kandi and Emmett's imperfections did nothing more than display my own. What fears are you trying to conceal by putting others' shortcomings on display?

I spent years making jokes about the people who had wronged me. Anytime I saw my raw emotions coming to the surface, I would cover their tracks with slams. Even in meetings with attorneys and detectives, it was easier to mock Emmett's and Kandi's mistakes...than to let them see the pain that had built a colony right in my heart.

Laughter isn't always about what is funny. Sometimes we laugh because it helps us not to cry. Fear and pain can be suppressed for a long time...but they always find a subtle way out...or eventually explode through our screams. The pain I had buried deep inside of me raged its way out through hurtful words about the tragic events of my past, and mocking jokes about those who had wronged me.

The emotions that drive our actions are larger than they seem. They are powerful, they are blatant, and they are self-destructive. Spend less time putting others down, and more time letting out the real emotions you have buried deep inside of you.

Our bodies were not made to be storehouses for pain. Our bodies were built to be the receptacles of beauty and light. When we hold in our pain...it hurts. It doesn't feel at home, because it was never meant to reside inside of us.

This mortal journey we are on is more than just a road full of painful bumps, it is a rollercoaster of excruciating exhaustion and fear. It is a river of whitewater rapids that can toss us back and forth. We were each sent to earth with a body. That body is a gift to serve as a vessel for our spirit as it navigates the bumps and feels the pains of mortality. Our end goal is not merely to see how much pain we can store inside and take back to heaven with us, but to see how much of the pain we can overcome...how many of the mountains we can cross without harboring the pain all the rocks create under our feet. We have to learn to let go if we want to return back to God. Those pains that are still a part of us when we die will not be left here with our mortal bodies. If we haven't let them go, our spirits will hold onto them. That is why this earthly life is the time for us to learn to live and let go.

Each one of us has been given our own roadmap, but our final destination... our end goal... is the same for all of us. When we left the Spirit World, we knew that the things we would endure were to help us return to live with God. He sent His Son to die for us to make that possible, but He also commanded us to forgive all men... and not harbor the pain inside of us.

When life feels like it is trying to bury its darkness deep inside your soul, fight for the light of Christ to carry it away. When others are sent to hold your hand, let them do their part in helping you release your pain. When memories of the past cloud your ability to live today... pray for the power of God's love to lighten your load.

I know that Christ is the one being who has walked this earth, who has seen firsthand exactly how each day has felt for me.

When those around you are singing about the "Big Dreams" of the future, let it be a reminder that the sorrows in your heart can be transformed into peace. It is good to hold onto your dreams, even when the dream you are living feels dark. There are brighter days ahead. Don't give up on the big dreams and the little memories about eggs... for when we stand at the gates of Heaven, searching for the acknowledgment of the one true God who gave us life... remember that we will be judged on the days we are living now.

Heavenly Father doesn't care if you are a bread maker or the owner of the entire bread company. What He longs to see for us, His children, is that our road of life was lived to its fullest. He longs to hear the stories of when we overcame the darkness that tried to bury itself in our smiles. God desires to see us sacrifice, and love, and work hard to fulfill the mission He sent us here to perform.

Whatever mission He has sent us on... we cannot see its purpose when we are busy hiding from it. I have found that in the moments when

I have let it all go, it is then that He has been able to speak to my heart.

If your heart is clouded with the secrets and pain of the past, and you can no longer feel or hear Christ's tender whispers, now is your time to unclog your connection. *He* isn't the one preventing Himself from coming to heal us, *we* are the ones preventing Him from coming.

When you feel like you've buried yourself deep in the sorrow of your past…you are the only one who can allow that sorrow to be set free, but He can carry it away. He stands waiting for you to ask for help. Deep inside of you, under that pain, are all the answers you are seeking. Clear the view and you might see the perfection waiting for its voice to be heard. You are more than the pain others have left in your heart. What is buried even further down, deeper than the pain… is you.

CHAPTER FIVE

# *Holes*

**I NEVER KNEW A GUN COULD LEAVE** so many holes. Emmett was left with the wounds that Rob's bullets made in his forehead and heart, but my holes were not as clearly visible. I had holes in my heart that didn't cause me to lose blood or die, but their penetration had caused me to lose my very sense of life. That gun left holes in my family and an empty space at my table, but it also left holes in my mind that blurred my vision of who I was, and who I wanted to become. Those holes impacted all aspects of my life... especially my parenting.

When I was in seventh grade, I had a rough year. My parents' divorce had become an excuse, in some ways, for me to lash out. I found myself using it as an excuse for doing some of the things I did, or for getting out of doing things I didn't want to do. At church, I had a teacher who seemed to hate me. Every chance she got, she called my mom and complained about something I was, or was not doing. The sad part is... she was usually right. My behavior warranted complaints and I deserved being disciplined for the way I was acting.

My mom was good at handling these constant complaints. She always managed to find a punishment that fit the crime. She took away privileges that were important to me, and it worked. It helped me admit my shortcomings, instead of making excuses that the teacher was just picking on me. My mother was always very loving in her approach, but she never allowed any of the circumstances in my life to be used as excuses for bad behavior.

[ 39 ]

One day, I was out in the hall at school working on a project. My group had gone back into the classroom, and I was still out in the hall alone, cleaning up our mess. My church teacher—who was also a substitute teacher at my school—walked by. She didn't say hello, so I didn't bother to speak to her either.

That evening, my mom asked me to come into her room. She told me that my teacher had seen me "in trouble" again in the hall. The story she told was elaborated, and for the first time, it was not at all true. I became emotional because I feared losing a privilege for something I hadn't done. I looked into my mother's eyes and said, "Mom, you know...I've been making some bad choices at school, and at church...and almost every story you have ever been told, is true. I accept responsibility for the things I've done, and I can see why this teacher is frustrated with the fact that she has to deal with me...but Mom, I promise you, this time...this time I did nothing wrong, and I would really like you to believe me. I was in the hall doing a group project, and I was not in trouble for anything. This time, she is just picking on me because she hates me...and I deserve that...but please believe me, this time I didn't do anything wrong."

I know my mom must have prayed hard at that moment, because she didn't doubt me for a second. She gave me a hug, and I left her room. She didn't question my story—she just believed me. I'm sure it got so old hearing about all the mistakes I was making. I'm sure at times, I was a burden for my poor mom—a single mother raising five children. As if she didn't already have enough on her plate, there I was giving her added challenges.

There are times when we go through trials for our kids, and other times, our children themselves become our trials to bear. Even if we don't see our children as a burden, it doesn't take away the fact that their challenges become our own.

In the months following Emmett's death, almost everything that could have gone wrong with my children did! One week in particular,

I remember Teage walked into his room, and for no particular reason, he broke a bunch of toys and destroyed some books. Bostyn and Bailey pushed a boy down the slide at the park, and his parents yelled at all of us. There was so much anger in Kaleeya that she was biting holes in all of her binkies. I wasn't ready yet to wean her off of something that gave her comfort, so I had to run to the store multiple times a week to buy more. Tytus was still having allergic reactions to all of the formulas we tried. It felt like the list of problems with each of my children seemed to be getting longer and longer.

I was overwhelmed by the task of raising grieving children, and I was unaware of how to help them. One afternoon, I left Tiffanie with the kids and I got in my car and went on a drive alone. I stewed about all the heavy burdens I felt were destroying me as a parent. The ease and joy I once saw in parenting seemed to be fading, and it scared the crap out of me. *How can I parent these children, when those around me are treating me as if my children are freaks? Why do I feel so embarrassed when my children make mistakes, like somehow I am at fault?*

Anytime someone complained about my kids or gave me dirty looks, it almost destroyed my day. I internalized all the perceptions I figured they had about my children and my parenting—or lack thereof. I became so enmeshed in my children's negative behaviors that I almost didn't want to take them out in public for fear they would embarrass me, or cause yet another stranger to look down on me as a mother.

As I continued to fret about the week's negative events, I drove and drove, with no purpose or final destination in mind. I continued to brood over memories and talk out loud about how obnoxious the kids had been all week, and how pissed off I was that I no longer had any control over them. I was humiliated because I felt like I was failing to raise my children properly... and others were seeing all my shortcomings.

I turned down a street, and right in front of me was a park I knew well. I hadn't paid attention to where I had been driving because I had been so wrapped up in my own pity-party. As I drove slowly past the park, I could almost picture my little family sitting on a blanket having a picnic there. That was one of the good memories I hadn't thought of in some time. Emmett had met us there after work one summer day for a picnic dinner. I was pregnant with Tytus. Abbey and Alex, who were dating at the time, where also there with us. It was a perfect evening spent eating, laughing, and playing with the kids at the park.

Instantly, I snapped out of my feelings of embarrassment and anger over the children, and I just missed Emmett. I missed his smell. I missed his kisses, I missed the feeling of having a complete family, eating dinner at the park. I missed having someone to talk to when I needed to find answers for the kids' struggles.

I began to talk to him as if he were in the car, "Em, I can't do this with out you. I don't want to do this alone. We were supposed to work together, and grow old together. Why do I have to be here alone, trying to figure out how to help our children? Why did you have to leave me…Why wasn't I enough for you? Why can't you come back and take care of me and our babies? You promised me you would take care of us…Emmett…"

Suddenly, the sorrow I felt because I missed him was transformed into a wave of anger against him. I began to scream, "Emmett…WHY WASN'T I ENOUGH for YOU? Why did you leave me here alone? WHY do I have to do all the dirty work because of your freaking mess? These kids are so hurt, they are crazy, they are almost an embarrassment to me! They can't function in society. I don't know how to help them, and it's all because you are not here. It's because you are dead. WHY did you LEAVE us? Why didn't you fight for us, Emmett? I *hate* you, you know that? …Yeah, I don't miss you at all, because…because I HATE YOU! So there. Now you know, I don't miss you, Emmett. I hate you for leaving this mess for me. I hate you for leaving me alone. I hate that I miss you so badly my soul hurts. I hate that a "bad guy" came and destroyed our family. I hate that it was Kandi holding you when you took your last breath. I hate that you left me ... I was begging you to stay, but you left me all alone. And now, I am still alone. You never came back to me. You said you were just going to run to Walgreens. I waited for you all night long ... I called you. Why didn't you answer your phone? Wasn't I worth answering your DAMN phone for? I worked so hard to make you happy ... I would have gone to the ends of the earth to see you smile. I hate you for that, too! You had me, I was right there waiting for you ... and you couldn't even see me. I was right there. I was ... I miss you Emmett. I miss your smile. I miss making you your stupid eggs. I miss your toothpaste all over the counter, and your wet towel on my side of the bed. I miss your stinky socks all over our room. I HATE you for doing this to me, but I ... I still need you. I still want you ... I still love you. What am I supposed to do now? The kids have asked me a million times what they are supposed to do without you, so now I pose that question to you as your wife: What am I supposed to do without you? How can I help our children fill the holes that are left in their hearts, and how will I ever fill mine?"

My contradictory words came out like the floodgates had just opened. I missed him so badly that it hurt, but I was also so broken because of his actions, I didn't know for sure where to even begin: with anger or with love.

It wasn't just Rob's or Emmett's fault that my children were having issues, it was my fault as well. Never before in their lives, had I been embarrassed about their imperfections. I had spent years laughing when they made mistakes, and loving them through them. Now, all they could see of me, was that I was ashamed of them. I was trying so hard to fill my own holes, I was overwhelmed with the thought that I had to help them patch their own holes. I was not being the mom they deserved. I was allowing others' views of my kids determine how *I* saw them.

They had to learn to forgive and move forward, but the principal way they were going to be able to do that was ... by watching me. I had to show them how to let go, and I was not being the example they needed.

Forgiveness. Such a simple word, and yet its meaning is so strong. Not long ago, as I sat in church and listened to others speak of the lessons they had learned about forgiveness in their lives, I was humbled to my knees. Tears would not stop flowing as I thought of all the heartache I have read in messages sent to me by unfamiliar names who wanted to share with me their own stories of pain. I have felt humbled to be the ears to which some silent hearts have turned to share their deepest pain.

Why do we hurt each other? The thoughts of tender voices who cry in the night, all alone, break my heart. My eyes have wet my pillow on many nights as I have prayed for some of my brothers and sisters whom I will probably never meet.

This world is huge. Each of us has our own story, but the darkness that tries to destroy hope, and the fear that causes us to live in pain...is in us all.

Forgiveness is the answer to that pain, but what most of us want to know is...HOW? What my children needed to SEE was HOW.

One afternoon, I heard the kids upstairs screaming that the toilet was overflowing. As I ran upstairs, huffing and puffing as I skipped steps, I angrily thought about all the times I had pleaded with my children to stop using so much toilet paper. When I reached the cresting toilet bowl, the kids were staring at it, horrified at the nastiness floating around inside. I let them have it! I repeated the demands I had been spewing for weeks. "Why can't you guys stop using so much toilet paper! Doesn't anyone ever listen to me?" They all scattered, leaving me alone to let out my anger on the toilet.

I grabbed the plunger and began forcing it into the water over and over again, all the while emitting angry words about everyone using too much toilet paper. I worked for about five minutes, but the clog would not budge. I continued to abuse the toilet with the plunger and my words. Still, nothing happened.

All of the sudden I stopped. I held the plunger over the toilet and watched the nasty water drip down into the full bowl. I realized how stupid it was that I was grunting out my anger onto a porcelain toilet bowl, and I was humbled to realize I was going about it all in the wrong way. I said a quick prayer in my mind, "Heavenly Father, I am sorry for the way I have gone about this challenge. I cannot get this toilet to work, and I really need Thy help. I'm not plunging this toilet for fun. I'm not doing it for myself. In fact, I really wish I didn't have to do it at all. It is disgusting, I am ticked off, and I have to figure out how to fix this. I'm not doing it for me, I'm not even plunging this toilet for my children... I am doing it for Thee."

I pushed the plunger back into the water, and within three seconds the bowl drained. It was so simple, and yet, such an eye opening moment. That toilet didn't matter to anyone... including my children. They didn't care if they used too much toilet paper, because I was the one who would be there to clean up their mess! There wasn't a person on the planet who gave a crap (no pun intended) about that toilet in my upstairs bathroom. At that moment, I didn't even care what happened to that toilet. For all I cared, we didn't even need it anymore. I was trying so hard to make it obey ME, but as soon as I found purpose in what I was doing, the real reason I needed to plunge that toilet... it flushed.

That plugged toilet was a learning-lesson for me. Its imperfections— though they were inconvenient for others—didn't really matter to them. And so it was with my children. Their imperfections didn't really matter to other people—only to myself. I had to stop worrying about what anyone thought.

Other people are going to put you down about how you are raising your children. They may even call and tell you about all the things your little ones are doing wrong. What really matters is not what others think, but the way your love can help your children through their hard times. As hard as it feels for you as the outsider to have them struggle, try to remember how hard it is for them. Our children already know they are not perfect. Others remind them of that fact, and they also discover their own weaknesses by themselves.

The only way we will find the right answers for them personally is through Heavenly Father. In the same way I couldn't get that toilet to work properly on my own, we cannot properly mold our children without the help of God. The minute I included Him in my plunging, the problems I faced were solved.

We may hear stories and think that our kids are just like someone else's, but the answers we need for each one of them are unique. Sometimes the only "self-help" we can receive will not come from a book, or from a phone conversation with a friend. No, the answers we are seeking may only come through heartfelt prayer.

All of these responsibilities weigh us down at times. They feel as though they are heavy burdens and immense trials. Due dates loom, and children complain. Teachers share concerns, and coaches degrade. Cars need cleaning, and laundry takes over every empty space in our homes. The list of hard things will never end. Heavenly Father didn't ask us to complete all the hard things we have to do in one day. He never said that He only sees our worth when our children are perfect, when no one is disapproving, and our houses are clean. He has asked us to take on these responsibilities, and do our best. He has pleaded with us, as we pray for his counsel, to do ALL things for Him. With that request, He promises that if we ask … He will send us help.

If you are overwhelmed with the heavy burdens of daily life, give them all to the Lord. He knows the list never ends, and He has seen that the trials get heavy. I have looked at my life when I tried to carry my load alone, and it's a joke. I drove around in my car overwhelmed with the messes I had yet to clean up, and I splattered poop all over the bathroom trying to fix things on my own. In the moments, when I transferred the burdens of my responsibilities from my own hands into the hands of my Savior, He picked them up and helped me find the way.

He may not literally grab the plunger out of your hand, but He will send you the light to know how to use it.

Sometimes when life feels the heaviest, we are too bent over from its weight to see the light shining at the end of the tunnel. I challenge us all to look for the good. Maybe you are lying in a hospital bed with a heart condition, maybe you are alone in an apartment full of emptiness, maybe you are buried deep in laundry and your babies are screaming, and you ... are just trying to remember who you are. Wherever you are today, I want you to find reasons to smile.

Right now, as I sit at this computer, I can see a picture of my children. They are all at school right now, or taking naps in their beds, but they are the first priority on my list. They make me smile with the funny things they say and the happy voices they spread throughout our home.

I can see a few piles of their misplaced toys, and I am thankful for the sweetness they bring to my children's imaginations. I am thankful that I have the ability to teach them the responsibility of hard work.

I can see a sink full of dirty dishes, and I am so thankful I have enough food to feed my family. I am thankful for the clean water that pours into my cup at the simple turn of a tap. I am thankful for my dishwasher, because I have no idea on earth how I could keep those dishes clean without it.

I can see a pile of bills. How thankful I am to have electricity and heat to keep my house warm in the winter and cool in the summer. I am thankful for a cell phone that helps me communicate with my loved ones. I am thankful for warm showers, and garbage days. All of the blessings, that come from the bills I pay.

I can see a gash in my table made when one of my children took a fork and imprinted thirty little indents in it that will probably remain there forever. I am so thankful that I have healthy children who enjoy spending time with me. I am thankful for their creative minds that have brought me many works of art ... some not so convenient ... yet quite creative, like the artful patterns made in the wood of my table.

That table may look like it needs to be replaced. My windows sure as heck need to be washed, and my dishes are rarely clean...but how amazing is it to be surrounded by so much beauty? My children are not mine...they are on loan to me by Heavenly Father. The bills sitting on the counter are His. I am just His steward as I take care of the responsibilities He has blessed me with.

Parenting, dating, school, work...wherever you are...ask for Christ's hand to enrich the little moments when you stand with a plunger in your hand, unable to find the answers as to how to solve the riddle.

It is my prayer that we can be the putty that fills the holes made by others in our children—and the holes in all our relationships—and we can let Christ choose the pieces we use to build the foundation of who we are, so that He can fill the holes inside of us.

We can be the constant in others' lives to help them see their roles; we can be the love that holds them together when others try to bring them down. And we can put our faith in them when they need the benefit of the doubt.

Many eyes have whispered a million words to my heart, and many voices have pierced my soul when my children have made mistakes. Let them watch; let them talk. Pray for the guidance to be the stability your child needs. Others may cause you to believe that the people in your life are burdens...but you have the power to find the good.

Sometimes we *are* in the wrong. Let us teach our little ones to take responsibility for their own actions and not to use others as the excuse for why they are being "picked on." Then other times, when they really *are* working hard and trying their best, let us remember to believe in them, even when others do not. My mom believing in me was empowering as she let me walk away without punishing me. Her silence spoke stronger to my soul than any words she could have scolded into me. I knew she believed in me. She had drilled and drilled me that I had to own up to the role I played in the scenarios of my life. And this time, I had played a role I could be proud of...and she trusted me.

It's okay that our children aren't the star athletes. It's okay that they are sometimes less than mediocre. Luckily, they were not sent here to be perfect for us. Just as Christ loves us with all of our shortcomings, we must see the worth of our loved ones...even when they are covered in holes. Christ never said it would be perfect, He only promised that it would be worth it.

The relationships in our lives are no different. They will not be perfect, but when we desire our part to be better...we can pray for His love to guide us in the roles that WE play.

As children we have a different job to do. Mothers and fathers will not always do everything right. Hopefully, our children can still love us when we fall short as their parents. Even parents fail. We react poorly to a situation; sometimes we even hurt those we love. Physically and emotionally we get stretched to our max...and in those moments, sometimes we don't respond with love. All the while, our young children still love us...because we are their parents. Their love is not contingent on our perfection.

How dare I feel sorry for myself for raising "broken" children, when I myself was just that. Heavenly Father never saw me as a burden or trial He was merely trying to overcome. He saw me as His daughter, no matter how messed up my actions seemed to Him, or to the onlookers who went to Him with the problems they were having with me.

Emmett's children had holes in their hearts because of their father's death, but as Heavenly Father's children...we can become whole because of Christ's willingness to die on the cross for us. Death is the ultimate teacher. It teaches us about who we want to be; its lessons ring through the lives of those it impacts. But death can also be the ultimate healer. Christ's death was not in vain, as Emmett's seemed to be. Our brother Jesus died so that all the holes that have been shot through our lives...can be made whole—even the wounds unseen, discreet holes, left by a gun.

He was resurrected so we can one day live again...complete and whole from the sins of this world. All wrongs can be made right, and all debts can be paid. He may have died on the cross for us...but the thing we can never forget is: He lives again, and so can we.

CHAPTER SIX

# *Heal*

**IN THE WEEKS FOLLOWING EMMETT'S DEATH, I** received
many priesthood blessings. One in particular—given to me on a very
trying day when I was exhausted—stands out in my mind. My body hurt,
and I didn't know if I could take another minute. A spiritual leader from
my church, my Stake President, put his hands on my head and blessed
me with many things. The phrase that stuck out in my mind for weeks
after the blessing, was: "There is a man who has been preparing to come
and help heal your family." I knew when that sentence hit the air... that
one day I would meet a man who would have the gift to help heal my
family, and I could only hope that meant that I would be a wife again in
the future.

I put that thought in the back of my mind for safekeeping. It didn't
seem to be an idea that could pertain to me in any near future. I had a broken family to put together, a murder trial to go through, and let's be honest... a body that JUST had a baby. There was no way I would be ready for
said man to come our way any time soon. I knew in my heart that even if
a man was being prepared to come and help me heal our family, he was
going to need to see some hope that we were fixable... and I saw no apparent timeframe for that happening... EVER.

One afternoon, I had an appointment with a partner of a friend of
ours to discuss some changes in a health plan policy. I had met him a few

times, but really didn't know him personally. We sat on the couch in my living room chatting about his line of business, and he offered me some great long term advice. As he got up to leave, he turned and said, "I know I don't really know you…and this is super awkward…but I feel strongly I need to tell you this…I was randomly listening to a talk this morning with one of the General Authorities talking about when his wife died. He was saying how he felt lost and like he could never love again…but then he met a woman whom he felt inspired to marry quite quickly after his wife passed away…and the whole way here I have felt really impressed to share this with you.…You will probably never feel prepared to love again, just like the man in the talk, but Heavenly Father might send you someone who will come to help you heal."

The minute he said the word 'heal,' I thought back to the blessing I had received containing that very same word. Heal . . . that is what I planned on doing long before a man would ever get to know me again. I appreciated this health insurance agent's willingness to share those thoughts with me…but inside, I was almost laughing. Like I really needed to worry about someone ever wanting any part of my crazy life.

Some weeks after our talk in my living room, I found myself once again sitting alone in the Celestial Room of the Temple. I spent a lot of time there trying to find peace. This day, my tears were a plea for healing. In silent prayer, I begged—not for the impossible 'do over' for which I had spent weeks wishing—but for true healing. I didn't want to be broken any longer; I didn't want to feel alone. I wanted to be free from the void enmeshed in my soul. I prayed for healing that when the time did come, I would be able to stand worthily and be prepared.

I knew that, one day, I would be given the opportunity to love again… but I began to have a very strong opinion of what *I* had to be first, and what I had to *have*.

What if there *was* someone prepared to come and be my partner? My mind wandered to my internal list of requirements. I wrestled with my thoughts and began setting high standards and criteria for this imagined man's personality traits and qualities. I reflected back on Emmett's virtues, but also on his imperfections, which I had come to blame for my current situation. I began to panic. I could not accept anything less than perfection if I were to ever love again. Emmett and I had seemed to be a dream couple... he had so many of the qualities I had looked for in a spouse... and yet here I was, sitting alone... and feeling even more alone inside. If I were ever to do THAT again... I deserved perfection and ease... and that was FINAL.

As I sat in the Celestial Room, I let Heavenly Father know exactly what I expected this man to be. He wouldn't be able to come into my life for a few years, because I wanted to be "whole" first. Like me, he needed to be a widower. Other things I was certain of as well: he would not have attended Centennial High School, he would not have a tattoo, and he would not be a convert to our Church. I listed off every one of the background facts about Emmett, which I had come to blame for his bad choices. I told Heavenly Father what I would be able to put up with this time around... and informed Him what I expected of this next man... PERFECTION. I had been through anything but... and I was not about to think of allowing myself to settle for less than that.

When I got through with my check lists of "Do's and Don'ts" I sat there silent, embarrassed that I had just given God a list of what I expected Him to do for me. I could almost picture Him sitting there with His arms folded saying, "You about done daughter?"

I looked around the room, feeling uncomfortable for having just stubbornly rattled off all of *my* expectations. I was about to stand up to leave when I felt the calmest feeling of peace come to my mind, along with this message: "His mission in life will be to heal this family."

Now I was not just embarrassed, I was ashamed that instead of spending the last half hour listening and praying for counsel, I was demanding and elaborating on what I would and wouldn't accept in a possible future husband. What was wrong with me? I was too ashamed to stand up and leave on that note.

His mission... what did that mean? Did that mean he would not have served a full-time mission as a young man? Well that surely didn't fit the mold I had just created, but yes... that seemed to be exactly what the message meant. He hadn't served a mission... but taking on my crazy clan would be just that for him: a full-time mission! That realization settled deep down inside of me and brought a tear to my eye... and a smile to my face.

I drove home with a new sense of hope that day. Maybe I didn't have to have it all figured out... if this poor fellow needed to serve time to fulfill his mission, maybe my broken family was good enough just the way we were right now! I walked a little lighter as I opened the front door and looked around at what some might look at as a broken group of individuals. All I could see was beauty.

One night, a few days later, Tiffanie, my sister Ali and her boyfriend at that time, Will, helped me put all the kids to bed. As we sat down on the couch, they started talking about how much work it was for me all alone, and how I needed some help. Somehow the idea of going online and checking out eligible bachelors became a reality. Tiffanie, Ali and Will spent hours laughing their guts out at the idea of "lining me up" with some of the men they found on the internet. I humored them by laughing... but inside, I began to grow scared just thinking about the process of dating again.

I stared at a few of the photos thinking... there is no way I will ever trust a single one of them. First of all, I just had a baby... who would ever want to take out a chubby widow with five kids whose husband was murdered because he was cheating on her? The odds were certainly not in my favor. After deciding we were done for the night, I felt discouragement set in as we turned off the computer, and I headed to bed.

I lay in bed, a little ticked off at myself for even looking at those men online, but I was even more overwhelmed by the idea of putting myself out there in any way again. I resolved that I would never again look at another online profile.

However, without my knowing it and as it turned out, luckily for me, those three had a greater scheme brewing. They had entered my e-mail address onto the site!

Over the next few days, every time I checked my e-mail, there would be a million messages from the dating website where we had been browsing. I hated the reminder that I had been looking in the first place. It was hard enough for me to check my e-mail as it was … the last thing I needed was to be stalked by this dating website, or to have to pay a fee or give them any more information about myself.

One afternoon, I had had enough. I opened one of the e-mails from the website and scrolled down to find the 'delete me from your records' button. However, as I scrolled, I came to a section called NEW IN YOUR AREA. A row of photographs stared out at me, but all I could see were two blue eyes.

I kept scrolling down, then found my way back up to the big blue eyes and happy smile. Wait … I didn't remember this face from the other night as we had laughed our way through the profile pictures. I knew this guy hadn't been on there then, and there was something about his eyes that drew me to him. I couldn't stop staring at his photo.

I clicked on the photo, which led me to his profile. What was I doing? This was not what I wanted to do … but as I read and gazed at a handful of his photos, I couldn't help but smile. I sat at my computer staring. I tried to send him a message, but since I hadn't paid the sign up fee, the site wouldn't allow me to send a message. So I got out my credit card and paid the fee.

I think my message said something like, "Hey … yeah … so I am not going to do this whole online dating thing, but looks like we are from the same town and I don't know, you seem normal and if you ever want to chat my number is ..." (I later came to learn that he had to pay the fee to sign up as well, just to receive my message!)

What was I doing? I felt ridiculous and yet...I felt so confident. It was exactly what I was supposed to be doing. There was something in this man's eyes that reassured my heart.

That weekend, some of my friends kidnapped me and took me on a two-day girls' retreat. It was the first night I had spent away from the kids, and I was so nervous to leave them. The first morning I didn't even wake up until noon! It was a relaxing and beautiful getaway up in the mountains with great food and nothing but calm. It was the perfect weekend.

On the last day, I was in the middle of a massage when my phone received a text message. The therapist asked me if I wanted her to hand me the phone. I said, "No thanks...I'm half asleep and don't want to talk to anyone at the moment."

When my time was up, she left the room and I lay face down for a while, tears streaming from my eyes. I loved getting away, and being so relaxed, but I missed my children. I missed their sweet faces and the safety I felt when they were in my arms. I hated being away from them. What if they needed me? What if they felt frightened or alone and I wasn't there to help them? What if I needed them? They always made me feel so loved. I always knew that I was enough for them. I missed them so badly.

My face began to hurt...but I didn't move. In that moment, I felt the reassurance that my kids were all I had...and I was okay with that. I couldn't wait to get home to tell them about the feelings of peace I had found over the weekend, and I couldn't wait to go home with a renewed sense of who I was and everything that I saw we could be.

I finally stood up, got dressed and began to head for the door. I pushed the button on my phone to see what time it was, and there it was ...

"HI. This is "Lakersfan24." You gave me your number and I just thought I would say hello. How is your afternoon going? I just got done with my daughter's dance recital. It was super fun. Anyway, I was just thinking of you and wanted to say Hi."

I sat back down, with butterflies in my stomach. I read the words over and over. I started to text back, then I paused. What should I say? I erased everything I had written. For a few minutes, I tried to decide what I should write to someone who didn't even know my name. I vowed that I wouldn't give any specifics about myself until I knew for sure that this man was not a crazy person.

I went downstairs to join the rest of my friends, who were having fun in the game room. I kept putting my hand on my cell phone, in an attempt to text back, but I just couldn't do it. Every time I reached for my phone, guilt would set in, because Emmett had only been gone for a few months. I was insane to even think about talking to another guy, let alone a stranger. As I sat and talked with my friends, my mind churned with this internal debate about whether or not I should respond and if I did, what should I reply.

I went in the bathroom where I could be alone and decided that it was time. I took out my phone, and typed out my message: "Hello there. Sorry it took me a while to reply. I was getting a massage. Dance recital huh? That sounds fun."

We texted back and forth throughout the day. He was so refreshing and seemed so real, and I genuinely enjoyed our conversations. He even sent me a picture of his cute daughter in her little ballet tutu. Everything seemed to be going great. I couldn't wait to read his next text. He was adorable and funny and the smile on my face seemed to grow with every word he typed.

Then it came…I got the text that almost became the deal-breaker of a lifetime.

"Well," he revealed to me, "I grew up in Eagle and went to Centennial High School! I live here in town. I have been divorced for two years."

I put down my phone…NO! I had resolved that there was no way I would ever go out with anyone who went to the same high school as

Emmett. Couldn't I just get away from people who knew anything about me? I didn't want to have to tell him that I was the widow from the horrible story he had read about in the news. He would run for sure if I gave him any of that personal information. Plus, I needed someone who didn't know Emmett, someone who would be emotionally unattached to anything from my past. AND... Divorced? I had enough baggage on my own.

I didn't reply for a long time. I was debating about whether I should just never text him back, or if I should make up some kind of a story. So, I would pick up my phone and start typing a lie... then I would feel guilty and erase it. I didn't want to give him any reason to reject me, so I thought maybe I should just get it over with, not let him know anything more about me, and just end this conversation once and for all. Again, I wrestled inside of myself about what to do. Then all of the sudden this burst of 'what the heck' came over me, and I decided to just rip it off, like a band aid.

I picked up my phone and let it all out, "Well... my real name is Ashlee Corrigan. I have five kids, and I was recently widowed. My husband's name was Emmett Corrigan... and he went to your high school. He was the man who was murdered a while back at Walgreens." SEND ...

I knew that would be the end of our conversation, and I was okay with the fact that this would probably be how my dating life would be... for a long time. In that moment, I truly knew in my heart that I would never hear from Lakersfan24 ever again.

I put my phone away and tried to enjoy the friends who were all around me. Auna and I did a 'Dundee' awards ceremony and awarded random mugs—which she had found at thrift stores—to each of our friends for a specific funny reason. It was hilarious. I laughed so hard... actual deep belly laughs. It felt so good to be laughing and having a good time, but in the back of my mind, I was really wondering what "lakersfan24" was thinking.

As our night came to an end, I finally got the courage to pick up my phone. I had a message. It was him. "Wow," he wrote "I had no idea. I read your entire story in the news. When I saw your picture, you looked so familiar, but I didn't put any of that together. I am so sorry for everything you have been through. I can't say I have any words to describe how sorry I am. I know a lot of people who knew Emmett. I never met him personally, but everyone who knows you has raved about what an amazing mother you are. I would like to take you to dinner if that is okay with you."

What? He knew how crazy my life was, and he texted me back? I didn't know this man, and I didn't know if he would ever really take me on a date, but just the fact that he texted me back, after hearing who I was, healed something inside of me. It gave me hope that my broken life didn't have to define who I would become. It healed the fear inside of me that led me to believe I would never go out on another date.

As we all went to bed that night, I couldn't sleep. Again, I offered up prayers to my Heavenly Father. This time, I thanked Him for sending me a new friend. I didn't question His timing, and I didn't even question why this friend had so many of the traits I had put on my "Unacceptable List." Instead, I just told Him how grateful I was to have a friend who was willing to look past the crazy life that was mine, and try to see *me*.

I thanked Him for the healing I had felt that entire weekend. I begged for a continued road to reconstruction as I went home that next morning to a family who needed my love.

We left the country to go back to the city, and as we drove into town, I could see light infuse every landscape we passed. It was Mother's Day. I went to church to celebrate myself as a mom, surrounded by my babies. They seemed to glow, and so did I.

I knew that day that we were going to heal. Someday, we would be set free from the darkness that had tried to destroy us. For the first time since their father died, my children had a real light in their eyes. They were looking to me to help them find peace, and I was watching the hand of God send me my own. He had a plan for us, and I could feel the power of His plan. I was no longer going to fight it. I was going to let Him steer my course, and I wanted to show Him that I had faith that He would not lead me astray.

On the road to moving forward, the steps to healing are different for each of us. Sometimes, we need years to heal ourselves before we begin to think about moving forward, and other times, God has a greater plan to help us heal. He asks us to leap.

Whatever dark roads have caused you pain, there is a path that can lead you to the healing you seek. I thought my job was to heal myself, and then search for a way to find love again, but Heavenly Father seemed to have a different plan in mind for me. That text message was not just some random message from a man I didn't know, it was a gift from God reminding me that maybe my past was dark, but I was not broken. There was hope that someone might be able to look past the crooked road I had traveled, and help me find the way to the new road He had planned for me. The thought of love became less scary as I felt the loving hand of God reassure and inspire me to follow the spirit, which led me to a new friend.

Healing, is not something we can always do on our own. Some of us need the help of professionals, some need medication, but we all need each other. We were not sent here to earth to do everything on our own. As a bull-headed woman, I didn't always comprehend that. I could do most things on my own, and I didn't always like to rely on someone else.

Even before Emmett died, I didn't really NEED him in parenting. I did most things on my own, and though I really longed to have him with me, a part of me enjoyed doing it all my own way. It wasn't until after he died, that I realized how much I really did need him. At that point, I also learned that I had to rely on others. It was a humbling time when I learned that I *did* need others in my life when I fell short. Emmett's death was humbling in more ways than one. I learned that when I felt insignificant by myself, it was okay to ask for help.

It wasn't until after Emmett's death that I truly realized how much I really *did* need Heavenly Father, Jesus Christ, and the Atonement.

Healing was not something I could do on my own. I needed Heavenly Father, I needed Jesus Christ's love, and I needed the power that was available because of His life on earth and His death on the cross. I needed to have Them steer my course…and I needed to have faith that when They told me to have patience…I needed to wait. When They asked me to jump in with both feet with faith…I needed to leap.

There had been so many moments when I had prayed for help in my life when the answer always seemed to be: "Be still, and have patience." And, as a woman who constantly needed a reminder to wait and have faith in God's timing, I had counted on those lessons in patience continuing. Little did I know, that for once in my life…at a time when all I thought I needed was patience…Heavenly Father would ask me to take a giant LEAP of faith.

We all need each other when it comes to healing. We need to support each other, we need to help others through their hard times…and we need to allow others to help us through our own. This answer to my prayer, through the text message of a stranger, would not be the last time that Heavenly Father would send help to me on my road to healing.

I didn't need a list of what would be best for me, because God's list was what I really needed. There wasn't going to be a "perfect man" sent my way, because frankly…I was not a perfect woman. I was in no way ready to "move on," but I wasn't about to fight the peace that came to me as I did.

Sometimes we will be humbled by the "I will nevers" of life. Just when we think we have it all figured out, that's when we are sent the deal-breakers! When his text came with the description of his childhood that had parallels to Emmett's, I wanted to run away. I had made it clear that I had my own plan, and I had my own perfect list.

One of the greatest teaching moments in life is just when we think we have it all figured out, we are sent trials or opportunities to exercise our faith. We will be asked to have patience through sickness; we will be reminded that we are not invincible. We will be asked to love others through their addictions, and shown that we can have the power to help them heal. We might be asked to carry the heavy load of others' pain as they learn to heal. And then other times, we might be asked to be humble enough to let others come in and fulfill their missions as they help us reconstruct ourselves.

We have to have faith that sometimes—even when the conditions we have created are not met—our Heavenly Father's blessings are even greater than any we could have imagined on our own.

Nonetheless, His timing and His blessings will sometimes come in imperfect packages. Sometimes, the very thing we have put our foot down about, will be just the thing He uses to allow us to show Him that we can still have faith.

Wherever you are on your road to healing, watch for the little blessings being sent your way. Allow them to be the tools they were meant to be, even if they are as simple as a feeling of peace that comes to your heart, or a text message that reminds you that you are lovable, just the way you are.

On the other hand, even though we all need those around us in this journey, we can't always wait around for others to heal us either. Sometime, ours is a road that is personal and only God will be there for us, but when He does send the little moments to remind us that He is there...we can't forget to thank Him for those reminders.

He loves us. He loves you when you are face down in a massage chair crying tears and missing a life you once had. He loves you even when you think you know what is best for yourself. He loves you when you feel confident that, even though you've gone through hell, you will fight your way out. He loves you when you are broken and on your knees in your closet. He loves you when you are rattling off demands about what you will find acceptable in your future, and He loves you even when you are trying to plan your life without His help.

He doesn't ask us to be perfect, but God does ask us to carry on through our imperfect lives.

We cannot fight His timing. I was in no way—in any shape—ready to start looking at online profiles. I didn't go looking online because I felt I was ready to find love, but I was guided to a place where two blue eyes waited to help me heal.

He will send you whispers of His love; He will send you earthly Angels to write you messages that will help you find peace. Don't try to heal yourself alone. Watch for the signs flashing in your face, and for the silent peace that comes to your heart when you are exactly where you are supposed to be. Healing a life that was once broken, is not impossible. With Jesus Christ as the foundation of your path to healing, you will find a way. He can guide you there.

He believes in you, and in the peace you seek. Only He can send you along the road to help you heal, and His plan is always going to be greater than your own. Only He can direct you to the hidden blue eyes waiting to help you on your road to peace.

CHAPTER SEVEN

# *Your story*

**WELL, AS MY NEW ON-LINE FRIEND HAD** promised, he asked me out to dinner, and before I knew it, the day had come. I was as cool as a cucumber as I got ready and kissed my kids goodbye. I had picked the meeting spot to be in a public place, an eating establishment only a minute from my house, in case I needed to make a quick getaway.

I was the first one to get there, so I went to the table alone waiting for him to show up. As I sat there, I looked around the room. Emmett and I had been there so many times. It was one of our favorite restaurants, and it felt so weird to be sitting here waiting for someone else. Every other time I had sat in these chairs, I had been with my husband. We had shared the very table I was sitting at not too long ago. I tried very hard to banish from my mind the memories of my times there with Emmett. It was also hard for me not to think back to the scripts I had written in my head when I was a little girl… about how my life would be. I had lived some of those storylines, but the ending of my marriage was certainly not in the story I had written.

I could remember as plain as day the first time I began 'writing' my story. It was the day when going on a date with a boy finally became a reality: my sixteenth birthday. It was the first day of what I considered to be the "beginning of my life." I planned out in my mind all about the many handsome young men who would take me on perfect dates. I pictured the years I would spend being adored by the man of my choosing.

That birthday, I drew the map of my life as I planned out my future. It was the story of what was to come. Every detail was considered in my mind, and every day was written to be perfect. I would marry young, and I would become a mother. I pictured my children, and vowed that I would have at least have two boys, because, of course, every boy needs a brother.

And so at the age of sixteen, I had already written my story. All my "t"s were crossed and my "i"s were dotted. All I knew back then, is that I wouldn't give up until every aspect of my story came true.

And it did. As of March 11, 2011, I had checked off nearly every item on my storybook list. I had just given birth to my fifth child... our second son, giving Teage his promised brother. We finally lived in my dream house, and my husband had the dream job every graduating law school student hopes to achieve.

I had written the perfect story, and I thought I was living my perfect plan.

Every book ever written has an ending. However, in real life with the stories we write... we don't always get to choose the ending. Sometimes, life throws us an alternate ending. The timing is never right, and the plot can sometimes be one that no one would intentionally ever plan.

My story with Emmett had ended, even though cleaning up the mess he had made of my past would continue on for years. I sat alone in that restaurant. I had no hope for a second date; I had no expectations... I had little faith that I would even be able to enjoy myself that night, but I *was* determined to be myself.

The door into the restaurant opened and the sun flashed into my eyes. I tried to squint through the light to see who had entered the room... and there he was. I could see the blue in his eyes from where I sat. There was a sparkle in them, like one I had never before seen. When the sun pierced my eyes, all my fear of the past seemed to be swept out of me. I held my head high and watched him as he came toward me.

He walked to the table with a confidence in his step, and he was just as cute as his photos. He sat down and introduced himself: "Hello, I'm Shawn ..." As he spoke, it felt as if I had always known him. My eyes didn't leave his during our introductions.

Not a second went by that night when we weren't talking. We spoke about everything and anything. I told him parts of my story that I hadn't told anyone, and he opened up about his. It was almost like poetry as we buoyed each other up and shared the pain—and the joys—of our respective pasts. In some ways, he had been in my shoes, and it felt reassuring to know that he had felt the same type of pain that was in my heart.

Our stories were not the same, but my soul felt safe as he reassured me that I was not alone in having suffered through serious pain. We talked and talked. In what seemed like just a matter of seconds...two and a half hours had actually passed.

For the first time since Emmett died, I spent an entire evening feeling completely safe. I felt safe in sharing my feelings, I felt safe having Shawn sit at the table with me, and I felt safe knowing that I was exactly where I was supposed to be. Not one single time did I think about the murder trial, which was always at the back of my mind. I didn't talk about Kandi or Rob, or for that matter, even think about them. That night, the sick-to-my-stomach feeling I usually felt was replaced with peaceful butterflies.

Shawn and I walked out of the restaurant together, still talking with every step we took. It was raining, so I told him about my curse: that my hair controlled the weather. He reassured me that my hair couldn't possibly have that much power...but I stood firm in the belief that my curly hair chose whether or not it would rain. I insisted that because I had straightened my hair that day, it rained. It was my tried and true method to forecast the weather. He laughed at my weirdness, and humored me by admitting that I must have pretty powerful hair! We were about to say goodbye and part ways, but I didn't want to leave. I looked into those blue eyes of his and said, "Do you want to go for a drive?" He smiled back and said, "Heck ya!"

We got into his car and drove around town in the rain. He was so witty and funny. He almost made me forget about all the mountains I had been scaling in recent months. I felt filled with life, and even through the rain...I could see light.

While we were driving, he received a phone call and answered it. When he hung up he said, "I'm so sorry, but I have to go pick up my little girl. I don't usually introduce her to women I'm dating, but I need to get her right now. Would you be okay with that?"

We pulled up to the arranged meeting place, and his daughter Jordyn hopped into the car. She was so sweet and cute. I started asking her questions, and during the rest of the drive Shawn sat quietly while Jordyn and I got to know each other. She reminded me so much of Bostyn and Bailey. She was not at all shy, and she talked to me just like my own children did. She opened up to me about her day, and about what she had been doing all evening. We laughed and joked together.

I felt reluctant to leave as we pulled up to the parking lot where I had parked Tiffanie's car (yeah, I made her lend me her car for the night in case *Lakersfan24* turned out to be a crazy person—in which case, I didn't want him to know what I drove)!! When we stopped, I just wanted to bottle up the evening and take it back home with me, in hopes that the peace that had surrounded me would carry me through the rest of the night.

Shawn got out of the car. He looked a little baffled. He stared into my eyes and said, "Jordyn usually doesn't say a word to anyone she doesn't know. I have never seen her talk to anyone the way she just opened up to you. Thank you for taking the time to talk to her and appreciate her."

He gave me a hug, and I started to clam up. Slowly he pulled me in a little bit more. I didn't want to let him... and yet, I didn't want him to ever let go, either.

I looked into the car at Jordyn's big brown eyes and black spiral curls. She looked exactly like the Cabbage Patch doll I had received for Christmas when I was four years old. She was smiling from ear to ear. I waved to her, and let go of Shawn, not sure when or if I would ever see them again, but hoping I would.

That night, for the first time in a long time, I felt hope. Hope that I could be me. Hope that some day, my story would have some bonus chapters written with a new alternative ending—and most of all hope because I had felt so much peace. Before that night, I had come to believe that for me, a true sense of peace was just going to be something I read about in other people's stories. But that second, I saw a glimmer of it in my own.

I drove home in reflective silence. I felt good about my decision to meet Shawn that night. I didn't feel frightened anymore. I could feel the peace that God had sent to bless and heal me... almost to the point where I felt that my healing was nearly complete! I thought of the incredible promise I had received in past blessings: that a man would come to heal me... and somehow hoped that meant... it would be in the blink of an eye.

I didn't know then that I still had a very long journey of healing yet to come... but that night gave me the hope that healing was actually possible. My story—which had not played out as I wrote it—might possibly have a chapter about finding peace!

Each of our stories is unique. God has written a different storyline for all of us. Don't be afraid to embrace *your* story as you climb the mountains and jump the hurdles in your life. They were made just for you. As you reach a little higher, each jump might get a little easier. When you fall and scrape your knee, it might take a while to get back up and enjoy the hurdles again, but at least you will have learned that it is easier if you learn how to jump over them correctly and make it over the first time.

The broken pieces of our dreams that surround us, are there to remind us to keep moving forward and jumping high enough to clear even the tallest hurdle.

Your story may not be the one you wrote in your journal when you were sixteen... but it is yours. Embrace it.

I have learned that hope has to come before faith. Have hope for a brighter day and use your faith to jump with all of your heart.

What is your story? Wherever you are right now, your story is unique. The night Emmett died, I felt like my story had ended...as a tragedy. I frantically searched for hope...before I could find my faith again.

Hope comes in many forms, like in boxes filled with letters addressed to "the people of Japan." My hope has been restored when a special song has been sung just for me. My hope has grown as angels have sewn blankets for me in which to wrap my precious babies.

Heavenly Father sends you the little reminders of His love to help you build your hope, because He knows that until you see a glimmer of hope...you will not be able to feel or see your faith.

At the end of the *Book of Mormon,* Moroni almost pleads with us to find hope. He shares one of his last desperate cries as he writes in *Moroni, Chapter 7:*

> [41] *And what is it that ye shall hope for? Behold I say unto you that ye shall have hope through the atonement of Christ and the power of his resurrection, to be raised unto life eternal, and this because of your faith in him according to the promise.*
>
> [42] *Wherefore, if a man have faith he must needs have hope; for without faith there cannot be any hope.*
>
> [43] *And again, behold I say unto you that he cannot have faith and hope, save he shall be meek, and lowly of heart.*
>
> [44] *If so, his faith and hope is vain, for none is acceptable before God, save the meek and lowly in heart; and if a man be meek and lowly in heart, and confesses by the power of the Holy Ghost that Jesus is the Christ, he must needs have charity; for if he have not charity he is nothing; wherefore he must needs have charity.*
>
> [45] *And charity suffereth long, and is kind, and envieth not, and is not puffed up, seeketh not her own, is not easily provoked,*

*thinketh no evil, and rejoiceth not in iniquity but rejoiceth in the
truth, beareth all things, believeth all things, hopeth all things,
endureth all things.*

*⁴⁶ Wherefore, my beloved brethren, if ye have not charity,
ye are nothing, for charity never faileth. Wherefore, cleave unto
charity, which is the greatest of all, for all things must fail—*

*⁴⁷ But charity is the pure love of Christ, and it endureth
forever; and whoso is found possessed of it at the last day, it shall
be well with him.*

*⁴⁸ Wherefore, my beloved brethren, pray unto the Father with
all the energy of heart, that ye may be filled with this love, which
he hath bestowed upon all who are true followers of his Son, Jesus
Christ; that ye may become the sons of God; that when he shall
appear we shall be like him, for we shall see him as he is; that we
may have this hope; that we may be purified even as he is pure.
Amen.*

When we miss the light sent our way each and every day...we will fail
to have the faith required to develop or feel the pure love of Christ. When
we are surrounded by darkness, and we let it prevail...we cannot see the
good that is also trying to play out in our stories.

We have all been hurt, and at times, each one of us is frightened. Unfortunately, the righteous desires we planned in the stories we wrote for
ourselves when we were young are not always achieved. When that happens, we might lose the hope we have in our own story. We begin to see
our life as a failure of the one we had planned.

However, the hope that we must never lose is the hope that the story
we are living will be enough, and that will happen only if we are certain of
who is writing our story.

I have a brother who I felt pushed all of us away for a long period of
time. We, as his family, were often not a part of the life he was living. We

all missed him, and for many years, we were totally and completely separated from him.

I remember one Christmas—as I watched my mom bundle up a care package for him with a sweet letter enclosed—I asked "Mom?...What are you doing? Why do you even care any more? Why don't you just give up and let him go. He obviously doesn't need you any more, or want you to be part of his life...so please just get over it and stop trying. I don't get why you are still fighting for him."

She looked at me with tears in her eyes and said something I will never forget. "Ashlee...your brother is still my son. He has pushed me away, he has let me know that he doesn't need me...but sweet daughter...I end every letter I write to him with 'I hope you are finding the happiness you are searching for.' Ashlee, one day, he is going to be searching for that happiness he hasn't found elsewhere, and guess what?...He's going to know right where he can come to be safe. I am not going to give up on this boy because I believe in him. I love him, and one day, he's going to remember that I have always been right here."

My mom had a hope I knew nothing about.

A few years after Emmett died, I received a phone call late one night. It was my brother. We had rebuilt our relationship over the years, especially since Emmett died, and I had seen him come back into our lives, but this call was different. He said, "Ash...hey, so I...I just prayed for the first time in eighteen years. I spoke to God, and He was listening. Ash, I think He has missed me."

A few days later, he sat in my living room and with tears in his eyes, he bore his soul to me about the type of love he had been missing in his life. He said, "I don't know much, but I do know this...every single person who has been a true hero in my life...has something that I have been forgetting. I need that light back."

My mom was right. I had no idea that her love had carried him, even when she hadn't physically been around him all of those years. He was standing at the crossroad she knew would come. . . and her hope in her son had been the anchor he needed to know where to turn.

Sometimes, we search for happiness where it can't be found. Sometimes, we frantically rummage through boxes of crap in our garage, or skim through e-mails searching for peace. Real peace doesn't come from anything we can tangibly touch here on the earth. Real peace comes through the healing power of Jesus Christ.

In the same way my mother waited patiently for my brother, our Heavenly Father sends each of us quiet notes and care packages to remind us that He is right here when our search for happiness elsewhere fails. When we have finished sorting through all the phony substitutes for genuine peace and happiness... He is quietly waiting on the sidelines for us to return.

When we finally do turn to Him, He doesn't stand there reminding us of all the things we did wrong. No, He stands with open arms, ready to pour out His love upon us... and help us write the rest of our stories.

Genuine happiness comes from relationships: friends, family, service... but first with God. NO matter what other relationships we have, our relationship with God has to be our anchor. In marriage, as in single life, Heavenly Father has to be the author of our story, and it is never over... until it is over. Every day presents a new opportunity for us to increase our hope in ourselves, in others, and in God.

We need faith. We need to find hope. Hope cannot come in the form of another person, place or thing... for all of those things can be taken away. Hope has to come from our relationship with God, and our reassurance that the story we are living is being written by Him.

Maybe your story has more bumps in it than you had planned. Maybe everyone you have ever loved is gone. God is still there. He hears your prayers and He has numbered your tears. You are not crying alone.

The story He has written for you may be far different from the one you wrote on your bed on your sixteenth birthday... but you have to live the story that is being written right now. Live your own story, and find hope that it is enough for God. His version of your story is what leads you to your own 'happily ever after.'

CHAPTER EIGHT

# Free Pass

**IT DIDN'T TAKE LONG FOR SHAWN TO** call again. Before I knew it, we were sitting on my couch spending another evening in non-stop conversation. The kids were asleep, and he hadn't met any of them yet. I wasn't really ready to introduce them to him, but I enjoyed talking with him for hours as we sat together on the couch.

Before coming to see me, Shawn had spent the evening playing basketball. He warned me that he was all sweaty and stinky, but I didn't even notice. He looked so cute in his basketball shorts and T-shirt.

We shared with each other more of our personal stories that night; I shared things with Shawn that only the detectives knew. I told him about the night Emmett died, revealing the details of the emotions I'd felt leading up to the hour of his death. I shared the explosion of relief, and the other waves of emotions I'd felt since that moment I had sat with the detectives...on the very couch where we were now sitting.

It was getting late and as we talked about his need to go home and get to bed, I leaned in and kissed him. For a few seconds, our lips touched and I could feel sparks fly. For me, it was a perfect kiss accompanied by happy butterflies in my tummy.

I was smitten.

The next day, I was out with Tytus for a doctor's appointment and I stopped by the pharmacy on the way home, which just happened to be right across the street from Shawn's work. I texted him and asked him if he would like to come and meet us there.

While waiting for him to come, I walked around the pharmacy filling my cart with random things, a little nervous at the thought of being seen in public with Shawn…but mainly scared to have him meet one of my children. Tytus was all smiles, and I talked to him gently as we strolled down each aisle.

As I was trying to decide on what color of nail polish to buy, I looked up and saw Shawn walking toward us, with a huge grin on his face. When he got to our cart, I introduced him to Tytus, who was now almost five months old. He smiled and cooed at Shawn for a few minutes, and then started to fuss. "Man," I said, "he is so tired…It has been a long morning." I took my pointer finger and, starting between his eyes, rubbed it down the bridge of his nose. As I reached the tip of his nose, his eyes closed and he was fast asleep.

Shawn looked at me in surprise. "What in the heck was that? Is that how he always falls asleep? That is so unfair!! I've never in my life seen a baby fall asleep so fast." We laughed about it for a minute and chit-chatted while Tytus slept in his car seat.

It felt surreal to have my two worlds coming together. I didn't know how I would be able to be in both: being a single mother, and learning to love again. I felt awkward as I smiled at Shawn, and then looked down at my little sleeping infant. I never pictured that such a day would ever be a part of my life. In my mind, dating and parenting were worlds apart.

When I went out on a date with Shawn, or sat with him on my couch after the kids were in bed, it was easy to momentarily step away from the darkness always lurking in my world with the trial pending…but it was overwhelming and frightening bringing both of those worlds together. I feared they would collide, and that one would destroy the other.

The next weekend, Teage left on an outing with some friends, the "Fathers and Sons Campout" for our church. It was his first time camping, and his first "father and son" outing. I tried hard to feel okay about the fact that he was not going with his own father and I choked back tears as I packed his bag and buckled him into his friend's car. I was grateful for the chance for him to go, but longed to have him share such a weekend with Emmett.

The night after Teage left, Shawn brought his daughter Jordyn over to meet my girls. We all watched a movie and the kids enjoyed laughing and playing together. In the middle of the movie, I started getting choked up as I witnessed the mixing of my two worlds, which was taking place before my eyes. I looked at the twins who were almost squishing Jordyn between them. I looked at Kaleeya with such a sweet smile on her face, and Tytus cuddled in Shawn's arms. It was a perfect moment, and the spirit was so strong as I looked around the room. It didn't feel complete without Teage there, but it felt amazing to see some of the holes—that usually gaped open with darkness—filled with so much light.

The kids started complaining about being hungry so Shawn and I got up to find them a snack. I opened the pantry to look inside, when all of the sudden, Shawn grabbed me and pulled me into the pantry and pulled the door shut behind us. There in the quiet of my pantry, we smooched. I could hear the kids giggling out on the couch, and I could smell food surrounding me, which since Emmett's death had been so hard for me to prepare. The darkened pantry—which just weeks earlier had witnessed me spilling tears of sorrow—now held me quietly wrapped in the arms of peace.

All of the sudden, the door opened and Jordyn said, "I think my dad was kissing your mom!!!!" They all ran off giggling and squirming.

That night, as I tucked the kids into bed, Bailey very matter-of-factly stated, "Mom, we don't have a dad anymore…and Jordyn and Shawn, they need a mom…so I don't get why we don't just ask them to be part of our family." I gave her a squeeze. "Bay, I wish that life were that easy. They are great friends, and it is fun to have them here spending time with us, so let's just be really grateful for that!"

My two worlds seemed to be merging into one, more easily than I could have imagined.

We spent the next few weeks enjoying our time together. Shawn and Jordyn met Teage when he got back from the campout. We had lots of fun days and everyone got along great. For the first time since Emmett died...we laughed more than we cried.

One morning, I got a call from the detective on the case, and reality set in once again. I don't remember why he called, or what he said, but I do remember the lump that settled in my throat as I imagined making Shawn and Jordyn go through this horrible nightmare with us. I got the kids ready for the day, and I headed to the temple. I needed to clear my head. The excitement of my new friend had almost made me forget about the trial that still loomed over me.

As I drove to the temple, I thought about all the times I had laughed that week. How unfair it was of me to make Shawn think I was happy. What kind of deception was I perpetrating on this poor man? I *wasn't* happy. I was scared, I was broken, and the reality was...I still had a life to clean up before I could start living a new one.

I walked into the temple with my stomach tied in knots. During the entire session, an internal battle was raging inside me between my desire to move on and heal, and my need to stay stuck in my pain so I could somehow bear the murder trial that would be coming. I felt strongly that I couldn't do both at the same time.

For the millionth time, I sat in the Celestial Room praying for peace. I knew in my heart, that I was wrong to turn my back on this new possibility...but I struggled to see how I could—in good conscience—ask this innocent man to crawl through the trenches with me. I knew what I had to do. I knew what he deserved...he needed a free pass. He needed me to tell him that I didn't want or need him so he could go on and live a normal life without us.

As soon as I got back in my car, I called him and asked him to meet me at my house. I drove home still feeling very unsettled and full of despair. I walked into the house almost in tears, knowing that what I had to do was going to be very difficult. Shawn arrived soon after I got home. He came to the door, knowing exactly what my intentions were. I didn't even invite him to come in, but I just grabbed my phone and asked him to come and walk with me.

We walked to a little waterfall at the entrance of my neighborhood, found a bench and took a seat. I looked up into his big blue eyes and let it all out. "So...I like you a lot, but I am in no way ready to be in a relationship. I think I have been forgetting about the reality of my life...and I, um...you...you don't deserve this. I wish I could say that I could sit around and date you, but this isn't fair to you. I'm scared and I don't know how to make this work. My world is so different than yours." I didn't have the courage to look in his eyes any longer, so I stared out past the green trees, and continued with my explanation.

"We are broken, see...and we haven't even begun to process everything we've been through. Teage is a raging ball of anger. Kaleeya bites holes in her binkies and punches the baby in the face, the twins are so sad some days that I don't even see them smile...and then you just walk in like you can't see how broken we are. Come on, you don't deserve this... and one day you're going to realize what a storm you just jumped into and you are going to want to run as far away from us as you can."

I started to get choked up, so I tried to get right to the point. "So, here is what we are going to do. You are going to walk me home, and then you're going to get in your car...and you are going to pretend that we never met. You go find a normal girl who has the ability to love...who wants to have a normal family with you...one who won't drag you through hell in the next few years trying to figure out how to exist. You deserve a woman who doesn't fall down at the park in a panic attack because an ambulance drives by...one who knows how to love. So you go find her... and be happy forever. I can't let you stick around and be disappointed for the rest of your life that you settled for a broken widow and her five broken children. You are going to find a normal girl, one who knows how to love … one who actually has the ability to make you happy. Find a young girl who doesn't have any baggage, one you can start a real life with … one that isn't just pretending to be normal … and when you find her … don't look back. I'm scared about what the next few years are going to bring. It's going to be hard. I … I talked to the detective this morning and just hearing his voice reminded me of all the mess I have left to live through. I can't do this to you, and I'm scared to let you even try to ride along with me … because eventually it will be too much for you … and you'll leave. So, I'm asking you to leave now, so I don't have to wonder when you'll go. I just can't do this … again. I … I don't … I just need you to pretend you never met me, and just let me figure this out on my own."

I don't think I even took one breath.

I looked back toward him. There were tears falling down his cheeks. He sat quietly for what seemed to be an eternity. He finally began to speak as he looked into my eyes. "Ashlee, I … I have dated all those so-called 'normal' girls you talk about. I've tried to picture my life with each one of them. It … wasn't just you I fell in love with during the first five minutes I talked to you. No, I've fallen head over heals with you *and* your children. I have never in my life felt what I feel when I am with you. I know the road that has brought you to me has been very hard, and I will never pretend that it has been easy for you … but right now, I need you to believe me when I say … you are beautiful. You are beautiful inside and out. Maybe Emmett couldn't see that when he died, but I am sitting right here in front of you … right now, and I see you. I know you have a difficult road ahead of you with the trial, and with the other challenges and responsibilities that are yet to come because of Emmett's murder, but I am not going to walk away … not after seeing everything I've always dreamed of … right here … right now. You may feel broken, and I get that because I've felt that way myself, but I … I love you Ashlee. I love all six of you … just the way you are."

As I watched Shawn wipe away his tears, I knew in that moment that he wouldn't let me talk him into walking away. I felt relieved. I had given him his free pass, and here he was... still able to see the me that had been hidden by so much tragedy.

But the possibility of this relationship going somewhere still wasn't quite as easy for me as it was for Shawn. It was as if I was trapped between two worlds. My dreams were still of Emmett, but my real life was trying so hard to piece itself together and move on. I was holding the hand of one man, while trying to figure out how to let go of the other.

My anger at Emmett pushed me into easily finding Shawn, but my pain held me back from giving Shawn my whole heart. I missed Emmett, and yet I adored Shawn. What kind of hell was this supposed to be? I lived in two worlds: one where Shawn loved me and the kids... and another where my heart was constantly racing in anticipation of the trial, and feeling Emmett's presence in my dreams. I didn't know how to let go so that I could take hold of something new.

In spite of my confusion, that day was when I understood that in spite of having set Shawn free, in spite of having given him a way out of our crazy world with no strings attached, he had still—and without any reservations—chosen us... just the way we were... broken and all.

Sometimes, even when we are broken and trying hard to hide all of our imperfections, people see the good in us anyway. I did all that I could to push Shawn out of my life so that I could continue being fractured... all by myself. I didn't want him to spend his life trying to fix me. I thought it would be easier for him to go and have a 'normal' life, but he stayed anyway.

We are all given a 'free pass' at one time or another... a pass given to us because Jesus Christ died for us. He sees that we are broken, and yet He still loves us unconditionally. The pass He shares with us, is only possible through Him. He died on the cross so that every day we are given the opportunity to use our 'free pass' to heal, to forgive and to repent of our sins.

Shawn's decision at the waterfall that day changed the course of my life. His ability to see me, even when I couldn't see myself... built me up. I didn't need him to survive, but to truly be whole again... I had to let him in. He was a blessing sent straight from Heavenly Father. He has sacrificed for me, he has given me courage when I couldn't find it on my own, and he has shown me that even in my empty state... I was still lovable.

I was being given a 'free pass' to a new life. My happiness had not ended permanently. I had given my all to Emmett, even when he didn't deserve it... and somewhere inside myself, I still had the ability to do the same for Shawn.

It would not be an easy journey. It would not always be smooth... but just like many times in my life—it was being made possible for me.

When I was in high school, I suffered from some mental and emotional problems. I had a very unrealistic view of myself, and at different times, I went through various phases of eating disorders. It was embarrassing, it was humiliating, and it was a painful battle I had to fight every single day. I struggled with many of the relationships in my life, and failed to see the role I played in many of those struggles I was having.

My parents ended up sending me to a therapeutic wilderness boarding school. I learned more about myself in those two and a half months than I had in all the previous eighteen years of my life. I learned I had been carrying a shadow of incorrect beliefs around with me, and I came to understand the power they had on the view I possessed of myself and how I thought others viewed me. I learned about personal virtues and why each one played a role in the person I wanted to become.

I even made it through a three-day solo period. I set up my camp, and without being allowed to leave that site... I had to spend three days in a row all alone—by myself. Up until that point in my life, I hadn't even spent a few hours alone without another person close by. At first it was strange—then I began to enjoy it. I laughed, I sang songs, I cried. Those were three of the hardest days of my life... and yet, I had never felt so alive and empowered.

Through that experience, I learned a lot about the roles I had played in my own life at home, which contributed to my failure to develop authentic caring relationships with my family and friends. I thought about the ingratitude that had diluted so many of my words, and so many of the hurtful decisions I had made without any regard for the people who loved me. I seriously pondered my own contributions and responsibilities in the negative scenarios of my life.

When my time at that camp came to an end, I was almost afraid to return to real life. It was my senior year, and I didn't feel ready to go back to that reality. However, when I got home, I realized something...those two and half months had been a free pass for me. I didn't have to be afraid any more to step back into real life, because I had finally found out what life was all about.

It was hard to go back to the relationships I had taken advantage of as a snotty teenager. As I stepped back into life with a new found knowledge of what it was all about, my eyes felt as if they had been opened.

My 'free pass' to change the direction my path was heading...saved my life. I no longer viewed the world as something to manipulate in order to get my way, or as an excuse to be selfish or mean. I saw it with the beauty I had found inside of myself.

Sometimes our 'free pass' is offered at a time when we need to change our course, and other times it is given to remind us of the things we already have, which we are fighting so hard to keep.

Shawn didn't want to walk away from the path we were starting to travel together, because he knew he was exactly where he was supposed to be. He saw the pathway long before I allowed myself to find it. His free pass, given by me, didn't make him want to leave...instead, it gave him even more reason to fight for what he knew was right.

On the other hand, there are free passes that are not for our good. These are the type of false 'free passes' Satan offers us or we offer ourselves when we want to step away from reality or when we have a secret we want to hide. Emmett took a 'free pass' offered to him as an enticing gimmick. He must have honestly believed that with his 'pass,' he could come and go in our marriage as he pleased, and that no one of importance would ever find out that he had taken it...but he did, and ultimately...that is what changed the course of all of our lives.

Use your 'free passes' wisely. They can, and will, change you. The course of your life can be destroyed if they are used to indulge your own selfishness or lust. The easy way is seldom the Lord's way. Shawn showed me an example of that as I gave him an easy way out, and he chose the right way instead.

God doesn't expect us to walk each step in life with ease...but when we walk it with Him, our burdens can be made light. If you are being tempted to manipulate yourself into thinking that you need a 'free pass' to distance yourself from the broken pieces of your life...make sure that it is Christ who is offering it to you. Satan will try to make his 'free pass' sound as if it will change you for the better, but in the end...he will not stand with you. Depending on the dealmaker, a 'free pass' can either help you rise above your pain...or cause more pain to follow.

In reality, there are really no 'free' passes in life—even the ones from Heavenly Father have been paid for by Jesus Christ through the Atonement. Shawn had no idea of the hard work he had yet to endure as he decided to continue dating me. He would have to work and sacrifice and find patience and love, even at times when I was not at all lovable. Just like our Savior, Shawn's pass didn't come without a price. And just like Jesus Christ, Shawn would have to go through pain of his own as he worked hard to make our journey together work.

Being in the right place at the right time doesn't mean that it will be easy!!!!

Wherever you are in your life, there will be times when a free pass sounds like it will save you from the difficulties of mortality. However, nothing can take all of your hardships away. There is no way around the pain of this world, just resources to help you through them. Spend less time trying to dodge them, and more time building yourself up to have the power to stand strong even as the storms rage around you.

That bottle of liquor may mask your pain for the night, but the fear will find its place again in the morning. That shopping bag full of new clothes may numb your loneliness for the afternoon, but your despair will not be washed away as you put them on. That trip to Disneyland may disguise the pain in your family for the week, but it will not fix the fractures in your marriage. The 'free passes' that just offer a temporary fix, do not change the problems or take away the pain…they merely postpone the suffering.

So many of us are hurting and longing to find a free pass from our pain. But, there is no pill to take, and there is no magic wand to wave. Hard work and diligence in respecting the truths we know will provide us with a foundation of strength and give us the courage to face our pain. Learn and study the genuine truths in the world. Search, ponder and pray about which of the principles you learn about are true. There is truth all around us, truths that can help us along our pathway to healing.

Be selective and only use the 'free passes' that come from God. Sometimes even the hardest trials ARE the 'free passes' we need to become the person that we long to be.

Waiting for, or fearing tomorrow only stops us from living today. Don't wait for another day to bring you peace. Search for peace, as you live through each day. The perfect calm in life may never come. In fact, even when you think you have gone through all of the hard times, more trials seem to find their way to you.

The good news is—we are not alone. All of us are trying hard to figure out what paths to choose and what storms to navigate. Don't let the good days pass you by as you wait around for the 'free passes' that lead you to what you think is your desired state of perfection. Sometimes, it is merely life itself that is the true gift you fail to recognize. Your time is now. Don't let it pass you by. Let each hour be the reason you choose to stand. Your 'free pass' might come to help you change your path, or it might come to remind you that you need to fight to stay on the pathway on which you are already traveling. Life is too short to spend it waiting. Live it and love it, wherever your free pass takes you.

# CHAPTER NINE

# *What if . . . I jump?*

**I WILL NEVER COMPREHEND HOW I WAS** able to move forward or why Heavenly Father asked me to become okay with the thought of finding love again so quickly. I can only say that I didn't do it alone. *I* wasn't ready. I wasn't prepared, and I didn't feel able to do it ... but I knew it was exactly what I was supposed to do.

On the Fast Sunday before going to Emmett's grave for Memorial Day, I fasted for my little family to be blessed with healing in our hearts so we could one day move forward. My fasting and prayers were answered ... more quickly than I ever thought possible, but I wasn't quite emotionally prepared for that immediate response.

Let's be honest. Throughout most of my life, God had constantly been reminding me to have patience ... and that was just exactly the lesson I needed to learn in every one of those instances. I think I was finally beginning to understand the platitude that patience is a virtue and I had almost mastered it; patience in His timing and patience in His plan. I felt like I had finally begun to get the hint ... because He kept taking the time to remind me to slow down and wait.

Then one day he threw a man into my life, and told me to jump with both feet; a leap of faith. He asked me to stand, despite my fears, the opinions of others, and regardless of the rational thoughts that were racing through my mind.

The first time I saw a photo of Shawn, I knew there was something special about him. The light in his eyes drew me in. On our first date, it felt like we had been lifelong best friends. There was never a dull moment in our conversations. I told him my story, and he shared his with me. We knew a lot of the same people, but we'd never met before.

I knew when I met him for the very first time that Heavenly Father had sent me someone special. I felt peace in my decision to take a leap of faith and go out with him. Little did I know, as the weeks passed, I would be asked to "jump".

It's funny that in those moments when we think we have all the answers...the Lord asks us to be patient and wait. But in this instance—when it had been drilled into my mind so often that I knew nothing—He asked me to show Him that I could still have faith in His timing.

Shawn and I got engaged, and with all the opinions of the community pouring in, I began to panic. I worried about everyone judging my decision, and I struggled as people told me about the timing *they* thought I should be respecting.

One night, I called my mother. I didn't even say hello, but just went off on a rampage of questions: "What if he cheats on me, or what if he dies? What if I give him my whole heart and he breaks it? Mom, I know what I'm supposed to do, but I have no idea how I can do it. I keep getting calls from all sorts of people telling me what I'm supposed to do, and it is making me doubt the answers I know I've received for myself. What if...what if he cheats on me, and someone shoots him in the head?"

With her usual wisdom, Mom spoke the words I needed to hear that day..."Ashlee, what if everything happens that has already happened? You have been where most of us will never be. You have felt more pain at your young age than most people who walk the earth will ever see in all their years. You loved Emmett, and he broke your heart, but he didn't break *you*. You are capable of still living all the dreams you have ever had. Even if Shawn walks away and leaves you, you will be the same person you are now. You will still be standing."

I ended the conversation with my wise mother and called Shawn. "I need to marry you, and I want to marry you. We are supposed to do this. Let's just do it. Why sit around and plan, and have the world tell me all the reasons why we shouldn't get married? What do you say I call my bishop and we just get married this week?"

He laughed, thinking I was joking, then said, "You know what. As long as you and the kids, and my parents are there...that is all I care about."

So our mission to plan a wedding came to an end. I called my bishop on a Monday, and by Thursday afternoon we were standing in front of him saying our vows. Surrounded by our children, some of our siblings, my Aunt Diane and cousin Tiffanie, and our parents...we committed to each other and our family that we would give our marriage all that it deserved...for better or for worse.

My mother, who at the time lived some distance away, told me she wouldn't be able to make it to the wedding, but to my surprise, she showed up a few minutes before it started. She walked into my bathroom as I was putting on the last of my make-up, and I was so excited to have her there that day.

I felt calm and collected. I wasn't scared. I didn't doubt, and I didn't fear. I walked down the aisle on my father's arm, feeling completely confident about this new family unit Shawn and I were about to create.

It was a beautiful day, one I will never forget. It was simple. The twins begged me to wear my wedding dress from my marriage to Emmett—and Shawn said it didn't matter to him—so I did.

My friends Brittany and Lindsay couldn't stand the fact that I hadn't arranged for any flowers, so they did some flowers for us. They even snuck in and decorated the clubhouse. It was beautiful.

When it was time to exchange the rings, Teage and Jordyn were our ring-bearers. The sun was shining, and in fact, it was so hot that we were all sweating in that tiny room.

Shawn didn't take his eyes off of me. Tears rolled down my face as I thought of the years that had lead me to this moment. I had flashbacks of the last time I had worn that dress, but my heart made room for the new memories I was creating in it.

Just as with the first time I had worn that dress, my hopes for my future soared out of that hot room and on past the sun. I considered the six children who I now called mine. They were no different from the ones I had pictured on my bed on my sixteenth birthday. They were sweet, and kind, and respectful. They were beautiful, they were loving...and they were mine. I didn't have to wait for that dream to come true. This time around, I wasn't going to be a first-time newlywed...but a wife and mother— living a life that looked as if we had been building it for ten years.

Although Shawn and I had not walked down all of our roads together, we deserved each other. We had no idea of the hard work that lay before us to blend our two families and to clean up messes from the past, but quite frankly, on that perfect day, we didn't care. We were just happy to call that family ours.

We took a three-night honeymoon to a local hotel. Neither of us wanted to be too far away from the children since they had so many adjustments to make, as did we.

Our honeymoon was relaxing and wonderful, and it gave us the opportunity to get to know each other without any other cares. In fact, it was actually fun to pretend to be young newlyweds. In every restaurant we went, someone would inevitably ask us if we had just gotten married, because apparently, we were a bit dreamy-eyed!

I enjoyed those three days, but I also couldn't wait to get home...back to real life. I couldn't wait to have a husband to call my own, and I longed to snap out of the funk that had put me in a state of panic every time I cleaned, did laundry, or tried to prepare food. I was just certain that all my cares would be soothed, and all my triggers would be mended...now that I was a married woman again.

I felt certain that the healing Shawn would bring, which had been

promised to me, would now be complete. After all, we were a family...
that was all the healing I would need, right?

I wish that one 'I do' would have been the answer to all the pain Emmett's murder had planted inside of me. I think a part of me thought my
new marriage would fill all the holes inside of me, as they were filling the
holes in my household. My bed was no longer empty, my nights were no
longer lonely... but inside, there were still wounds gaping open and parts
of me still screaming. I had so many questions still left unanswered, I had
so many wrongs to forgive, and I still had mountains to climb to find the
peace that I still sought. But, I had no regrets about taking that leap of
getting married.

What if? Two little words that we, especially we women, can spend a
lifetime asking ourselves. We hallucinate. We map out scenarios. We try
to find answers to our recurring states of panic. We search for peace inside
ourselves because we fear going through what another person HAS lived.
What if he doesn't call back? What if I get in a car crash? What if this cancer is my final test in life? What if I get hit by a car? What if I never meet
Mr. Right? What if...the girl I am supposed to marry already married
the wrong guy? What if my child chokes on an apple? What if I give my
whole heart, and it gets destroyed?

So many 'what ifs!'... and there will always be something. There will
always be a reason to fear. Cars can crash, dogs can get sick, babies can
drown, cancer can spread, spouses can cheat, and people will die. But
'what if' we never jump because of all our fears?

What if every single 'what if' we fear all came true all in one night?
Where would we be? Who would be left? We will never know until we
jump. And when we jump, both feet must jump together. We cannot have
one foot in one world, and one in the other.

Jumping with both feet may hurt. There are always risks with jumping. And even if it doesn't hurt immediately, it may hurt later. It may cause
you years of new battles to fight in the future. But that doesn't mean you

didn't leap with faith in the first place.

What if? What if I never took another breath for fear I might get hurt? Life is too short to not live it fully because it may hurt. We will not grow if we do not feel the growing pains that are sent to refine us. We don't know what pains lie ahead, or which pains from the past have actually purified our souls ... but with the two soles we use to tread along our path in life ... we also have the power to jump. We can't be afraid to use our power to jump because of the risks—but we have to use that power wisely and choose to jump in the right direction.

A jump in the wrong direction can be fatal.

Emmett and I lost a lot of family and friends in the years that followed our marriage. Almost every year we found ourselves at a funeral of someone who was very close to us.

One hot summer Sunday while living in Washington for law school, we got a call that one of my best friends had committed suicide. Everything inside of me went weak. It broke Emmett to the core; he was very close to her and her husband. Emmett had summer school that he couldn't miss, but we got in the car and drove straight down to see her husband and the two beautiful children she had left behind.

She had been suffering from a severe post partum depression that eventually caused her to end her own life. Little did I know as I held her husband and we sobbed together that night, that Emmett would be joining his sweetheart in just a few short years.

After Emmett's death, I had a dream one night about Emmett and our friend. In the dream, they were talking to each other as if they weren't aware of the fact that I could hear them. They discussed their respective family members who were still living. She was saying how proud she was of her husband who was working so hard to raise their children and who was moving forward and finding love again. She also told Emmett how brave he was for helping me to find love again. She told him how happy she was that her husband and I were both finding ways to move forward from our tragedies.

Emmett began to cry and she put her arms around him. She whispered into his ear, "I wish I could do it all over again too...but *they* still can."

I woke up from that dream unable to fully understand what it all meant at first. It took me some time to process. She had taken her own life because of an illness that compelled her to take a leap in the wrong direction. She felt the weight of her pain that came as a result of losing control over her actions. Emmett had also taken a leap in the wrong direction. He had jumped over the edge of the cliff he had been scaling, and the decisions that followed his leap...ultimately got him killed.

My dear friend's message to me in that dream rings so true. She and Emmett were suffering from the pain of their past mistakes that ended their lives, and unfortunately, neither of them had the mortal 'do-overs' that are still possible for the living. In spite of their regrets, my friend and Emmett could see the value in their spouses' search for peace and continued progress in their mortal lives after they found themselves alone.

We have all had the occasion to approach the edge of a cliff. We know there is a great risk in getting too near, and yet...so many of us continue to tiptoe closer and closer. Some of us willingly choose to flirt with the edges in life. We seek cheap thrills, and purposefully find our way to uncharted waters. However, the way doesn't have to be life-threatening if we would just remember to stay as far away from the edge as possible.

My dear friend and Emmett have taught me so much. Although I loved them both with all my heart, my heart also aches for the years they are missing with their families. They have moved on past mortality, but their desires for us are no different than their desires for themselves. They have taught me the importance of putting one foot in front of the other and continuing to move forward. We must endure to move beyond our pain, and we must jump with both feet—not in the wrong direction— but into the good things of this world.

Even if all of your leaps so far have resulted in your falling on your face, you have to develop the faith that as you practice jumping with both feet in the right direction, one day, your feet will get a little lighter... and you will no longer fall. Some day, that same faith may require you to take a giant leap, and you will want to be certain it is in the right direction, and that both feet are equally committed. And even with that, there is no guarantee of a soft landing.

"What if I get hurt?" You will.

"What if I get rejected?" Yup... that too!

But 'what if' you never jump? It is only when you leap with faith that you will find your wings.

CHAPTER TEN

# *Triggers*

**BY DEFINITION** the word trigger is:

*Noun: a small device that releases a spring or catch and so
sets off a mechanism, especially in order to fire a gun.*
*Verb: to cause (an event or situation) to happen or exist.*

On March 11th, 2011 a trigger was pulled that sent my life into a
whirlwind. I had never thought much before about the power of a trigger. It is an important mechanism for a gun to function properly. The gun
cannot fire unless the trigger is pulled; a gun's power is useless without
that little mechanism.

After any traumatic event or major moment that has negatively impacted your life, you carry around memories of that event. Whether or not you
are aware of them, they stand ready to re-ignite a state of fear or panic.

For me, I have learned that the memories themselves also have triggers. Some of those triggers have been surprising and others, not at all.
For example, I had no idea that such a simple thing as a doorbell ringing
could send my body into a state of shock.

Each individual in my household has had a different experience with
his or her own personal triggers. For one, it has been a boy with a fake gun
in the front yard. For another, it has been something as simple as flowers
sent by a friend.

One night, I had to be in a building not far from the Walgreens where Emmett had died. I had always parked on the other side of the building, without realizing it, but this evening I decided to take a leap. I parked closer to the Walgreens and went inside, feeling very brave, as if I had finally overcome my personal battle.

When the night came to an end, I said goodbye and started out to my car. As I opened the door and exited the building, I stepped outside to a view of Walgreens with sirens and lights flashing everywhere. (There had been a car crash). My body went into a state of shock, and I felt as though I was standing and witnessing first-hand that dark night that had changed my life dramatically—just three years earlier. I ran back inside, shaking and crying. Luckily, I was greeted by familiar faces who didn't even have to ask any questions about my state of panic. With time, they calmed me down and talked me through my attack.

I had no idea those emotions were still so easily accessible inside of me. I've been through many similar situations in the last three years, but somehow I thought I was over the extreme reactions. As I lay in my bed that night, I thought about all the triggers that have stopped me in my tracks during the past three years. It all started with the trigger of that gun being pulled... and now I am still being paralyzed by the triggers in my mind.

A trigger changed my life back then, and triggers continue to disrupt my life when I least expect them. And unfortunately, it seems like there is no way to prepare for them. That night I was next to the Walgreens, I had no idea that a trigger would be pulled for me. It was just an average night, but walking into that one scenario sent me spiraling back in time.

For a long time, going into grocery stores and preparing meals were triggers for me. I have spent many moments in my pantry hyperventilating... completely stuck, because flashes of the night Emmett died would sink down deep inside of me. I would picture myself preparing all of his favorite food that night and just waiting for him to come home.

Every time a siren whirls by my house, I freeze. So many triggers: fireworks, babies crying, my security system going off, lights flashing on the ceiling when a car drives by, knocks at the front door, people whispering when I walk into a room, a song on the radio, smells, a lockdown at the kids' school on Valentine's Day—and no way to be let inside to make sure my babies are safe. For a long time, not a day would go by without a trigger firing inside of me.

One of the greatest triggers I have faced has been at weddings. Not long after Shawn and I got married, my little sister Ali and Will were sealed in the temple. Walking into the sealing room, my mind flooded with memories of the past. I sobbed and sobbed through the entire ceremony. The pain in my heart was a trigger to the pain that Emmett was not only gone—but the eternal marriage he had committed to live with me... felt like a lie.

A few months later, my little sister Abbey and Alex decided to get married. The entire drive to Utah I tried to calm my mind and focus on my wonderful children and husband. By the time the morning of the sealing came I felt totally prepared—to focus on the beauty Abbey and Alex

Little sisters Abbey and Ali and Mom

were being blessed with. I kissed Shawn and the kids and went into the temple. I felt strong, and was so excited for my little sister. I found the rest of my family and we all walked into the sealing room. Trigger. The tears began to fall and I sobbed the entire ceremony.

It was hard to understand why something so exciting and beautiful could bring to my remembrance so much pain and heart ache. I was so proud of them and so happy to be apart of their day, but that didn't stop my trigger of pain from igniting. I just never knew when, or how, a trigger was going to fire.

A while back at church, we were having a lesson about when Joseph Smith was killed in Carthage Jail. Someone was reading in our manual about the men who came and shots were fired. It was like I actually heard the gun go off... my heart started racing and every rational thought was erased from my mind. I grabbed my purse and ran into the bathroom. I sobbed and shook in the bathroom stall for the rest of the hour, unsure of how to get rid of my panic. Nothing was wrong, but there was no way to logically talk my body out of the state of shock it had gone into.

I have no idea why our bodies have such a drive to bring back to our minds the fears of our past, but they do. These triggers are like mechanisms in our lives that set off fear or a remembrance of pain.

Our first Fourth of July after the death was filled with triggers—like the flame that would ignite the fireworks, each pop brought us back to the sound of the gun. I remember holding Teage in his bed as he sobbed about the "guns" that were going off outside his window. I remember the twins running down to my room in the middle of the night hardly able to breathe.

I had no idea that triggers could ignite fear—but when those fires would start, they always brought us back to that gun.

A few days after Shawn and I were married, we were sitting in our giant bathtub. We were talking about the kids and the events of the day. I was trying hard to relax and enjoy the quiet hours in our home. All of the sudden, an ambulance turned on its siren nearby.

Another trigger. I had not fully prepared Shawn for these moments—because I truly believed they would disappear with his presence. He had no idea of what to do to help me. My panic attack lasted a few minutes, and the whole time, Shawn just held me. I didn't have to say a word. He just let me cry.

About a week after that, Shawn surprised me by bringing home a movie he had been told was amazing. He brought home dinner as well, and we had a quiet date night while the kids were all asleep in their beds.

As the movie began, one of the first scenes was of a murder. A trigger fired again, spiraling me back to the night of the trauma. It was getting embarrassing, and I began to feel sorry for this poor man who had married me.

That night, after my heart finally stopped racing and we lay in bed, I turned over to him and said, "I gave you a chance. I warned you I was broken...you should have run away when we were sitting at the waterfall, and never looked back."

He reassured me, calming my fears as he kissed my forehead, and whispered, "NO, I am right where I belong."

A few weeks later, I decided to surprise Shawn at work. I grabbed him one of our favorite strawberry lemonades from McDonalds and headed to his work. His car wasn't in the parking lot. Another trigger fired.

I pulled into a stall and began to sob. He wasn't at work? Then where could he be? My thoughts went to the worst-case scenario, which for me was: he's either cheating on me, or he's dead in a parking lot somewhere.

I grabbed my phone and dialed his number. He didn't answer right away, which only helped confirm my worst fears. Finally, once he did answer, with all of the anxiety built up in my heart, I let him have it. "Where are you? Why aren't you at work! You said you were going to work...and I finally get brave enough to come and visit you...and you know how hard this stuff is for me, that you even have to work with other women... and I am here, and you aren't even where you said you would be. You told me you were going to work. So where are you? Am I not enough for you, or what? Can't you even call to tell me you aren't going to be at work, so I don't have to worry? Do you not want to be married to me anymore? Is there another woman?"

Every possible insecurity I suffered from spewed out of me in one breath. I didn't even wait to hear where he was, or what he was doing. As the words were leaving my mouth I was embarrassed for myself, and yet, there was almost no other alternative to handle the fear boiling inside of me.

This wouldn't be the first time Shawn had to pay for my having one of my triggers go off; and in that particular moment, he just listened and reassured me rather then getting defensive. He calmly told me about the errand he had run, and reassured me that he loved me.

My heart calmed down after hearing his kind words. I apologized for taking out on him all the pain from my past, and I ended the call. My head fell into my hands, and I sobbed hysterically. What was wrong with me? Shawn had never done anything to lose my trust, and yet here I was treating him like he was the bad guy in my life.

The poor man! Anytime Shawn did anything that Emmett used to do (AKA...being a man) it set off a trigger of fear inside of me. If he came home with an energy drink, like Emmett used to drink, my heart would start racing as if he had come to tell me he had found another woman. If he took Nyquil so he could sleep when he was sick—which was the reason Emmett had given me for running to Walgreens that fateful night— my head would pound with memories of the past. None of the triggers ever made sense to me, or to Shawn, but they were so real.

One summer day, Shawn asked the kids and me to come down to a car show he was participating in. When it was over, I told Shawn we would meet him back at home, since we had driven separate cars. I assumed he would beat us home because I had to spend extra time loading kids in the car.

A few miles from our house, the traffic had come to a stop, and I tried hard to see what the hold-up was. As I veered my car over to the side, to look past the line of cars waiting in front of us, I could see that there had been an accident and that one of the cars involved was a black SUV that looked just like Shawn's.

I called his phone. No answer. I called again. Nothing.

This time the trigger that went off inside of me was not just pulled, it was blown! I threw the car into park, knowing that my panic attack was going to leave me light-headed. I could see ambulances creeping up in my review mirror, and I could hear sirens coming from all around us.

My heart sank, trying to brace for the truth of what I thought was happening—Shawn had been in that wreck. He had left a few minutes before us, and now this was going to be my next hill to climb. I began sobbing; the kids became concerned about what on earth was making me freak out.

Bailey could tell I was losing it and suggested that we say a prayer. Her tender voice began to quiver as she spoke to God. She prayed that mommy would be able to calm down and get us home safely. She prayed that Shawn had not been in that accident in front of us, and she asked that we would all be blessed with a feeling of peace.

As her prayer ended, I knew we had to get home. I did a U-turn and went down the nearest road I could find to get us home, all the while praying that I would be able to breathe and get our car home safely.

We pulled into our driveway, but no Shawn! I called his phone again. No answer. I called his parents who had been at the car show with us to see if he might still be there, but they said they hadn't seen him since we had all left.

Worst case scenario. Was I living it again? The kids ran inside, and I stayed in the car. I continued to pray, this time out loud. "Please, let him be safe. Please bring him home to us. I am so scared." I begged and pleaded in the quiet of my car, hoping with all of my heart that Shawn had not been in that wrecked SUV I had just seen.

I tried his phone again. No answer.

I said one last prayer before I got out of the car. "You know I may seem strong... it may look to some people as if I have myself all put back together, but I am so broken. With all my heart, I pray that Shawn is okay today, but Father... if he isn't, please help me to be strong again. Please help me to stand... I feel like I am falling. Please help me to know what to do."

As I opened my car door, Shawn pulled up.

This time, I wasn't mad. I was just plain relieved that he was okay. As he got out of the car, I ran over to him and jumped into his arms, "I am so glad you are okay. I am so happy you are home."

Progress. This time, my trigger had been pulled... but I had won the battle. I didn't have to yell and scream just because I was scared. Even though I was upset, Shawn hadn't done anything wrong. It didn't matter where he had been, or why he hadn't answered his phone... I was just glad he was home. (It turned out he had stopped for gas, and his phone was in his bag in the back seat.)

Triggers. They are not just mechanisms on guns; they are mechanisms we each have inside of us that bring forth fear and anger. We cannot control when they are fired— but I have learned that I can control what I do with the emotions that follow.

I have seen others' triggers go off when they are cut off in traffic. I have read stories about shaken babies who have died because of their parents' desperation to have them stop crying. We have all seen fights happen over something that later seems insignificant.

When triggers fire, the aftermath can be devastating. A gun may fire a bullet when a trigger is pulled; but what triggered the man who fired the gun?

We have to learn to control our fears and our pain when our own personal triggers ignite. Acting on them never brings peace, and carrying out their plan never brings happiness.

There have been more triggers in my life since that gun's trigger was pulled, but I have found that I can determine who I am in spite of their power.

When those situations arise, and the dark cloud envelops your entire being... pray for the power that can help you win. We do not have to fall victim to the triggers in our lives. Rob's gun had a trigger. It was pulled in anger. Emmett fell victim to its power. I fell victim to that trigger in my life, but I will not fall victim to its power in my heart.

The flames that have ignited in me, have only been put out by the grace of God. I chose to stand up to the triggers that have tried to destroy me. I will not be a victim, but a survivor of the powerful triggers that have brought me to my knees.

Whatever dark triggers have been pulled in your life... it is not your fault. Whatever triggers have ignited in your heart... you are not broken. We may seem like victims to the world, but each time we stand, despite our pain... we are survivors of all the triggers that have tried to make us fall.

CHAPTER ELEVEN

# *Still Here*

**A FEW WEEKS AFTER WE GOT MARRIED** I was reading Shawn's patriarchal blessing. I came to a line that said, "Your mission on earth will be to help heal your family." The same exact words I had felt in the temple before we met were also a promise he had read hundreds of times about himself. It seemed so simple that God would have an antidote for our family's past. He had given Shawn a gift to receive answers about how to help us heal. I got chills all over my body as I reread that line over and over. I felt reassured and lifted by that promise my Heavenly Father had sent to me—and had another confirmation that it would come true.

A few days later, we were running some errands as a family. On the way home, we drove past a Walgreens. One of the girls asked if that was where their dad was killed. I got a pit in my stomach, and considered pretending I didn't hear her. "Nope," I replied, "that is not the Walgreens. That is just a store... see all the people going in and out?"

I had heard these questions while driving alone in the car with the kids, but with Shawn by my side, I had a whole new apprehension about how I should answer them. I was nervous that he would tire of their panic-stricken questions and eventually wouldn't be able to take it anymore.

And then came the question that always inevitably followed, "Well, Mom, then when can we go to the one where Daddy died?" I blew her off and finally reached the point where I pretended I didn't hear what was being asked. There was no way I was going to entertain that idea.

The questions seemed to disappear as that Walgreens faded from our view. I settled in my seat, grateful that no one pushed me further to answer the request.

However, all of a sudden, another Walgreens glared at us through the car windows and a similar conversation from a different child began. Shawn leaned over to me and calmly said, "I know you don't ever want to go to THE Walgreens, but maybe we should stop and show the kids which one it is so they can have their questions answered. Maybe it will help them relax and not ask you about it every time we pass one of their stores."

Now the pit in my stomach seemed to be eating my insides, and I freaked out. "NO... Shawn, we can't go there... we... that is so not happening... EVER. Please just be quiet about it, I can't... we aren't... that is... NO... I don't want to ever go there. That is a stupid idea, and we will not be doing it." I folded my arms in anger and turned my body toward the window, so he wouldn't be able to see my face.

In his patient wisdom, Shawn grabbed my hand and said, "I really feel that it might help the kids find some peace from their fear of all Walgreens... Hey it might even be good for *you* to see that it is just a store... like we keep telling them."

Tears started to fall down my cheeks as I pictured stepping foot onto the ground where Emmett's body had fallen. But, I knew Shawn was right, and in that moment, I almost hated him for it. I stared out the window as we drove a few more blocks, my eyes brimming with fear-filled tears. Instead of my plan to avoid and pretend that THE Walgreens didn't exist... now Shawn's idea was to take all of the kids there? It seemed preposterous to my poor heart, and I couldn't even wrap my head around entertaining the very idea.

I envisioned the Walgreens that now haunted my dreams. I could almost see the yellow tape surrounding the scene of the crime. I pictured Emmett's and Rob's trucks and Kandi's car parked nearby. I pictured the gun; I could almost hear the sound of it blasting through the air. In slow motion, I pictured the bullets piercing Emmett's flesh; I could hear Kandi screaming. I could see Emmett's body lying on the ground covered in blood. I could hear the sirens and see the people rushing everywhere, trying to piece together all of the facts. I pictured the roadblocks with cop cars lining the streets. I could almost hear the detectives talking about their preparations to come over to my house to tell me that my husband was dead. I could imagine the fear that stirred inside them as they left Emmett's lifeless body to come and find me—wondering how to break the news to me.

I thought about the urgent knocking on my door and carrying my heavy body towards it. I pictured opening it to see three strangers who held inside of them all the answers to my past questions...and the truth about my future. I could almost hear them again, describing in bits and pieces the events that had transpired at THE parking lot.

All the details of the power that Walgreens had over me that night were replayed on the movie projector in my mind. It was as if someone had flipped the switch that turned it on, and once it began, there didn't seem to be any way to turn it back off. Like a flame held to a firework, the thought of that store brought an explosion of every emotion I had felt on that dark night.

The thought of going to Walgreens on purpose was *so* scary. How could that help me heal, when just the thought of it brought me so much pain? I had vowed I would never go there; I had no desire to even entertain the thought of going there as long as I lived.

I wiped away a few more tears, which were now being shed along with my pride. How could I allow myself to let it go? I was so scared that Shawn's idea was exactly what I needed. As much as I was fighting it, I knew he was right. I looked over at my new husband and as the tears continued to fall down my cheeks, I humbly made a decision. "You are right, Shawn. WE have to go. I am so scared, and I don't want to do this... but they deserve to see where their dad died...don't they? Since he died,

I have told them that we will never be going there, and there is no reason they should even think about that place...but we do. It's all we think
about some days, like it's controlling every decision I make. It isn't going
to go away, is it?"

He grabbed my hand again. "Jordyn and I will wait in the car. You guys
can get out and take as much time as you need. We will be right here."

Within a few minutes we were parked in the Walgreens parking lot. I
wasn't sure exactly where Emmett's body had fallen, but I had been given
enough facts to know which side of the building was the site of those grim
events.

Shawn parked the car. My heart wanted to fight its way out of my body.
I could not breathe. I felt as if I had stepped back in time to the night
the detectives sat with me on my couch, and I had a one-million-pound
weight sitting on my chest. "What if Rob WAS still there?" The question
that had been asked a million times by my children now danced around
inside of me. "What if SHE was still there?" My eyes darted around the
parking lot to scan it for any sign of her.

My foot hit the pavement and soon I found myself opening the doors
on each side of the car so the kids could hop out. Ty was asleep so I left
him in his car seat; and Kaleeya said she didn't want to go. One by one,
Teage, Bostyn, and Bailey piled out of the car. We held hands and crossed
the parking lot. There were a few cars, but for the most part, the lot was
pretty empty.

Emmett's truck was not there, as I had pictured it in my mind. There
was no yellow tape to barricade us from the scene of the murder. I couldn't
see "Kandi's" license plate parked in any of the stalls. It was just a big,
empty parking lot. To the normal person...no one would ever suspect
that someone's world had been shattered on that very pavement.

The kids started picking up papers and rummaging through anything
they found on the ground. They were speaking a thousand words per
minute. They said things like: "Look, here is a bag...maybe it got shot

out of his hands. Look here is a piece of paper, maybe he left us a note on it. Put all this stuff in your pockets … what if it was his?"

They looked all around the concrete for signs of his blood; they circled around any stain on the ground they could find, and talked about it belonging to him. They shuffled together around the building looking for any clues Emmett might have left for them.

Tears fell down my face as I watched my little babies searching for a sign. They didn't cry, or get mad … they weren't even looking for Rob … they were just looking for hope. They were praying that they could find something of their father's to hold on to.

I finally started to wonder about exactly what they were thinking, and I gathered them close to me. "Hey guys. What is it we're looking for?"

Teage yelled out, "MOM … maybe he is still here?"

I fell to my knees. By this time we were at the back of the store, far from the location where their dad had died. They all moved in closer and I scooped them around me with my arms. "Sweethearts, Dad is not here. He is not going to be here. This is where he died, but we aren't going to find him no matter how many times we walk around this building. I am so proud of you guys for being brave enough to come here today. Daddy isn't going to be here, but I bet you his spirit is here with us right now watching us miss him so much."

Each of them had tears in their eyes. We found our way to the backside of the building and sat on the ground with our backs against it. The twins began to whisper, "Daddy, this is where you died … and we have wanted to come here so we can find you … but you aren't here Daddy." Teage chimed in, "Dad … I don't know if you can hear me … but I found your bag … and I will keep it safe for you. Your bag is safe now Dad, there are no bad guys here anymore. Nobody has a gun. I think it is just a store now."

We each took turns talking about what we missed and loved about Emmett—good memories from the past. They talked about Shawn and Jordyn and the new hope we had been finding as a family. They whispered messages to their dad of the love they had for him, and the love they were finding since his death.

They continued sharing their thoughts with him for a few more minutes: "Daddy, we miss you…Why did you have to leave us?…I am sorry you got shot here, Daddy…We wish we could talk to you and see your face…We love you Daddy."

On the backside of the Walgreens—where their dad was murdered—I sat and cried with my babies. We did not fear as we searched for hope. All the anger that still raged inside of me seemed to leave for a brief moment as I listened to the loving words my children whispered to their dad. We didn't talk about Rob's or Emmett's mistakes…we cried for the pain that our fear of that store had brought us.

A part of me healed that day. Walgreens WAS just a store. Kandi and Rob weren't there. There were no bad guys with guns waiting for me. There was no yellow tape mapping out where the crime had taken place. All the questions that had stirred up my home were answered. For the first time my children's question, "What if he is still there?" had an answer. Rob wasn't still there, Kandi wasn't still there, and neither was Emmett.

That parking lot didn't hold on to the fear of its past; it just carried on as if no one had ever tragically died there. If that parking lot could let go of all it had seen, I hoped that one day we could let go of the painful story it had written inside our hearts.

My children truly thought Emmett was going to be waiting for them. Like in a video game where the hero resuscitates after dying, I think they thought their dad would just pop up again. They had hoped that he would be lying there, and that their love would give him the energy he needed to breathe again. They wished that the genie from Aladdin would come and grant them a wish to undo their past.

No miracles happened that day to bring anyone back to life or to erase the past, but the miracle of healing a dark pain began its journey. That day, I realized that my little angels were not only going to be brave enough and capable enough of finding true healing from our tragedy...but that they were also going to pave the way for me to do the same.

Just like their box of hope to send to "The people of Japan," they still searched for hope in this world. Their faith was powerful and their encouragement for me to be brave...was empowering.

That night as I tucked my three older children into bed, I asked each of them the same question: "How did you feel when we were at Walgreens tonight?" Bailey said, "Sad. I miss Daddy so much." Bostyn said, "Sad and happy. Happy to know that Walgreens is just a store, and there are no bad guys there, because every time we pass one I feel scared." Teage said, "Happy. I always wanted to see what it looked like. I felt scared not knowing what it was. I am so happy Dad left his grocery bag there so I could find it."

Fear of the unknown can make us feel scared. Sadness can build up into anger. When we find a way to let out our emotions, fears, and thoughts, it can make us feel capable of feeling happiness again. My children's constant anxiety about that store turned into relief just by doing the one thing I had been holding them back from doing all this time. I felt a release of fear in myself as well, and for the first time since Emmett died, the pain in my chest was a little lighter that night.

Sometimes life is going to feel like you are trying to wade through a giant puddle while it is still raining ...without any hope there will be an end. Just keep walking, eventually the rain may stop falling and you will find that those puddles were all just part of your journey.

Whether we are making all the right decisions, or all the wrong ones... we will struggle. Satan had a plan in the pre-existence before the earth was created. In his plan, no matter what we did on earth, we would walk away from life with a free pass. The plan Satan proposed to our Heavenly Father before we came to earth was a plan of ease. There would be no struggle or pain, but in his plan we were not allowed to choose for ourselves. His plan would leave us to follow directions, without experiencing the highs or lows of this mortal life … and without experiencing life's joys. All of us would end up in the same spot, with no deviation as to how we got there.

In the plan we all chose—which Jesus Christ said He would fulfill for Heavenly Father—we get to choose what roads we travel. We get to choose the direction in which we put one foot in front of the other. We knew that we would be tested. We knew that others' agency would affect us. We understood that we were sent here to overcome obstacles and grow from them. We were aware that sometimes we would have to do big things that were hard and scary … but we still begged to come to earth and carry out that plan. We chose it because we knew that we could overcome the hard times to find the joy.

In Satan's plan, there would have been no hard times, but without darkness … it is hard to appreciate the light. True joy comes only after we have overcome our trials or been set free from the pains that have pushed us to find a better way.

We can walk in paths that always feel safe, or we can be directed to those that challenge us or help us grow … our own personal puddles.

In Satan's plan, we would never fall, but we would also never fly. We would have been in a state of "BLAH," never falling beneath an acceptable marker, but also never reaching our full potential. We chose a different plan because we all saw the potential that we had within ourselves to one day fly, and we knew it would only be possible through Jesus Christ's plan.

It is because we experience pain that we are motivated to push out of it. Fear and pain encourage us to ask ourselves the difficult questions like "What if he is still here?" I lived with that question constantly, and it hindered my actions. I worried that Rob was 'still here' and had a similar fate for me. I worried that Kandi would be around any given corner on any given day. My children's pain had caused them to ask the same question, but for them, it was about their father. "What if he is still here?" They had spent all that time wondering if he was still at Walgreens, and I had held them back from finding their answers.

It wasn't until we set foot in that parking lot that we truly learned that no one was there. Rob wasn't there waiting to kill me. Kandi wasn't there to take anything more from me, and Emmett wasn't still there, waiting for us to come and wish him back to life.

Shawn was right. We had to go there that day. We needed to release the fear, let go of the pain, and answer the questions inside each one of us. His encouragement for me to step outside of my comfort zone is what brought healing to me in a way I would have never been able to do on my own.

Sometimes the growth part of life really hurts. Getting out of that car took every ounce of energy I had...but walking around and sitting with my babies in the back of that building reminded me that even through pain...there is peace to be found.

Some days we might find ourselves just crying on our closet floors all alone, but sometimes we have to face the fears that hold us back. Don't fight against the things that can help you let go of your anger, your fear, and your pain. For us, Walgreens was a building we held accountable for our pain ... because Emmett and Rob were not around to be held accountable. We had to visit that building to let go of our fears.

If there is a 'building' that needs to be visited in your life, don't let it stand there waiting all alone. Let it be accountable for the pain it has caused, so you can let it go. If you spend your years hiding from it, or pretending it isn't real...you are not punishing anyone but yourself.

The Walgreens parking lot didn't care who I was, or what heartache I had faced because of it. It had no idea that I would drive a few extra miles, just to avoid driving by it. That parking lot had no idea of the number of times we said its name in our home, and it couldn't have cared less that just the thought of it sent chills down my spine. It just carried on, continuing to do the job it had always done. It was just a parking lot after all. It wasn't powerful or grand. It WAS just a store.

"What if he is still here?" can become a question that causes fear for anyone who has suffered pain … or it can be a question that brings relief if we ask it as we turn to our Savior and realize that He *has* been there all along. He *is* still there. During the highs and lows of life we knew would come, He holds our hands and carries us through. He sits in the Walgreens parking lot with us as we fight the fears and the questions that try to pull us down. He sheds a tear as we battle in our minds the decisions we face each day. He didn't say it would be easy, He only said it would be worth the fight.

We need to learn to fight only those battles that can truly bring about change. We only get this one life. If we spend it focused on questions about the past, without doing whatever it takes to answer them, we will not be able to move forward into the future.

We all have our own 'Walgreens' to overcome. We each have our own questions to which we need to find the answers. Stop fighting those questions and face them head on. When it is time to step up to the plate … hit a homerun. As you watch that ball fly over the bases, you may have to squint because of the sun to see it soar, but if you look hard enough, you *will* see it. When you are in the right place at the right time, and you let go of the pride that tries to prevent you from being there … that is when little miracles take place.

It is easy for others to say to someone suffering from pain: "Let it go," but for the one suffering … it is much easier said than done. In my case, the letting go has come through taking baby steps. But it has been in each baby step that I have seen the little miracles that have given me the hope to let it go.

What if He is still here? He is. You may not see Him from where you are standing … sometimes we never do until we fall. If you have lost sight of the truth because of the angle at which you are trying to see it, maybe it is time to change your position. He has been there all along, and … He is still here.

# CHAPTER TWELVE

## *Walk Away*

**KANDI HALL...I HAD MET HER MANY TIMES.** She had held my
baby and apparently been on dates with my son. She had willingly and
with perfect knowledge defiled my family. She had slept with my husband.
My anger toward her was boiling. There wasn't a day that went by that
I didn't stew about what I would say to her if given the chance. Every
time I was driving in the car, I would internally rehearse the conversation
I would have with her. I knew our paths would cross eventually. It was
inevitable. We lived in a fairly small town, and our houses were only a
few miles apart. I had many friends tell me they saw her here or there,
or that they were in line behind her at the grocery store. It *was* going to
happen...and I was going to be prepared.

Well, that day inevitably came. I craved it like a lion craves its prey. I
dreaded it—and yet I needed it to be. I felt it coming every day for a week.
Everywhere I went, I could feel her getting closer. I searched stores for her
and checked the driver of every car I passed.

Tiffanie called that week and said she was on her way to our house,
and that Shawn and I needed to make hotel reservations so she could
come and spend time with the kids. In other words, she was kind enough
to realize that we needed some newlywed alone time.

It was fun having a weekend to get away and not think about parenting, or any of the daily tasks that occupied so much of our time together...or the trial. It was like a two-day-long date, which made up for the

months we had hardly been alone for a second.

While on our getaway, Shawn and I were out for lunch, watching the big Boise State football game at THE RAM. We hadn't been there long and hadn't even gotten our food yet. I was looking around for a bathroom, and as I turned to look in the other direction…there *she* was. She was walking into the restaurant with a friend. She looked exactly the same as she did the last time I had seen her at Emmett's office, and she was smiling as if nothing in her life had ever gone wrong.

I flipped around and almost screamed at Shawn, "She's here!" He looked over his shoulder and let out a few swear words. Both of us huddled down in our chair in shock. I started shaking and hyperventilating. My whole body went cold and limp. I couldn't breathe. Once again, it felt just like the detectives were sitting on my leather couch telling me the whole story of my husband's murder. Her, him…the affair. My chest stopped working and my heart tried to stop beating.

Shawn rubbed my back as my panic attack took over. I was so lightheaded, I thought I was going to pass out. How was this real? As much as I had craved the chance to give her a piece of my mind, how was I going to spew it out if I couldn't even breathe?

Shawn put his arm around my shoulder and whispered into my ear. Over and over again he said, "It is going to be okay, Ash. Breathe…everything is okay. I am right here. I promise I will protect you. Breathe. Please take a breath. Be calm, Ashlee. I am right here. You are okay. Nothing is going to happen to you. Breathe."

With the help of Shawn's words, I calmed down enough to take a full breath. I leaned into him and said, "Shawn, I have been waiting for this. I will be right back." I got up to go confront her and Shawn grabbed my arm. "Ash…this isn't the time. Your anger at Kandi is not going to change anything, and your going over there in this restaurant is NOT going to end well. Please, let's just leave and forget that we even saw her."

I looked him in the eyes, my body still shaking. "Shawn," I replied, "I have been waiting for this opportunity every single day. I have rehearsed in my mind exactly what I'd say. I have been given this chance, and I am not about to let it pass. She *has* to hear what she has put me through. She needs to hear about the pain my children have endured. She needs to know exactly what I think about her, and about what her selfishness has done to my family. She just got seated across from us in this restaurant, and I'm going to take that as a sign that she needs to hear about all the emotions and pain in my heart. I am not leaving here until every word of it is said today."

His eyes didn't leave mine. "Ashlee. I love you. I can't imagine what you are going through, but I don't think you should do this. However, I am here for you and I support you."

I was still trembling, uncertain about what I should do. "Shawn, I am going to go into the bathroom, but I promise you, I'm coming back out and I'm going to let her have it. She deserves this, and I deserve to give it to her."

I went into the bathroom without her having seen me. I ran into the stall, hoping to let my tears out so I wouldn't break down in front of Kandi. But no tears came. All I felt was anger towards her. In that moment—I couldn't even think of the gun, or my husband's role in his own death. I prayed for the words to say, the words that had been storming around in my mind since the day of the murder. As if she was the only one who had screwed up, I whispered out loud the pleas of my heart. "Heavenly Father, I know that I need to forgive this woman who has wronged me, and yet... my entire body is shaking because of all the hate I feel for her. Because of her, Emmett stepped out on me. Because of her, Father, I was made a widow. Because of her, I have had many sleepless nights, sometimes because of the taps on my shoulder from my children paralyzed by their own fears. Because of this woman, I have felt immeasurable pain and heartache; and because of her... Emmett got shot. And today she is here before me, and she needs to be held accountable for all the pain I hold in my heart. This is my chance. This is a gift I've been given to let her know of all the wrongs she has done to my family and me. Please give me the words to say and the power to address everything she needs to hear. Please let me have this chance to put her in her place. I need this moment to help me heal. I have craved it every day. She needs to hear the words that have built mountains inside of my heart. Please let me have this moment today."

In the silence of my bathroom stall, I didn't receive the peace I thought would come about my proposed plan of action. The only feeling that came to my heart was, "Ashlee BE STILL. She didn't care then, and anything you say now won't change a thing. She will not be affected by your pain."

I almost stomped my foot in rebellion. "No…please. I need this! I need to scream and slam things on the table. I need to tell everyone in this restaurant of the heartache she has caused my family. Please. I am going to go out there, and I need to let this out, so I can let it go."

Nothing. Silence.

I had made up my mind, and regardless of the impressions I'd received…I knew I would regret it if I just walked away from her.

So, I marched myself out of the stall. I was not going to let this chance pass me by. This woman had to hear from me about the mess she had made, and I wasn't about to spare anyone's feelings, including Shawn's.

I walked over to her table and our eyes locked. Her friends began to laugh. Kandi had a look of fear on her face, but there was also a defiant look of "you can't hurt me!" She didn't say a word. We just continued to stare at each other.

Chills covered me; Shawn said he could see my heart beating in every vein of my body. I have never felt so much fear, sadness, anger, hatred, and pure disgust in my entire life as I felt as I stared at the woman who had not only slept with my husband, but whose husband had shot bullets into the head and heart of my children's father.

Just staring. A minute went by. Shaking, staring. Just as I felt in the bathroom, I realized that this woman didn't care about me. I felt hopeless as I stared into her eyes and saw nothing in return. Still staring...waiting for the words I thought she might say; hoping to release all the pain I held...waiting for her words.

Nothing. Silence.

I threw my hands up in the air, and without a word I turned back toward my table. Shawn—patiently waiting and hoping that I would finally take a breath—had our food all boxed up and ready to go. He grabbed the bags and motioned for me to follow him. I did not take my eyes off of Kandi the entire way out of the restaurant. I walked away with all those words I had scripted out in my mind still stored in my heart.

Forgiveness was walking away.

All the words in the world weren't going to change the past. My forcing her to see my pain was not going to release it from inside of me. I was just going to add one more thing to the list of things I still had to overcome. The last thing I needed was to add something I needed to repent of to my list.

Regret. I knew I had done the right thing, but where were all those words supposed to go? For the next two hours, Shawn drove us around as I screamed out everything I had wanted to say at the top of my lungs. Everything that woman deserved to hear...but which wasn't worth my spouting off in hatred.

Forgiveness for me was walking away. Forgiveness wasn't going to come to me by making a scene in a restaurant full of people. And though in that moment, it is what I wanted to do almost more than anything, I would have regretted it.

Forgiveness doesn't come to our hearts through angry words, but it would start to come to me as my Heavenly Father blessed my heart with peace for doing the right thing in that moment when I wanted to carry out my own will. It came through trusting that God had the power to heal my soul. It wasn't Kandi's words that would help me find peace; it wasn't the screaming and yelling I craved to do that would help me let it go. God had the gift to bless me with power from the Heavens in a vulnerable moment when I felt like crumbling and screaming and making sure that woman knew what was in my heart.

I grew a little taller that day, knowing that *I* had the power…not her. She would no longer control my thoughts. I was going to live with a purpose…and that was no longer going to be spent searching the town for her. The power I had been giving her had only brought me more heartache. She didn't own any part of me. That power was going to be for me. That energy was going to be used for good.

Being able to forgive doesn't come just from hearing the words "I'm sorry." Kandi Hall will probably never say those words to me. It is not through *her* actions that I can forgive her for the pain she has caused in my life. Being able to forgive is a gift from God that we can only receive from *Him*. As we seek to follow His counsel and rely on His timing, we can feel peace no matter how or by whom we have been wronged. Forgiving is a process and not something we check off a list. We will find a need for its power over and over again. It is not a magic pill or a one-time event. But each time we do it in our Heavenly Father's timing, we will gain a testimony of its power and feel its healing in every aspect of our lives.

Sometimes forgiving is confronting our fears at the Walgreens parking lot; then other times, it is walking away from something we want more than anything else in the world.

I never knew how much strength I really had inside of me until that moment I walked away. I saw myself as a warrior laying down my weapons of war. I have never lacked knowing exactly what to say when confronted or put on the spot. My weakness has always been knowing when the heck to shut my mouth.

Warriors don't always fight battles with guns and bombs, or even harsh words. Each one of us has a warrior inside of us. We put on our armor as we leave our homes every day. We know that we may be confronted with a temptation. For some of us, that temptation may be as simple as spouting off our mouths anytime we have an opinion. For others, the temptation might be to remain the shy girl in the corner who never makes a friend, and never sticks up for herself. Some of us are tempted to bully others and put people down; others are tempted to laugh when someone else is the brunt of a joke.

We have all been in these situations. Sometimes we are the top dog, and other times we are the one being shoved in the locker. Wherever you find yourself today, you are not alone. You have mountains to climb in your pain, but also waters to tread in your river of learning to forgive. We all do.

If you are barely keeping your head above water, and waiting for the other person to throw you a life raft…stop. There is a life raft already keeping you afloat. You do not need anyone else to help you find peace. Jesus Christ's atonement is as real for the sinner as it is for the abused. It is our life raft. Whether or not the person who has wronged you ever comes to you with an open heart to ask for forgiveness, you CAN let it go. You do not need their life raft to keep your head above water, and you do not need their "I am sorry" to heal your heart.

In the New Testament (John 8) we read the story about the woman taken in adultery who is brought before Jesus by the scribes and Pharisees. The Savior says to them, "He that is without sin among you, let him first cast a stone at her." Jesus doesn't look up, but continues drawing in the sand. As the accusers all depart, the woman is left alone on the ground waiting for Jesus to condemn her. He finally turns to her and says, "Where are those thine accusers? Hath no man condemned thee?" The woman looks to him and replies, "No man, Lord." Then Jesus simply says to her, "Go…and sin no more."

We are all sinners waiting for Christ to forgive us for our sins so we can let go of them and become better people. And yet, we have also at times been among the accusers, waiting for permission to cast the first stone, unable to forgive those who have wronged *us*. However, many of us are waiting for someone to come and show us how to let go of our fear, and to trust, love and forgive the sinner. In this parable, Christ didn't say go and harbor all of your pain and never forget that you messed up. Furthermore, He didn't send off the accusers with the idea that they should throw stones at this woman every time they saw her. He didn't ask them to stand above her. He simply reminded them that they, like her, were also imperfect.

That day at the restaurant, the words I had planned to speak would not have been kind, and all my eyes could see was hatred…but I chose to walk away.

As we go about this life, sometimes we will be the woman taken in sin. We will be the one waiting with tears in our eyes for someone to still be able to see our worth. We will mess up, and at one time or another, we may lose sight of our goals. Our mistakes may even make waves in the lives of others, or they may just cause us to struggle without impacting anyone.

We will snap at our partners. We will get frustrated with our two-year-olds. We may fight with our fathers, or sneak behind our mothers' backs. We will say unkind words, we will think degrading thoughts. We may even lie, steal and cheat at times to get what we want.

Whatever it is in your past that has humbled you to your knees, look to the Savior's encouraging words for hope that even *you*, in spite of your imperfections, can change the course of your life. "Go and sin no more." Even if you tripped over your shoes today, tomorrow is a new day. Take one step forward and be a little bit better tomorrow. Today, you may have slid down the mountain of your life, but tomorrow, you can still try to keep working your way up to the top.

It may be words that help you forgive those who have wronged you, or it may be silence that reminds you that you have the power to forgive. Even in the moments when you don't want to stand tall…do it anyway. Sometimes standing tall takes courage, and other times it only takes humility. Walk away.

# CHAPTER THIRTEEN

## *Blood*

**ONE AFTERNOON, I GOT A CALL FROM** the detectives letting me know that Rob had requested the release of his truck after it had been held as evidence. I stubbornly shot back my response to that information. "Well, then I request the release of Emmett's truck as well." I wasn't sure that I was really ready to have his brand new truck returned, but I certainly didn't want Rob to be getting a privilege while "out on bond" that I myself wasn't receiving as a law-abiding citizen of our community.

Within days, my request was approved and the detectives called to say they were on their way to deliver the truck back to me. I was nervous to see it again. I was afraid of what I would find inside, and I was scared of how my body would react to having that truck parked in my driveway again. Most importantly, I was nervous to drag Shawn through another reminder of my past.

I paced around the house, trying to mentally prepare myself. Soon, there was a knock at my door. My heart pounded as I opened it to the familiar faces of the detectives from the police department. I walked outside, followed by Teage. Kaleeya and Tytus were asleep and the twins were at school, and we didn't have Jordyn that day. So it was just Teage and me.

The detectives and I chit-chatted for a few minutes while Teage peeked inside the truck's windows. They told me they had run it through a carwash on their way over to make certain that all of Emmett's blood had been washed off before I saw it. Just the thoughts of his blood being on the side of the truck made my own blood grow cold. Shivers ran down my spine and goose bumps popped out all over me. I glanced over toward the truck, trying hard not to get emotionally involved as they talked about the blood that had been on it.

They were very thoughtful and caring as we talked for a few more minutes, and then they headed out. As they drove off, I stood near the vehicle with the keys burning my hand like hot coals. Teage begged me to let him get inside the truck to see what he could find. At first, I resisted to protect my son and myself. I stood frozen, with a million thoughts running through my mind.

That truck almost stood there mocking me. It had seen it all. It had carried the victim straight into the line of fire. It was as black as the hole it made in my heart.

I thought back to the day Emmett had first pulled it into the driveway. He was so proud to finally have his dream car. He had talked about it for years, and finally the time had come. He walked me through every detail of his new prized possession. He showed me how to push every button, and talked up all the special features that were included in his purchase. He was so proud of it in every way.

I pictured the afternoon he had packed the back seat with kids and taken the three oldest to a BSU game. They were so excited to be going with their daddy. I thought about our date nights we spent driving around town. I pictured the false alarm nights we drove down to the hospital thinking Tytus was coming... and all of the long drives back home after being turned away. I smiled as I pictured my doughnut dropping crumbs all over that truck. It was a meager trophy for another rejection from the hospital, but it was all my prego belly needed to patiently wait for the next drive it would take in that truck down to the hospital.

I pictured that truck as it drove up to Walgreens on the night of Emmett's death. All of the sudden Teage tried to grab the keys out of my hands, which quickly snapped me out of my funk. I looked down at him,

ASHLEE BIRK | 125

remembering our cathartic day at Walgreens. That day had turned out to be a leap of healing, and I could feel this one was going to need such a blessing. I stared into his giant blue eyes. I could see the longing he had in his heart, to be in his daddy's truck. I almost chuckled to myself to think that I was ever going to change his mind, "You know what buddy? Here we go!"

I unlocked the passenger-side door and pulled it open. The truck still smelled new. Emmett's gym bag was in the back seat, and the entire truck looked exactly like it had the last time I had been inside it. I sat in the passenger seat while Teage jumped into the back. My breathing became heavier, and I could feel myself begin to panic. I asked Teage if he was ready to go back inside the house, but he replied that he wasn't ready. I tried to remain calm and then asked him a few more times.

Teage wouldn't get out. He refused to leave the truck. For a few minutes, I continued to calmly beg him to go inside with me, and then it hit me...I needed this too.

So now, I had a silent partner who craved the search for clues almost more than I did. He rummaged through the back seat, while I read every receipt and went through all of the console compartments I could find. I knew that all the evidence needed for the case would have been kept at the police department, but I searched for more clues anyway.

It was almost like I had been building a puzzle. Each bit of information and every new fact that would arise would give me another piece. Having that truck parked in front of my house was like finding a missing piece to my puzzle. I had run out of things to read in the box in the garage, and after my bad experience with Emmett's email account, I vowed to never go looking there ever again. The truck gave me a desire to search a whole new realm of the past.

I turned the ignition on and pushed play on the CD player. The music had Emmett's typical punk flavor, but with a romantic twist. It was a song I had never heard before—the words spoke of running away together. I pushed eject. The CD had been made the day of his death, and the date was written in his own handwriting. I cringed thinking about that. Had this CD been made for *her?*

Suddenly, my phone alarm went off, reminding me that it was time to go pick up the twins from school. I grabbed Teage out of the back seat and we ran inside to wake up the babies. They were both in a deep sleep. I disliked waking them up to go only a block to pick up the twins, but even more so on that day... I hated being forced to leave my search.

I got everyone buckled in their seats and we drove off to the school. I called Shawn on the way to share some of my emotions with him. He listened calmly and reassured me that everything was going to be okay. I got a little emotional and said, "This is so hard. I didn't realize it was going to be so hard to have the truck back."

The twins jumped into the car, and at the top of his lungs, Teage chirped, "Guys... Daddy's truck is home! Want to play in it and pretend that he is driving us somewhere, when we get home?"

My heart sank. Here we go again. I knew that we were going to have another interesting night filled with memories of the past, but nothing could have prepared me for what happened next. I ended my conversation with Shawn just as we turned onto our street.

We pulled up into the driveway and parked in the garage. The kids hurried out of our Yukon and booked it to their dad's truck, dropping their backpacks as they ran. They hopped inside, and for thirty minutes they rummaged through his stuff. They tried on his clothes, tied his tie around their necks, put his earphones in their ears, read all of the receipts, and pushed every button in that truck. They were having fun playing with his stuff, and I was actually enjoying myself as I listened to their laughter.

A short time later, Shawn's truck pulled up. I was surprised to see him home so early, and I knew he had come to comfort me. He stepped out and I was surprised to see that he was as white as a ghost. I had feared the return of this truck might affect him as well. In many ways, he already felt like he was a replacement for Emmett … and now here Emmett's truck sat in front of our house as a loud reminder of the past.

He began to run toward me. He grabbed me and pulled me toward the house. "Ash … there is blood all over the other side of the truck. You can't see it from this side, but it is all over the other side. Have the kids seen it?"

My throat began to close up. "No! What are we going to do? We haven't gone over to that side. They CANNOT see it! That is their dad's blood. I … I … can't handle this …" I burst into tears and ran toward the truck. The kids were so into their make-believe, that they didn't notice the tears in my eyes. I slowly walked around to the other side. Sure enough, the carwash had not removed the blood from the truck. As plain as day, Emmett's truck was covered in his blood.

My heart dropped. I lost it. I don't remember anything from that moment on, but soon I found myself running through my room and into my sanctuary. I was hysterical … again … alone in my closet. This time, I wasn't in there begging for a "do-over." I was begging for a "when is this going to BE over?"

I had been in that closet so many times, but never before with a visual of the blood that Emmett had lost. My heart had hurt for the unknown of the past, but never before because of what I had viewed with my own eyes. Having that truck back was hard, but knowing that it carried the blood stains of a man that I loved was almost more than I could bear. I knew the mess of the past was not over, but I hadn't known it was going to be so apparent on the side of that truck.

Here we were, trying so hard to move forward and gain ground from our past … and here was yet another bold, red, reminder of the blood that had been spilt. A literal reminder. I have no idea how long I stayed there in my closet, but I do know I was surprised that I could still shed so many tears.

I was again reminded that just because I had remarried and hoped for a new normal, that didn't mean it was an overnight process. Every tear I shed that day was just as hard as the ones that had come before I met Shawn.

Once I calmed down, I knew I needed to get outside to help the kids in case they were also having a hard time. I swallowed the last of my tears and started to make my way outside. I went to the front window to scope out the situation. I wasn't sure if anyone else had seen the blood, or how they were handling it, if they had.

I looked outside at a scene that is almost impossible to put into words. There was Shawn, covered in suds, along with all of the kids with scrub brushes in their hands ... and together they were scrubbing Emmett's truck.

No one was crying, and in fact, each child had a huge grin on his or her face. They were talking and laughing and having the time of their lives. For several minutes, I sat at that window with tears falling down my face. No mother has ever prepared to see a scene such as this. A moment that had initially seemed as if it were going to break me all over again, turned into a vision of hope and peace.

I watched out the window as my babies scrubbed their father's blood off of his truck.

Shawn didn't panic or run away. Instead, he jumped in and changed the course of that day. Not one of the kids ever saw the blood. Shawn didn't say a word about why they were cleaning the truck. He made it a game, and he included each child as part of his team. He told them that they were cleaning the truck for Emmett.

Shawn did *not* step in as a replacement for Emmett. He came to save me from the many moments that would come to remind me of the past and try to break me.

Blood. It has the ability to stain, but it also has the potential to sustain life. It is such a powerful substance, and yet, when it is shed ... it has the power to end a life and change the course of the lives of everyone around the victim.

Blood. It is the topic of so many courtroom proceedings. It is the focus of so many TV series and movies. We see it on our screens as if it is just a substance that can easily be replaced or removed. It's not until we experience the shedding of blood in our own lives that we realize those characters on the big screens also have pulses. Those actors in the movies or television shows make it seem so simple. But in real life, when people die in cold blood, they also have families. Some of them are parents, and all of them are sons or daughters. They do not just have blood that falls to the ground; they also have communities surrounding them that suffer. Their blood isn't the only thing lost as they fall.

In so many homes in our world, we play video games where we shoot guns at people as if it were a fun joke. It isn't until blood is taken from us in real life that we truly realize that these games that cause us to view the shedding of blood as a sport... in reality, only minimize the sanctity of life.

Guns are real. Blood is not make-believe. Without blood, a person cannot survive.

What if, in our world, we were to view every life as important? What if we were able to see the soul of everyone we meet? What if we were to always think about our actions... before we act? I believe our world could be a lot different. If our lives were not taken for granted, then we might not view death as a sport.

Everyone has a story, and everyone has a past. Even your old crotchety neighbor was once a young carefree kid. Maybe his screams about your dog taking a crap on his lawn seem outlandish and over dramatic... but maybe that green grass is all he has left. Maybe he has seen the blood of someone he loved fall to the ground, or lost them tragically long ago. When we are alone or scared, it isn't about the poop on the grass or the fly in our water. Reacting to those small irritants is usually merely an outlet for our pain over something else much more significant.

Take a step back. Watch for the panic in the eyes of those around you. Some may be running to their closets with nowhere else to go. They might have literally found the blood that has stained their heart. Some may be blind to the blood that is flashing in their face. Sometimes, you may be able to see the blood they are scrubbing off their father's truck, and other times, you may just see the smiles that result from learning a new skill. It all depends on your view.

Nothing is as simple as it seems, and not everything is as monumental as it feels.

Blood has been spilt; mistakes have been made in all of our lives … be we mustn't miss the suds foaming up around us to wipe the blood away. The blood on that truck was Emmett's, but Shawn wasn't afraid to take Emmett's babies and teach them how to wipe it clean … for him.

I realized that day, even more than I knew it previously, that Shawn and Emmett were a team. Rob wasn't the only one who had messed up. Emmett had made serious mistakes that got us to where we were that particular day, but he had also helped me find Shawn to assist his family in cleaning up his mess.

From the window that afternoon, I watched it take place, and I have seen it every day since. Shawn wasn't sent to replace Emmett. No, he was prepared to carry us through in a way Emmett could not. He was there to help me clean up our past, so we could see the beauty that was all around us.

Shawn is not a perfect man. We have had so many bumps as a blended family that are yet to be told in our story. There have even been nights when we didn't think we would make it, but in many moments … he has perfectly shown ME how to stand.

When our Savior suffered in Gethsemane, He bled from every pore. He physically felt every single pain every single person who ever walks the earth has felt or will feel. He felt the pain I have carried since Emmett's death. He counted my babies' tears. He felt the pain Emmett suffered that night as a bullet entered his skull and sank into his heart. He felt the sorrow of Emmett's parents who have not only had to lose their son, but who have had to sit through a trial and hear every detail of how he was murdered. He has even felt the pain of those who sit in a jail cell all alone.

I know that not everyone will physically see with their own eyes the spilt blood that has caused them so much pain, but each one of us will, at one time or another, be wronged. Christ has felt the pain of every hurt.

He has fallen to his knees in pain. He has cried out, "Father, remove this cup from me." He has wondered, "When will this pain ever be done." Just like I fell to my knees praying for a promise that my pain would one day cease, our Savior has felt a hurt so excruciating that caused even Him to pray to see an end. He not only has felt our pain, He has prayed for a way out of it.

Knowing we are not alone can help us remember that even our pain will one day find peace.

He didn't suffer through that pain because it was easy, or because He wanted to... He did it because He loves each one of us. He knows each one of our names, He sees the honesty and sincerity of our hearts, and in the noble and honorable things we do, He smiles at our progress.

He sheds a tear as He watches his little ones scrub their own father's blood off of trucks, but He also smiles as He sees the willing "fathers" step up to the plate. He knows these challenges are not easy. He knows there are not many willing to take on "burdens" such as this... but that is what makes those who do so special.

We are each unique and special in the moments when we stand. Don't wait around for the world to change, find a way to stand strong regardless of its constant spinning. Sometimes, it might feel like it slows down just for us, and other times it feels like we may never catch up. We weren't created to march to anyone else's beat; we were made to be original.

No one will ever be right where you are, but Christ *has* been there. He has cleaned up the "blood" we have spilt through our poor choices, and He has bled from every pour... for us! Blood is real... and death is inevitable... but that is what makes life so precious. Never take a day for granted. The blood of this world has already been cleaned up by a loving Savior who has wiped it away for each and every one of us. All we have to do is ask, and He will willingly wipe our past clean.

You are not forgotten, and your past is not insignificant. He has seen your tears and heard your prayers. Even your blood is enough for Him to purify. Tomorrow might still bring reminders of the messes that have been made in the past, but they can be made clean. Turn to the only one who has the power to scrub even the toughest of stains. Heavenly Father will never let one drop of blood go unaccounted for, and He will never forget one tear. He is the light and life of this world, and because of his blood…we can have Eternal life.

CHAPTER FOURTEEN

# *Together We Stand*

**ONE DAY, JORDYN CAME BACK TO OUR** home after being away
for a few days. She struggled most of the afternoon and by bedtime she
was in tears. She shared with Shawn and me the challenges and struggles
she was facing because her parents' divorce caused her to go back and
forth between each household.

We did our best to comfort her and calm her down. We put all of the
kids to bed and headed downstairs to enjoy the quiet of the evening. We
talked for a while about how to help Jordyn, but began getting frustrated
with each other. Each of our ideas about how to help her were very different, and the tension it was causing in our marriage was becoming overwhelming. We sat on the couch arguing about each of the kids, and what
we each felt they deserved and needed.

After some time, we could hear voices upstairs. We tiptoed up and
perched ourselves outside the bedroom where Jordyn and the twins
slept. Shawn held his arm out to stop me from entering. "Let's just listen
for a minute," he suggested.

We sat outside their room and silently cupped our ears near the door
to hear our daughters' conversation. Through uncontrollable sobs, Jordyn was again talking about the struggles she was facing going back and
forth between her two houses. She was teary and emotional as she told
them of the pain it was causing her. She told them a few stories, and how
she felt so left out when she had to leave our house. She talked about the

events of her day, and how she hated having to share her time between both places.

We continued to listen. Soon the girls began to comfort Jordyn, trying to help her through her pain. Nothing they said seemed to console her. She continued to sob and go through all of the topics over and over again.

All of the sudden, Bostyn got a little emotional and said, "You know, Jordyn...I can't imagine how hard this must be for you. It would be so hard for me to leave you guys and go back and forth to another house. I bet that isn't easy, but something that was hard for me when Daddy Emmett died was that I don't EVER get to see him—ever again. I miss him so bad. Our parents didn't get divorced, but when he died, it changed our family too. I have wished so many times that I could go—when you do—to see HIM. So maybe it is hard for you to leave, but imagine if one of your parents had died and you never got to see one of them ever again."

By this time, Jordyn's heavy sobs had stopped. Bailey continued Bostyn's thoughts. "I would give anything to have the chance to get to go see Daddy Emmett. You are so lucky Jordyn, to have two houses full of people who love you. It may be hard to leave us, but how special it is that when you do...you always know you have both families? When you wonder if your parents love you, you get to wrap your arms around them and hear their voices. You are so lucky to have two places to go when you feel alone."

They talked for a few more minutes; by this time Shawn and I were the ones with tears running down our cheeks, our ears still pushed against the wall next to the cracked open door.

Shawn grabbed my hand and squeezed it. "Man, I love you. I am so sorry." He wiped a tear from my face and leaned in and kissed me. "We may be a broken group of individuals, but we are not alone."

That night, our wise twins didn't just speak to Jordyn and calm her fears, they reminded Shawn and me to have empathy for each other. He had been through the pain of divorce and single parenthood. He had done hard things. Even though his pain was different than mine, it didn't mean that it wasn't hard for him.

I realized that day that all of us struggle. My five kids were not the only ones that had been through loss. To the twins, Jordyn was the lucky one. She had two parents with whom she got to spend time. She got to see their faces, and touch their skin. They were jealous of her because she hadn't lost one of them to death. A part of them almost wished Emmett and I had divorced, because at least that way, we would both still be part of their lives. And for her part, Jordyn wished she had what her new siblings had. She longed for a time when she didn't have to leave any more. She hated going back and forth and craved the consistent home life that the other kids had. Neither of them had it perfect, but each of them were lucky in the others' eyes.

The grass may look greener on the other side, but that doesn't mean it is. We all stare at each other and wonder what it would be like to stand in another's shoes. We sometimes long for a story that is not ours. It is okay to wonder if the grass is greener somewhere else, but sometimes when we go looking for it...we may see that ours just needs us to give it a little love.

Just like death, divorce is a hard fact of life that almost every family has experienced in one way or another. I saw it as a young girl. I remember being where Jordyn was that night...wishing that I didn't have to go back and forth between my mother and father. I remember the pain of knowing that my parents were not going to spend their life loving each other any more; I remember feeling loss.

It isn't fair that we all have to lose things. I hated losing the consistency of my parents' marriage. As the years went on and with my mother's remarriage to a family that had lost a parent to death, I learned that there were pains that ran more deeply than my own. Her new husband's children had lost their mother to death. They shared the feelings in their hearts of the lonely road of learning to deal with life without her. Knowing of their pain didn't take away my own, but it helped me see that parts of my situation were a blessing. I still got to kiss both of my parents' cheeks and feel the embrace of their arms.

Life is not always going to let us win at everything. After the divorce of my parents, I grew up a lot. The day my mom announced she would be remarrying, I thought my chance for my family to come together again was over. I knew that her decision to move on would mean there was never going to be a way for my dad to live with us again.

At first, it was hard. I hated sharing my mom. I hated moving away from my friends, and the head cheerleader position I had just received. I hated selling my dog and leaving behind all of the memories we had created in our tiny little "single mom" duplex. I begrudgingly packed my things and got in the car on the day of the move. I thought for sure my mom had made a huge mistake, and that she was ruining my life as I knew it.

Going into ninth grade in a new school was not my idea of a good time. I didn't want to start over, or make new friends, or be a stepdaughter and stepsister. I didn't want to share a room with my new stepsister who was almost four years older than me. I just liked the way life was in our world. I was afraid of the unknown, and I didn't like the thought of change.

A few weeks into the school year, I woke up in the early hours of the morning. I was soaking wet. I rolled over and screamed, "Audra ... I had a dream I was in the bathroom and I ... I ... I peed the bed!"

My new sister, who was a senior in high school (I was in ninth grade and had never in my life wet the bed), started laughing hysterically. Relieved that she didn't want to disown me and never talk to me again, I began to laugh too. We giggled for an hour as we pulled of the sheets and put new sheets on the bed.

It was so simple, but in that moment I knew I had a sister. From that point on, she was one of my best friends. We could talk about anything. Together, we admired the Val Kilmer poster she had hung in our room, and we talked every night about our dreams for the future. I loved having an older sister for the first time in my life.

Our stories were not the same, but the more we took the time to get to know each other…we truly became sisters. Our two families had never planned to be together. We each began our lives on totally separate journeys, and yet as the years have rolled by, I have come to realize…we were always meant to be together.

I have seen loss, but after every loss I have learned that there have also been gains. I never hoped for my parents to divorce, but I have learned to love the blessings that have followed it. My stepbrothers and stepsisters are some of my best friends. My stepfather has been there for me in ways that nobody else has.

Stepfamilies may not always be our first choice. They present a different level of hard work that most traditional families have never had to face. The level of commitment to love someone who has already spent a portion of his or her life loving someone else, is trying on relationships and brings about new insecurities.

No couple kneels across from each other at an altar and makes vows with the thought that one day their marriage will end. We all plan our futures without factoring in the bumps that inevitably will come. Nobody ever plans on the day of his or her wedding, to divorce, to have a partner die, or to struggle to love.

Even if all the dreams you ever had for your family have been lost and you are forced to start over, don't get discouraged. If all of your plans have had to change, find a way to see it as a new opportunity to find empathy and love. I never knew I would have a new stepsister who would have to help me clean up my bed after wetting my pants as a fourteen-year-old girl, but that was the day I knew I was truly sharing a room with a family member. As Shawn and I listened outside our daughters' bedroom, and heard them helping each other through their sobs... it reminded us to be there for each other. It reminded us that even through each of our losses... there was much we had gained.

Nobody ever plans to lose, and when we do, it is hard to wait around for the gains that will follow. Our losses can, at times, feel like failures. The gains don't take away the pain of the loss, but the blessings can be sent to help us remember to keep standing together. When we have each other's backs... when we clean up each other's messes and wipe away each other's tears, we are never really alone.

Even if the people who surround you were not there the day you were born, they are there now. Don't let your original dreams stop you from standing strong together. Stepfamilies, adopted families, and even families that are just made up of true friends can be there in the moments you need them the most. Your original dreams of the perfect family may never come true, but the blessings of the family waiting for you may be even better than any you ever planned.

The truth is, no family is perfect. Families are all made up of imperfect people, doing imperfect and sometimes hurtful things. Even those families with the immaculate yards and amazing clothes and perfect smiles in public... sometimes experience tears and screams behind closed doors.

I used to look at the "perfect families" when I was a kid and longed to have what they had. Now that I am older, I can see that I always did have what they have. Even now, I have exactly what they do: I am an imperfect mother, married to an imperfect husband, trying to perfectly raise imperfect children. We are ALL right there. We *all* have insecurities in the family we are raising, the parenting we are doing, or the daughter or son we are trying to be. No relationship on this earth is "perfect," therefore neither is any family perfect.

So even if your family has been taken apart, or imperfectly put back together... enjoy it. Every smile you see around you... is right there with you. We are all one giant family, walking around blindly trying to do our best. Heavenly Father always knew that is exactly where we would be while here on earth, and He doesn't expect perfection. All He asks is that we serve one another with love.

"When ye are in the service of your fellow beings ye are only in the service of your God." (Book of Mormon, Mosiah 2:17)

Service is done in love, not perfection. Don't expect that no one will ever make a mistake, and don't hold yourself to a perfect standard. Our families will never be perfect, no matter how much hairspray you use or pleas you make. Watch for the tender moments. It is in them that you will see the perfect words needed in a perfect moment. Perfection doesn't come as an individual, or as a family... it comes in little glimpses—little moments—when you know you are right where you are supposed to be... standing together.

CHAPTER FIFTEEN

# Not Forgotten

**THE TRIAL DATE HAD BEEN SET. WITH** the knowledge that it would be just months away I felt our life, in our blended family, would be able to start *for real* once it was complete. I constantly longed for the day when I could walk in that courtroom and let my voice be heard, and I truly believed that our new life would really begin once it was over.

Since our marriage, all that I thought would change in our "new life" did not. Every morning I would sit on my bathroom counter and rehearse the words I would say at the trial in my mind as I applied my makeup. I still continued to scream at Rob, Kandi, and Emmett when driving alone in the quiet solitude of my car. I still had triggers that would ignite and throw me back in time. I still struggled with anxiety about leaving my house. I was insecure in my marriage, and in the role of being a wife. However, in my heart…I truly thought that the single moment the trial ended so would all of the issues in myself, and in our family.

We swept a lot of our adjustment problems as a blended family under the rug, as to keep our selves stable for the pending trial. We knew it was our biggest issue, so any others that would arise seemed to be so small. We had a few small arguments about the kids, but for the most part it seemed I was still running on autopilot in an effort to make it to court. Anything else was petty and trivial, and therefore left unresolved and pushed aside.

Soon the trial was only a few weeks away. I craved the moment when

I would get to read my victim statement and let that courtroom hear my pain. The silence I had forced upon myself was ready to break in that courtroom and I almost counted down the days when I could look Rob in the eye and tell him how his actions broke my family.

One morning the big kids were at school and the little ones and I were at the grocery store. We were almost done with our list when my phone rang, a blocked number...pit in my stomach. It was the victim witness coordinator, "Ashlee, hey...so the...the trial...they are going to have to move the date. We had all planned it being next month, but they are thinking they need another six months or so for everyone to collect more evidence and get all the tests back, like the gunpowder residue reports and the bullet wound specialists, and all the angles of the evidence. I know this is going to be hard for you to continue to wait for, but I hope you will understand why they...they just need more time."

We talked for a while about what this delay would mean for me. She was very thoughtful as she spoke and reassured me that they were working as hard as they could to find the truth in every aspect of the case. The truth, a desire I needed just as much as them. I felt confident in waiting as we hung up the phone and I continued in my shopping.

I walked around the store with almost no emotion, feeling brave and strong. I unloaded my groceries out of the cart and robotically bagged each one. After paying the clerk and getting all of my sacks back in the cart I could feel my tears trying to find their way out. I had a panic raging, but it was a new form of emotion. Not a panic of "is this ever going to end" like I thought it might be, it was like that phone call drilled a hole in my heart. It was a deeper despair than any I had ever felt.

Waiting longer for the trial was going to destroy me; I could feel it. Though the outcome wouldn't make a difference in my life, waiting for it created space for another void of loss to grow inside of me. I longed for that trial; I yearned to hear the full story and put all the missing pieces together in my head. I needed to hear from all the specialists, and witnesses...what they had seen and heard. I hoped that their stories would help feel in the gaps in my own.

As I pushed my cart full of food and children out to the car tears silently streamed down my face. Six more months until I could look Rob in the eye and ask him why? More mornings that I would try to apply mascara through my tears. Months left to wait to read my victim statement that now played like an old screeching record inside of my heart.

My despair sank deep in my soul. My life felt heavy as I drove home from the store and unloaded the groceries. Everything around me looked dark.

For the next few days I was a stone cold zombie. I didn't even know how to feel. I felt so disconnected from my family, and especially from Shawn. I tried so hard to push away the gloom, but nothing seemed to make me want to smile. I didn't want to wallow in it, but I didn't know how I was going to let it go.

That next weekend was the Relief Society broadcast for LDS General Conference. A few friends invited me to go, but in my self pitied gloom I told them I had other plans. I didn't really have anything else going on, except for my own personal pity party.

As the afternoon began to turn into evening on Saturday, the day of the broadcast, something kept urging me to let go of my bitterness and go with my friends. I fought it all day long. Shawn asked me all day what was wrong but I never opened up to him. After asking me what was wrong for the twentieth time I told him what I was struggling with. I was feeling too dark to attend the broadcast. As those words left my lips, I knew what I needed to do. I headed to my closet and threw on a skirt.

I walked into the living room where my family was playing. I could see their beautiful eyes, and I could hear their tender voices, but I could not feel an ounce of their love. They all gave me a kiss and I headed out to the garage and got into my car.

As the door shut I could again feel darkness sink a little deeper inside of me. I offered a small prayer, "Heavenly Father, I know it is so simple compared to the past but this date change for the trial is weighing on my heart. I can't seem to feel anything but utter despair. Somehow I am waiting to take my next breath when this trial gets over, and the thought of waiting to breath for another six months is going to kill me. I... I just... I need to know that you are still here. I feel so alone, I am so scared, and though this murder trial isn't going to bring Emmett back, I feel like... it has to come to help me heal. We aren't living life as we wait, so why can't it just be now, so I can let it go. I can't feel anything, I can't even feel the spirit today. Everything is like a black fog and I am scared that if I go another six months living like this, I am not going to be able to feel anything ever again. I just, I feel like, maybe somewhere along the way...you don't remember I am still here... I feel so forgotten."

My car pulled into the parking lot, and my prayer was cut short. I looked into the rearview mirror. I quickly swiped my fingers under each eye in hopes that no one would notice I had been bawling like a baby.

Everyone was still eating dinner in the gym. I walked in. I could see the friends who had invited me all sitting around a table in the back. I passed my sister-in-law and all of her cute friends. She came over and gave me a big hug and asked me to sit with them. I already felt guilty that I had told my friends that I had other plans and I had showed up anyway, so I decided to go sit with them.

After most of the girls had finished eating they headed into the chapel to get seats. It was just one other girl and me left at our table. I didn't know her that well and hadn't had a chance to talk much with her. She asked a few questions about me, and then about the trial. Like a broken dam had just burst I spewed out parts of my story that I had hardly told anyone. The single world, "trial" sparked in me all the anger I had about the postponed date and my new knowledge that I had to keep my pain bottled up even longer. She just stared at me in complete shock. She listened for a few more minutes. It felt good to open up and let out some of my pain.

I walked into the broadcast just as they were about to say the opening prayer. My sudden spew of emotion at the dinner table hadn't brought me any more feeling of peace, but a darker despair that seemed to be swirling even harder around my mind.

The speakers began. I listened, still without feeling, to each of their words. Hoping for a time when I could go back and reread their truths, I tried hard to take notes for myself for later. One talked about what she wants her granddaughters to know someday. Another speaker spoke about charity. The next woman talked about holding fast to our promises that we make.

The last speaker was announced. Uchtdorf! He had always been one of my favorites, so I was excited on this day of feeling emotionally numb to hear his words.

He began. He said he was excited to be speaking and how honored he was to be there. Then his talk began.

As he spoke about the tiny "forget me not" flower and picturing it surrounded by all the other large flowers in the garden, like it was pleading with the Lord, "Forget me not, O Lord" my ears perked up. The very plea I had just cried to Heavenly Father in my car. Just like that tiny flower, I had prayed for a glimpse that I was not forgotten.

Then he spoke about *Charlie and the Chocolate Factory*'s "golden ticket". He taught that when we wait around for a golden ticket, we miss the simple pleasure of opening up a candy bar and eating the chocolate. His entire talk he spoke about truths I had always known, yet somehow that week I had forgotten. He bore his testimony about how not one of us are forgotten to the Lord. Every minute of his talk was a like I was the flowering "forget me not" opening up and standing tall, being proud to be a tiny little flower amongst the beautiful roses. He reminded me that though my problems were overwhelming and seemed impossible, I was not forgotten. All the anger in my heart quickly faded with each word that he spoke.

I knew his words were not just for me because I wasn't even supposed to be there that day, but I had come that night just for them. His soul spoke to mine, as he reminded me that I was not forgotten.

The trial was not what was going to bring me to peace. It was not my "golden ticket" to happiness. The only golden ticket that would free me from my pain was Jesus Christ. Maybe the people in the courts had forgotten how this delay would affect me, but I was not forgotten by Him. Just because the moment I was waiting for had been delayed, didn't mean I was alone. For the first time that week, I felt His love surround me and I knew without a doubt I was not forgotten.

Just like the tiny forget me not flower, God knew right where I was no matter how small I felt. Heavenly Father wanted me to remember Him as my "golden ticket", and not seek for one in my life.

There is no "golden ticket" that will come our way. There is no golden ticket in forgiveness. Even when we feel we have we done all that we can to forgive others, another opportunity may come our way to learn a different angle of the virtue. We may also find that all the forgiveness we have done, has been just the tip of the iceberg on our journey to true forgiveness. One moment of acknowledging a road to forgiveness is not necessarily the "golden ticket" to the end of its path.

There is no worldly golden ticket that can free us from our pain. No amount of money, clothes, cars, or houses will bring eternal happiness. Not even another person's words or admiration can free us from the pain inside of us. The false "golden tickets" that the world will send us, may bring temporary relief... but they will not heal our hearts.

There is no golden ticket or free pass from fear. Fear and anxieties are real. I was reminded just the other night, that even when I think I have fear under control, it can find a new angle to try to destroy me.

There is no "golden ticket" from any of the hardships we will face. There is no grand event that will teach us all we need to know. Every day is part of our test of mortality, every hour a new lesson on forgiveness, patience, humility, and love. Don't spend your life waiting for your "golden ticket" of happiness when there are wonderful things all around you.

I couldn't feel my family's love, and it was right there in front of me. I was waiting around for the trial to come and be my "golden ticket". I thought its magnificent power would heal my broken heart, close my open wounds, uncloud my dark mind, and help me let go of my pain. As I waited for it, I lost the moments that were passing me by.

No day is going to be your "golden ticket". All of us are waiting for something: to be married; to be a parent; to graduate high school; to move to our dream house; to be free of health issues; to be done with college; to lose weight; to not be held back by fear of the past. The lists of things we wait for are never ending. What if today was our last day, and the only thing we had left was right now? I bet as we looked back over our lives, we would wish that we would have spent today enjoying all the little pieces of chocolate that were staring us in the face, instead of opening each wrapper hoping it held the secret ticket to our happiness.

If we don't enjoy what we have right now, we may never find happiness. It is easy to wait around for your dreams to come true, but not as easy seeing the dreams that are already being played. There is a golden ticket that can bring eternal happiness. It is the knowledge of the truth that lies in each of us. We all have the potential to find the light of the world inside our hearts: the truth that we are not alone; the truth that even though we seem small...we are never forgotten.

CHAPTER SIXTEEN

# Born To Fail

**LIFE BEGAN TO FEEL NORMAL FOR A** minute. Shawn and I grew closer, and for a time the past seemed to be so far behind me. I started to enjoy some of the things I had enjoyed before the tragedy.

One day, Shawn came home with a gym membership for me. I was excited because a few days after the shooting, I had cancelled the gym passes for me, Emmett, and ironically, Kandi. I had not spent much time at the gym earlier, but I had loved the convenience of being able to go there for some down time at night. So having a new membership to a new gym was exciting. I was grateful for the gift.

For a while, I went to the gym off and on randomly. Then one week, I really got into it and went several nights in a row. It felt amazing to be moving my body in a way I hadn't since long before Tytus was born. It was relaxing and soothing to turn on my video iPod and lose myself in a movie while exercising. I started a movie, which I then continued watching the next day from where I had left off the night before. On the third day, I finished that movie and the next film in my collection began. I didn't think much of it as the opening song began, and I soon found my-self walking on the treadmill to *P.S. I Love You!* It was a movie I had seen with Emmett for the first time, and one which I had also watched alone not long after his death.

I felt I should turn it off, knowing my emotions might get the best of me, but I kept watching it anyway. It sucked me in. After my time on the treadmill came to an end, I headed to the mats to stretch. I didn't take my eyes off the screen as I silently did my stretches with the earphones in my ears. As time passed, I was no longer stretching, but was engulfed in the movie. Subtle tears fell down my cheeks as I became more and more enmeshed in the emotion of the film's message. The main character in the movie had so much in common with me, and yet our stories were so different. She knew exactly what it was like to be a widow, but she also had the knowledge I longed to have: she knew her husband deeply loved her as he took his final breath. She didn't have all the feelings of regret and betrayal that I still carried, stored inside every part of my soul. When *she* looked back to the past, she longed to hear her husband's voice repeating the words of love he had uttered in his last days, while *I* longed for my husband's unspoken apology.

My mind traveled back in time to the "P.S I love you!" moment I had experienced in the Walmart parking lot after buying flowers to decorate Emmett's grave. I almost resented the movie for reminding me of all the other times I *hadn't* received such a validation. In my frustration, I realized there was no point staying at the gym to work out because I was wasting my time on thoughts and movies that did nothing for me. I looked at my phone. It was getting late, and I figured I better head for home.

I turned off the movie, secretly hoping to return to it the next time I came back to the gym, but also realizing I shouldn't do that to myself again. I threw my iPod into my bag and dug around for my keys. I started to stand up to head toward the stairs and something caught my eye. It was a woman who looked really familiar. She looked like she was probably a few years older than me and she was talking to a younger guy, probably in his mid-twenties. He had on a wedding ring and so did she, but it was clear from their conversation that they weren't married to each other.

I sat there watching in shock as they flirted back and forth with each other. Did she know he was married? Was he aware that she was taken? My blood began to boil. I threw down my bag and pretended to be stretching again. I listened to them for a few minutes and became sick to my stomach. I burst into tears, and silently turned the other way. An inappropriate relationship was taking place just a few feet from me, and there was nothing I could do about it! It was almost as if I was frozen in that corner, unable to get up to spare myself from watching the disgusting scene. From the way the blood boiled in my veins, it was as if I were watching Emmett and Kandi. I wanted to walk up to the man and grab his face, as I had Emmett the night he was killed, and scream all the things I still longed to yell at *him*. "You have a wife... go home... and find out what it is about her that you are not seeing. Turn around and walk away from here. Don't give into this temptation! Go home and show your family all the reasons you choose them!"

I didn't ever say a word, but huddled in my corner sobbing for a woman who was sitting at home, probably cooking his favorite food, wondering if he would be coming home that night. I shed tears for any babies that man was forgetting as he was being swept away by another woman's charms.

The irrational part of my brain kept begging me to go over and remind him of all the paths this choice could lead him to, but in an effort to keep myself safe, I remained silent. But somewhere in the back of my mind, I couldn't stop myself from picturing the woman's angry husband waiting around the corner.

Soon, I couldn't take any more torture and I grabbed my bag and ran past them, around the corner, down the stairs, and out to my car. Once inside the car, I sobbed like I had never sobbed before. I cried for all the husbands and wives who have ever felt betrayed. I wept for the heartache that their insecurities could make them believe. I prayed for all the spouses who had been duped into thinking they could live their lies in both lives and not have it affect anyone else. I cried for all the families who had been destroyed because of one partner's decisions. I cried for my own soul that still sought peace from the pain my husband's infidelity had brought me. I cried for my babies, who I yearned to protect from hearing the ugly details of the truths from their past. I cried for all the wives, husbands, and children who had felt broken. Yes, I cried for my own family...but mainly, I cried for our world.

And that is when the fear set in...What if that man had been Shawn? What if all men were the same? What if no matter who I was married to, the ending would always be the same? What if Shawn cheats on me, and one day finds himself dead in a parking lot? What if all marriages are doomed to fail, and I couldn't survive another one? What if this crazy life I asked Shawn to share with me becomes too much for him and he turns to someone else for comfort? What if I was born to fail?

It was as if a small match had ignited and turned into a raging forest fire, and my hallucinations reached the point of insanity. I sat in the parking lot for a good twenty minutes trying to figure out which way was up.

By the time I got home, it was late. I didn't say much to Shawn as we turned in for the night and went to sleep.

In my dreams that night, I found Shawn and Kandi in my bed. I woke up in a cold sweat, hardly able to breathe. The next morning, my mind still lingered on the thoughts that had overcome me the night before. I was almost mad at Shawn for the acts he had preformed in my dreams, and just looking at him made me feel angry...like he had actually done something wrong.

As he was about to leave for work, he finally questioned my coldness. "Hey...are...are you okay? You haven't said much this morning, and I...I am worried about you. You doing alright?" I broke. "It was just...I had a dream...and you and...her...and I am so mad at you...and Kandi...you and her...were in our bed...and I am just disgusted with you this morning for being everything that Emmett was."

No harsher words had ever been spoken between us. He stared at me and said, "Ash, I'm sorry about your awful dream, but I am *not* Emmett. I am never going to be Emmett. I am sorry you had that dream, but it isn't fair for you to hold something against me that isn't even real. It's not my fault that Emmett did what he did, and I don't deserve to be punished for his actions. You have to learn to trust me. Hopefully, some day you will see that not all men are going to cheat."

I apologized for snapping at him, but in the back of my mind, I was still really mad...not specifically at Shawn, but at men in general.

The feeling of disgust I felt towards men lingered with me throughout the morning and by early afternoon, I was again on the verge of a melt-down. I needed answers to the past to try to figure out how to let go of it. I picked up my phone and called the Attorney General's office to ask a few questions.

We set up an appointment and the next morning, I was driving down to meet her at her office. The whole way there, I could barely swallow because my mouth was so dry. I checked in at the front desk and received a visitor's name badge. Then, someone escorted me into her office.

I sat down, still fighting back tears. The lump in my throat felt like a hot coal. She asked about the kids, and how we were all doing. I replied with basic answers. She finally got to the point. "Okay, you said on the phone you had a few questions you needed answered. I can't promise I can answer all of them, but I am willing to try."

Then out they came, with very few breaths in between. "Well, I am just struggling with a few things. It still doesn't make any sense. Where did it all begin? With Emmett...I mean...was she the only one, or is there any proof that there were other women? Are they sure there was an actual affair or is it just a suspicion? Did it all start out with a porn addiction...or was this just a one-time thing to further his career? I just... it doesn't make any sense. Why wasn't I enough for him? Did you find that?...Did you find any letter that maybe he wrote to Kandi, saying that he just wanted me? Was there evidence as to why he would choose her... and not...and not us? Was there anything that showed that he knew... that he had made a mistake? Did he have other women? Were there other affairs? Do you have any answers for me that can help me let go of all the things I don't know? I'm trying to figure out how to trust and love again, and I can't even begin to understand how it all went wrong the first time. Am I just destined to fail again? ... I wonder that because I don't even know where it all went wrong ... and I don't know when I stopped being enough. And I don't know how to be enough ... without figuring out why I wasn't enough for Emmett."

By then, I was sobbing uncontrollably, hoping that she was able to understand even a single word of all the words I spewed out. She also had tears in her eyes. I could see that she could feel my pain, and it was apparent that she truly cared about my plight.

I received a lot of answers that day—none which helped increase my trust in men—but many that helped me see that Emmett had been struggling more, and to a greater extent, than I had ever imagined.

There were some facts I learned that did comfort a part of my heart that day. Emmett talked about me a lot in emails. He spoke highly of me to many of his friends. He bragged about the kids. Our attorney told me that day that she truly believed he adored me and loved our children, and that is why he fought so hard to protect us from his secrets. It didn't change much about our past, but it did brighten my spirits about myself a bit.

Emmett's soul must have been so tormented. He seemed to know exactly what he wanted, but at the same time, he had no idea. He wanted the life he had created with us, and yet something inside of him was pulling him away from us. He walked down dark roads in his journey, but he also did so much good along the way. But where had it begun? Where was I going to find the facts that helped it all make sense?

I walked out of that office with a lot of the answers I had gone in to seek, and yet ... I knew nothing. I still didn't know how to let it all go. I still had no clue as to how I could move past the urge to despise and hate, not only everyone else ... but myself. I wanted nothing more than to be able to move forward, but my soul was tormenting *me* by hanging on to the past and the pain that past had caused me.

I never went back to that gym again. Months passed and Shawn continued to patiently pay the monthly fee until the period of my contract had expired. Though he will never understand the struggles I have faced, he has been understanding in those moments when I got lost in them.

To anyone who has ever wondered where to turn when the days get hard, to everyone who has questioned if they are enough, I can promise you that you are not alone in your battle. Searching for answers in the past may not change the future, but it can give you a perspective as to where the problems all began. In my case, I felt that learning where it had all begun to go wrong would help me stop holding all men hostage for the mistakes made by one man. But I didn't find the answers to those questions, and I still had to learn to move forward.

To anyone who is looking for happiness in the wrong places... Stay true to the promises you have made. If you are trapped in a corner feeling yourself slip, get out of that corner! You do not have to go down those paths that will destroy your family, or the life you are living. You do not have to battle with the torment that will lead you astray from everything you have created, or which you hope to have one day. Having an affair may seem like a quick fix to the troubles you are facing, but it will not take away or change those troubles. It may seem like an easy road compared to the one you are on now... but I can promise you, that lie will only last so long.

When we come to those crossroads... those moments when we decide to continue on the path we are on, or to start down a new one... that is the time when we have to make certain that all the "doors" of the past have first been shut. All the relational "doors" behind *me* had been slammed shut by other people, and it was difficult for me to open new doors when the doors of the past had been locked and prevented me from finding the answers I sought.

Other crossroads are even more critical. The man and woman at the gym that day... they were at a different kind of crossroad. They were at a moment of decision. They still had "doors" open in their lives, but they were toying with the idea of opening new ones.

In relationships, and especially in marriage, we cannot open more than one door at a time. We were not meant to have secret doors that we have to hide from our loved ones, and I am sure that anyone who has them, has found their own personal torment in that secret.

If you find yourself in that moment when you are thinking about opening a "door" without first shutting the one behind you... please step away for a minute. Think about the first time you kissed your husband; ponder on the first time your wife held your hand. Picture the day when you knew for certain you wanted to plan your life around that person. Think about the commitments you have made. Before you reach for that handle for the new and exciting "door", pray to remember all the reasons you opened the first door to begin with.

Maybe you will find that you need to go home and shut and lock door number one, but maybe you will just remember all the reasons that door was worth loving and fighting for. Maybe you will even see why that door should always be your one and only.

There is not always going to be a tomorrow. Live today with your whole heart. Turn to the people who are waiting at home with your favorite meal just for you. What if today was your last chance to show them you care; what if tomorrow never comes? Now is your time to live true to the relationships in your life. Today is the day to stand up to those choices that will bring you down. Walk a little taller, choose a little more wisely, and let go of the torment that is blinding your path.

Everything begins somewhere, including secrets. Every life has a beginning and an ending. Every relationship has a beginning, but it does not have to end. With love and hard work, relationships can last forever. We were not created to fail. Maybe your past has proven that theory wrong, but it doesn't mean it is. My marriage to Emmett didn't have to determine who I was going to be as a wife, and it did not mean that Shawn was going to succumb to the same trials.

Each of us is unique. Maybe you have been hurt in your past. Maybe you have learned to withhold your trust from anyone and anything. Don't spend your life blocking out everyone because of a fear of failure. Maybe you have lost or maybe you have loved and received nothing in return. Don't stop. Love is powerful. It has no end and no beginning.

For everyone who has lost at love…you are not alone. Don't spend your life dwelling on it…because that will not bring it back. You may not ever learn where the destruction began, but you can start again. Begin a new chapter. Losing love does not mean that you lost your ability to do it.

Whenever you find yourself crying in your car for the world, remember that the world is only as strong and as good as each one of us in it. We do not have to fail. Even if our marriages don't last, people around us die, or a dream we were living ends…it doesn't mean we have failed.

I wish I would have known back then what I have now learned, which is that we were born for greatness. Greatness doesn't come through ease and perfection. Greatness comes as we stand tall when others do not. Greatness comes to us as we get back up when we fall. Greatness isn't born…it is made. Greatness is found as we stand tall…but sometimes even more when we walk away.

If you find yourself standing at a crossroad today, don't take the wrong path because you have come to believe that you were born to fail. No one was sent to earth to fail. We are here to find out who we were before we came, and who we can become, and where it is we want to be when we die.

Maybe the past has let you fall, but the only time you fail…is when you believe you cannot get back up and start again. You were born to stand. Stand tall and stand true…you were born for greatness.

# CHAPTER SEVENTEEN

# *Greater Miracles*

**I WOKE UP ONE MORNING IN A** funk. Nothing in particular had sparked my foul mood, but I could not seem to stomp it out. It was a normal day. The little kids and I played and cleaned the house while the big kids were at school. I tried hard to ignore the dark gloom that seemed to be tugging at me, and I carried on with my normal routine with it constantly hanging over me.

As morning turned into afternoon, I got a call that brought a smile to my face. Rob had had his bail revoked, and was heading back to jail. It was a miracle!!! I was giddy as I went about the rest of my day. Finally, something was going my way, and he was going back to where he had belonged all along. He had killed my husband and he deserved to be back in jail. Just knowing I no longer had the possibility of running into him on the streets brought peace to my soul, but on an even deeper level, I was happy justice was being served.

The alarm on my phone soon sounded to remind me to go pick up the big kids from school. I loaded the little ones in my car and drove to the school. I couldn't wait to tell the twins about Rob's new "home." I knew it would calm some of their fears, as it had mine.

As I drove, I thought back to the nights they had tapped me on my shoulder to ask about "the bad guy." I thought of the hours spent holding them as they cried in my arms about the father they would never again see, and about their fear of the man who had taken him from them. I thought of their whispers in the silence about a stranger they would never meet and never be able to forgive for the pain he had caused. I thought about all that Rob did to deserve his time in jail. I was happy he was getting locked up again. I was angry for the punishments my children had been forced to endure because of him, and I was grateful that the justice system was sending him back to the life he deserved.

I pulled up to the school. I could see the twins walking toward our meeting place. I jumped out of the car and with a skip in my step I ran toward them. Once their hands were in mine, I kneeled down to whisper the news. "Girls, so you know how scared you have been since you found out all those months ago that the man who shot Daddy was getting out of jail? Well ... guess what? Today ... he ... he made some choices that got his bail taken away ... and so, he has to go back to jail!" I was grinning and excited for my babies who had cried through all those nights, worried this man would somehow come into their rooms. I was happy to tell them that the man who had shot and killed their dad was back in jail, locked up. I was proud that I got to deliver this declaration of their safety to them.

They didn't look up; both of them still stared at the ground and didn't say a word. Almost in desperation to see their excitement, I announced it again. "Girls ... doesn't that make you happy to know that justice is being served ... that he ... is ... in jail?" I tried so hard to get them to make eye contact with me. "I thought this might make you guys happy that the man who killed Daddy is not going to be out of jail anymore. They are putting him back in jail! ... So ... he ... is ... not ... out ... of jail anymore." Still no response.

A few seconds went by, and finally a sound came from my silent crowd. Bailey burst into tears, and sobbed "But what about *HIS* kids mom? They still have a chance to have a dad. If he goes back to jail, they don't get a dad ... just like us." I was dumbfounded. This little girl I'd held in the night as she had sworn up and down she would never forgive "the bad guy," was now in tears for *him*?

Bostyn finally looked up at me. "Mom, Bailey and I have been talking a lot about this," she said as a small tear fell from her eyes, "and we...we will forgive him now. We just ...What about his kids? They might need their dad. If we could have Daddy back, we would...but they still can. If he goes back to jail, then all of us lost our dads."

My heart dropped. All the excitement that had gotten me through the day quickly faded. Because of my bitterness and desire for revenge, I had spent my afternoon excited that Rob had been punished for breaking the rules and was getting sent back to jail. I had anticipated that the moment I told my children about it would be healing and uplifting for them, but it wasn't. Not because they knew him personally, or would benefit from his remaining free...but because they had learned to have compassion.

It wasn't until my two six-year-olds took my hand and taught me about empathy and forgiveness that I realized how wrong my celebration had been. I had spent months building up more hate and bitterness, while my daughters had taken those same months to find love and compassion for a man who had wronged them—a lesson, I had taught them...but had forgotten to apply to myself.

What a humbling moment I had that day. I was not the exception to the lessons of truth I had preached. Maybe Rob had hurt me, and maybe his poor choices had gotten him where he was...but *I* had to learn to let it go. Though his actions had shattered my family, it was *my* hatred that was killing my heart. I had to become like my little daughters: patient, compassionate, humble, and full of love...even for the man who had killed their father and made me a widow.

We are all here on earth together. We are going to wrong each other and cause others to feel pain. Sometimes we will be the one in the wrong, and other times we will be the ones who are wronged. Does that mean we can't still have compassion for each other? I learned that afternoon that forgiveness is real, not just in words...but in our hearts. Empathy is possible, even through our pain.

My twins walked in Rob's shoes that day, and felt the loss his family was going to have to live with. *I* wasn't that strong, but their reminder of empathy was not just enlightening...it was humbling. *I* was the mother—and yet *they* were my teachers.

What does it mean to walk in others' shoes? It means actually trying to feel what they feel, and trying to see what they see. It means taking a step outside of ourselves to see another point of view. As adults, we have trained ourselves to think that our way is the best way. We have become stuck in what we can see, and we think that we have the only answers. It usually isn't easy for us to look at something from a new perspective.

Often, it's our children who show us what it means to have empathy: empathy for a family member, a friend, a stranger, and even a murderer. They can show us how to see the world while standing in someone else's shoes.

A lesson I had taught a million times with words became real that day. As I walked hand in hand back to my car with my babies, I felt strength from them to develop that empathy myself.

Forgiveness is real. Being able to achieve it *is* within our reach. Maybe it isn't as simple as it was for my two little twins, crying tears for the children of a man who had killed their father...but if they can do it—so can we.

Have compassion for those who have hurt you. Find love for those who have let you down. Seek to feel empathy for those who need it the most. God will be the ultimate judge. It is Him who will have the final say. We aren't required to be the judge for anyone...but ourselves.

In the Doctrine and Covenants 64:10, we read this commandment from God:

> *I, the Lord, will forgive whom I will forgive, but of you it is required to forgive all men.*

It is a lesson I am still learning, and one that hasn't come easily for me. To truly forgive, we must have compassion. To have compassion, we must be able to love. And to truly love, we must give God our whole heart. *He* is the only source of eternal love we will find on this earth. The power He can give us can strengthen all the relationships with which we have been blessed, and can help us develop love for complete strangers, even for those who may have caused us pain.

Jesus Christ has felt your pain. He has counted every tear. He died for you that even you can be forgiven for the wrongs you have committed. Even you can be forgiven for the times when you have been too full of pride, hatred or anger to forgive.

We may never forget our pain. Sometimes the scars run too deep to completely disappear...but we can rise above our pain. The atonement of Jesus Christ truly covers all pain. It diminishes the scars; it eases the burdens. It can bring miracles to our lives.

There is a song I have sung many times in my life. I love it for its simple message. Greater Miracles by Hilary Weeks. In it she sings about many of the amazing miracles that happened when Christ was on the earth. How He can heal any pain, and help anyone. But if we put our faith in Jesus Christ and find true forgiveness that is the greatest miracle of all.

The miracle that day was not that Rob was going back to jail. It was that my daughters showed me how to feel empathy. They taught me, by their example, about forgiveness and love. They showed me what true compassion is, and what I could strive to become one day. They reminded me that even the sinners deserve to be set free—maybe not into the world—but from the hatred in our hearts. They showed me that even I, a victim, could find a way to be a survivor.

And that was the miracle...the greatest miracle.

CHAPTER EIGHTEEN

# *The Sun*

**I KEPT EXPECTING THIS GRAND MOMENT WHEN** I would feel whole again. I pictured it would be like what I had seen in movies. I hoped for the rooftop scene in *Beauty and the Beast* when all of the sudden, light radiated from every pore as the Beast was turned into something beautiful. I watched for those moments often in the little glimpses of perfection that would come into my days. I secretly hoped that a powerful 'rooftop experience' would bring me the light I craved. I didn't realize that it would take a series of steps, sometimes in reverse, for true healing to occur. As time passed, and I never had my 'Beast to a Prince' experience, I came to learn that such an event was not going to come.

*Sometimes it is in the most simple moments that we find healing.*

One Saturday, I was working with the kids in the house. We were cleaning up all of our messes from the week. Shawn said he was going to run outside and mow the lawn. We kept up our hard work indoors.

After a while, I realized that Teage wasn't with us. I searched in all the bedrooms, and there was no sign of him. I walked through the kitchen toward the front room when out the window, I beheld the brightest view.

I sat at the window and with tears in my eyes, I remembered …

The summer before Emmett died, I came upon Teage sitting in the exact spot where I now found myself. He was also looking out the window, but he was watching one of the neighbor boys playing catch with his father. That day, I watched my little boy as he longed for what that neighbor boy had—a dad who put his son first, over the demands of work, and the endless hours of responsibilities. I wiped tears from Teage's eyes that day in an attempt to heal a void I could not fill.

Teage actually asked me that night if Emmett still lived with us. I reassured him that Emmett was just very busy with his preparations to take the bar exam and starting up his new law practice. All of that information—although very true—didn't take away Teage's longing for his father to take a moment out of his busy schedule to play with his son. Emmett was excelling at work, and in all of the other things on which he was working so hard … but he was failing at the eternal things that really mattered. He was putting off being a dad for another day.

I'm certain that Emmett never thought it would get to that point. He never planned to fail as a father, but the excitement of excelling and the enticement of acquiring 'more' kept him from us. He *wanted* to be a good father. In the beginning of his years as a father, his greatest desire was to be the man his children deserved. On many occasions in the early days of parenthood, Emmett had been just that— but his responsibilities at home continued to increase and eventually his efforts slacked. No matter how many good days as a father he'd had in the past, those days didn't make up for the fact that he needed to continue and even increase his efforts. He had become so consumed in his work and in 'providing for his family' that he actually forgot the *real* needs of the people who were in it.

*Being a parent is more than the work in life. It is the little moments that they will remember.*

Now on this day, my view of Teage was very different. I sat in the same spot where Teage had cried tears of disappointment for a dad who had forgotten him, but what *I* saw as I looked out that window was light. In the hot summer sun, my son was pushing a lawnmower. With Shawn right behind him, Teage was guiding the lawnmower over the grass as if he had just won a prize. He held his head high. His smile beamed more brightly than I had ever seen. He was like a baseball player who had just won the World Series and was walking in a parade for all to see. His trophy was not the lawnmower, or his ability to push it. No, Teage's trophy that day...was Shawn. He was proud to be in the front yard walking in front of his new dad.

I continued to sit at the window as tears of joy fell down my face. All my little boy had dreamed of in his life was playing catch in the yard, or mowing the lawn with his father—and he was living it.

Had Emmett known that his time would have been cut short, I don't think he would have let a Saturday of mowing the lawn with his son pass him by. I think he would have taken a few more afternoons to throw the ball in the front yard, or to sit on the couch and read stories to his children. If he had known he would die young, he would have remembered to live in each moment.

As I watched Shawn and Teage push that lawnmower up and down the grass, I had an overwhelming sensation that Emmett felt immense gratitude for Shawn. Shawn was giving Teage what Emmett could no longer give—the gift of fatherhood. This day, I wasn't watching my son long for a father out the window; I was witnessing him living his dream of having a father who took the time to show him what mattered most. Shawn

was taking the time to show his son what life was all about.

What *is* life all about? Sometimes we forget how simple it really is. We forget to let go of the little things that hold us back from the relationships we desire. We forget that all our kids really want is to know they are important and valued. We fail them over and over again ... and for what? A clean house? More money? A raise? A new car? One more TV show? One more game? Another drink?

As the sun shines down on us, and summer brings us its warmth, let us take the time to see it. There are bright things all around us, but we must choose wisely. Money shines brightly when held up in the daylight. Diamonds glimmer when light reflects upon them. Cars are made of metal that shines brightly in the afternoon heat. Many things can shine. Some light can bring us temporary contentment for a moment ... and other light can bring us peace and heal us forever. We need to discern between those two types of light.

Our relationships are the things that count. Take every chance you can to show the ones you love how much you care. Tell them you love them, and then show them. Show them that they are more important than the messes they make. Show them that they are more important than their mistakes. Let them see that your time with them is what can heal both of your hearts. Turn to your relationships as you search for light in this world. Show them that they are more important than one more show, another football game, one last high, or one more drink. Help them feel your love by saying no to a demand or an addiction that keeps you from them. Don't let another day pass by when you forget what is really important ... and don't just tell the ones you love what they mean to you—show them.

Money can only last so long, and jobs can be lost. Cars lose their value, and rocks can scratch them. Markets can crash, and diamonds can get stolen ... but families—families can last forever. It's true that we will all die, but even after death our relationships do not end. That is why we must cherish them now, because whatever they are today—is how they will be remembered. Our children don't want to hear that one day we will play catch with them in the front yard—they want to do it now. They are proud of all the hard work we do for them, but that is not what they will remember.

I wish I had the original version, but a long time ago, Emmett wrote a blog post on our family blog about Bo Jackson and the way he put his sons over his game. Emmett talked about how critical it was for all of us to remember what is really important in life. He challenged us to take a minute every day to make sure our children came before anything else. Emmett was in the middle of law school when he wrote that post. I knew at that time, he was fighting the temptation to put school over his family. Most of the time back then, he won that battle. He tried to choose us. He found little moments to come and spend with us. Unfortunately, somewhere along the line after that, he forgot to take his own advice.

None of us are exempt from that advice. The temptation to let our blinders cover the bigger view is powerful. Take the power. When you feel your eyes getting heavy with the view of what is not important—take a stand. You have the power to overcome every temptation even those that come in the form of "I'm doing it for my family." If you have to justify the fact that you aren't spending time with your family…by saying you are doing it "for them," make sure that is what they really want. If you work your entire life "for your family," but then at the end of it, you no longer have one—none of that work will mean a damn thing.

It doesn't take great sacrifice to be the person you always hoped to be. Once you knock down all the walls of darkness that are clouding your view, it is the Son who will shine through YOU…and you will easily remember exactly who you are. It may not be in a grand moment like it was for the Beast on the rooftop, but step by step, light by light—You can become the "Prince." The Beast didn't want to live in his pain, and neither do you. Let it go.

If Emmett had a voice today I know without a doubt he would say, "Son…I am sorry for all the times I didn't play with you. I failed when I let the moments slip by when I could have taught you about life. I am sorry for all the times my phone was more important than your questions. I am sorry for putting off being your dad for another day. I wish I could have really seen you when I had you in my arms."

Remember what you have, and don't let it slip through your fingertips. Our relationships can be made light, and the power of those connections can help us heal our pain.

Turn to a source of light that can help you see what is really important. The sun is a powerful source, but the Son of God is an even more powerful source of light in a world filled with darkness. Remember the sons and daughters who are waiting at the window for you to be that little ray of sunshine for them. Put down your phones, your computers, and all the other "responsibilities" that keep you from the most important ones. Be the ray of light your loved ones need. The Son of God lives, and His light can live inside of you.

CHAPTER NINETEEN

# *Fight*

**I REMEMBER BEING PREGNANT WITH MY TWINS** and thinking
I had it all figured out. I had a birth plan all written, and I pretty much
knew exactly how my birthing experience would be. I had been on bed
rest for contractions for months, and thought for sure that being induced
would not be a decision I would have to come to. We had spent months
fighting to keep them inside, so I figured they would just crawl out when
the time came. Boy was I so wrong.

Thirty seven weeks was our golden number. When that week came
my doctor was in shock that we had made it that long. He took me off bed
rest and told me to get out on the streets and walk my heart out. I probably walked forty miles in a few days. I was determined to get those babies
out naturally. I continued to have endless contractions in my journeys on
the streets, but every time I would go back into the office he would check
me and I hadn't even dilated at all.

By the end of the week, and with no progression, my doctor scheduled
my induction. Both babies were head down, I kept my fingers crossed
that my natural birth plan I had fought so hard for would be carried out,
despite my set back of being induced. I was frustrated as the next day
rolled around and my scheduled induction was up. I walked in the hospital a little deflated that the first bullet point in my designed birth plan
would not be happening for me.

It was early evening and my doctor began the process. He said it could be fast, but most likely I would see slow progression throughout the night. The next morning came and went; still no babies. My contractions were consistent, but barely any progression in my dilation. My desire to continue my natural birth plan kept me hanging on with no drugs other than the Pitocin to create stronger contractions. They would up the Pitocin every few hours in a hope to see more progression. The pain was almost unbearable by early afternoon. Every time the nurse or doctor would check me, they found I had progressed very little. Nurses would beg me to get an epidural or take some pain meds, but my stubborn nature kept me driving to keep up the fight for my natural birth.

By evening I was in so much pain that tears would roll down my face every time I had a contraction. The Pitocin was turned up so high that my contractions were only about a half of a minute apart, so I had little breathing time in between. There came a point when baby B began to panic. Every time a contraction would start, her heartbeat would plummet. It was like the contractions were causing her to go into a panic attack. Her heart rate would drop dramatically, and then would become very sporadic throughout the whole contraction.

My doctor finally came to check the baby and me. After finding out that I was only at a three he started to get serious, "Ash...I know that you have written out this idea of how today was supposed to go, and we have laughed and called you the iron cervix for the last few months...but this isn't working. I know you are against an epidural, but I really feel like maybe it would help you relax and allow your body to do its job. You have been fighting for this plan, and I don't want to take it away from you, but I really want to get these babies out without doing a C- section. If baby B doesn't start handling this labor better, I am going in after her. So you can keep fighting through this the hard way, or we can try to do something different."

Within minutes my birth plan was gone and the epidural was in place. With the pain taken away I started focusing on my struggling baby. Every contraction seemed to affect her. Every time I saw her monitor waver I chanted in my mind, "Please let her be OK, please let her be ok."

A half an hour after the epidural was in place I got the urge to push. I told the nurse who almost laughed, "Remember when we just checked you, and you were only a three ..." Finally I talked her into getting my doctor, and sure enough— I was at a ten. They rushed me to the operating room. Since we were having twins, it was that hospital's practice to deliver in the O.R.

As soon as I began to push baby B's heartbeat would almost stop. After a few more pushes my doctor started to panic, "We have to get that baby out of there!" He grabbed his tools and suctioned baby A's head right out. She was beautiful, she had a healthy cry, and she looked perfectly pink—well perfect except for the little red yarmulke that had been left by the suction machine.

He searched for baby B's head, "I feel a hand... and a foot ..." My heart dropped—TRIPLETS? "She has flipped... I am going in after her." And he did, clear to his elbow! He grabbed her by the feet and yanked her out. She was as dark as a blueberry. My heart stopped as I held my breath to hear her cry... Silence. The nurse could tell I was not breathing well and handed me an oxygen mask. I tried to stay calm as I could hear them flopping her around and trying to get her to breathe. As more time passed I could feel the tension in the air—something was wrong with our baby. I pulled the mask away from my face and screamed, "What is happening... she hasn't made a sound... is she ok... please, somebody tell me what is going on!"

For what seemed like an hour, no one said a word. All the nurses and the doctors were gathered around our baby. I felt like I was in a dream as my heart cried out, "Heavenly Father, please, help this baby girl. Please help her keep up the fight and make it through." I sat frozen with my head in my hands. Everything seemed to be in slow motion. All the nurses scrambling—no one looking me in the eye.

And then it came... the loudest baby scream I had ever heard. It was as if she was answering my prayer, "Mommy, I am not only here…I am a warrior, I wasn't going to give up that easy. I am a fighter!!!" The sound every mother waits for. They rushed the twins off to the NICU while I caught my breath.

As the doctor was getting me ready to head back to my room, he found something interesting. He held up the placenta, which was the last thing on earth I wanted to look at in that moment. He looked puzzled and walked over to where I could get a better look. He said, I have never seen anything quite like this before. Both babies umbilical cords are connected in different places, but baby B's cord was barely even hooked on to this sac. Can you see where baby A's cord wrapped around the whole right side of the sack? That is what it normally looks like. I have read about this many times, but never seen it so dramatic. I have no idea how that second little twin of yours even got any nutrients, let alone lived. Usually when it is this disproportioned, one twin ends up getting all the growth and the other one doesn't make it. You are so lucky. Obviously that little girl is a fighter."

She was a fighter—just ten minutes into her life and we had learned a lot about our little twin…Bostyn. She wasn't going to give up.

Fast-forward a few years. Emmett is in law school at Gonzaga. Bostyn is four years old. We were at church one Sunday afternoon and Bostyn

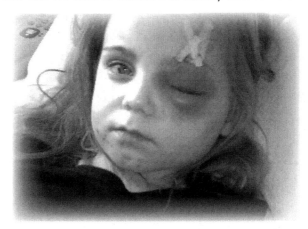

comes into my class crying with blood running down her eye. I took her into the bathroom and cleaned her up a little bit. A few nurses who attended our church took a look at her and suggest I take her to the little 24 hour clinic close by. I took her in, they threw some glue in her cut, and sent us home. Easy enough.

That night Bostyn woke up screaming. I tiptoed in and reminded her that her eye was just sore from her cut. She went back to sleep for a few more hours. At 1:00 a.m. she was screaming again. This time I flip on the light and run over to her bed. Her eye was the size of a baseball and totally swollen shut. Emmett ran her into the hospital, which was an hour away.

For the first few days they treated her for a MRSA staph infection. By the second night Emmett and I were sitting in the room watching the infection spread like wildfire down her neck, and over to her other eye. By this time she couldn't move her head, and could barely see out of her only open eye. Doctors kept reassuring us that it would start to go down, but as the evening turned to night we all started to panic. Doctors began coming in to schedule surgery for the next morning to start to drain her neck and try to get rid of the infection.

I remember at one point stepping out in the hall and pacing the floor. My baby, who had an identical twin sister, was going to have scars all over her neck and face, or worse... they weren't going to stop the infection and she wasn't going to live. I felt worthless— I was right there, and I couldn't do anything. I couldn't save my little girl. I paced the hall for twenty minutes searching for an answer inside of my mind. Nothing came.

In my pacing, I came to a dark hallway where the lights had been turned down. I rounded the corner out of plain view, and lost it. I burst into hysterical tears. Through my sobs I prayed harder than I had ever prayed in my life, "Please. The infection is spreading through her body. They are not finding answers and I feel helpless, there has to be something that can be done to save this little girl. I need an answer, and I can't sit here any longer. Please send us someone who can save her."

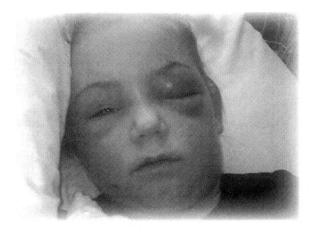

As I whispered in my mind my final AMEN, words began popping into my head. I almost ran down the hall. I wasn't sure where I was going, but I knew exactly what I was going to say. I finally made it to the nurse's station and with a power not of my own I began shouting out demands and pointing at people, "You are going to call the infectious disease specialist...You are going to go order this test to make sure this infection has been properly diagnosed ..." I don't remember much more of what I ordered that room full of nurses to do, but I do remember by the next morning many specialists had entered her room, prescriptions were changed, and Bostyn could move her neck and see out of her good eye. She didn't have to have the surgeries or have draining tubes inserted.

That day I fought...for my daughter's life. I fought for a power to send someone to help save her, and I was given the words to command the right people to come our way.

*Sometimes we fight for a purpose, and sometimes we fight for a fear.*

About three months after we got married, Shawn and I had our first big fight. He came to me one Sunday morning and said he was going to go to the drag strip to race his jeep while we were at church. The minute those words left his mouth, here is how my mind worked: *He obviously doesn't care about me; He is willing to break a commitment he made to me about how we would spend our Sundays; He doesn't care about my feelings. He doesn't care about the example he is giving my kid. If he can be easily swayed on our simple commitments to each other then one day some girl will talk him into walking out on our big commitments. He will leave us. He will cheat on me. Then he will be murdered in a dark parking lot for sleeping with another man's wife.*

Boom, boom, boom…Within a fraction of a second the scenario my mind created was flaring red flags through my entire body. He can't possibly choose a choice I don't agree with, or else he doesn't care about US. He can't use Sunday for racing his jeep, or he is not going to be a good dad. He is going to abandon us. My kids deserve a perfect example in every way; we don't deserve THIS. I guess he didn't want to marry me in the first place. If he can't even keep his word on something as simple as how we will spend our Sundays, he is never going to make it.

By the time he walked out the door to leave I was like a volcano spewing with all the fear of my past, and the imagined pain of my future.

I ran out into the garage and like an idiot rattled off every fear that had crossed my mind, "Shawn…I thought you were the kind of father that would give these kids a good example…I thought you were going put their need to see a good husband above your stupid ideas like white trash drag racing. If you can't even give up a simple thing like what Sunday activities you would rather do than go to church, maybe MY kids and I deserve better than this." My eyes burned with all the fear that was driving my words. Did he even love me? Did he really want to be their dad? In that moment I could not detach his desire to make his own decision about how he would spend his time that day, from his willingness to love my kids and me.

As he should have, after getting berated by his crazy wife, he left. I watched him drive away and I felt like a piece of me died again. My mind went back in time to Emmett telling me he was going to leave and run to Walgreens. I could almost feel my soul scream, "Don't go…please…

something is wrong. Please just stay here with me." I could feel the toxic shock of fear wave through my entire being. Emmett had left when I felt he should stay—and he died. How could Shawn do this to me again? Was he ever going to come back? Was today going to be the day when some normal, healthy, not broken girl would come and show him all that he was missing? Or would it be the day when deceit would come his way and drive him to his death?

The thoughts that overtook me seemed as real as the car that had just sped away. How could he say he loved me if he didn't even want me to be a part of his decisions? If he couldn't see how important it was to me for him to go to church with us, why would he not choose my choice? How could he come back and be a father now if he wasn't perfect in everything he did, or in the promises that he had made? If he was going to disappoint us, maybe it would just be easier to walk away. If I wasn't worth making good decisions and fighting for, maybe we were done.

My fear of losing him was trying to get me to believe I no longer wanted or needed him. I truly thought we would get divorced that day—either because of my unwillingness to accept his personal choices and imperfections; or because of his unwillingness to include me in his decisions and follow the simple commitments we had promised each other.

He was only gone forty-five minutes. He later told me that he drove to the racetrack, determined to show me that he could do whatever he wanted without "asking permission". He said as he pulled up to the track he sat in his silent car for a half an hour struggling with the internal battle of what to choose. He too felt the overwhelming feeling to just give up that day. To stop fighting for what we had been building, and stop trying to carry such a heavy load that had been placed upon us.

By the time he walked in the door we were both a heated mess of fear. We battled all afternoon back and forth. I was determined to show him that his stupid choices could ruin our family some day; and he was determined to show me that he had to be able to make his own choices and still be loved regardless of if they were perfect or not.

We both had very valid strong points, but on this day, neither of us could look through our own pain to see the other's fear.

The 'crazy cycle' is a wonderful definition of what we were in. My fear of reliving the past urged me to try to push Shawn into making all the right decisions— for *me*. His fear of feeling mothered and control caused him to want to make his own decisions— just to make sure he still could.

I don't know about other blended families—but for ours when a major argument would happen, it seemed our natural reaction would be to walk away. We both had felt like we had been through enough in our first marriage. This was supposed to be our easy one... right? Any heated fight we would have, even about simple things, would somehow end with one or the other of us thinking or saying that maybe we made the wrong decision to marry each other. Maybe we would be better off alone.

It was like no matter how many good days came our way, the minute contention showed up on our doorstep we would want to abandon any of the hard work we had made in our marriage. It seemed we would just give up the fight and walk away.

At times, blending two families is difficult. You both come into the marriage with fears from the past. Whether divorce or death— your past has been hard, and therefore your new marriage has many challenges right from the beginning. Fears are powerful, especially in new families that have come from a broken past. The power of your pain can ignite at any given moment. For us in the first few years... it happened often.

*Sometimes the strength of passion can help us overcome and fight through; but other times the weakness of passion can hold us back and hinder us in our progression.*

Shawn and I have come a long way since that day, but we haven't stopped fighting. But now, more often than not... we fight on the same team. We are passionate about our family, we fall victim of fears, but a few things have changed ...

One day our crazy cycle was in full force. The kids were all downstairs and we were up in our bonus room going back and forth over something about parenting. It was going nowhere fast, and neither of us was willing to compromise our stand. All of the sudden Shawn said, "Ash…stop. Get on your knees." We knelt down together and Shawn offered the sweetest prayer. He asked that the dark feeling in our home leave and that we could see each other's point of view.

By the end of the prayer I felt a peace surround us. We stood up and threw our arms around each other. He looked at me and said, "What were we fighting about again?" I replied with tears in my eyes, " I have no idea…but whatever just happened…was amazing. You are worth fighting for, I don't want to fight *with* you anymore, but I want to fight for you. We are not perfect people, but I don't want anyone else. This blending family stuff is hard. I never even had a clue how much extra work it would be to try to make our families come together…but I chose you. I chose us. I will fight for us!"

I wish I could say that that magic moment has cured us of the urge to nitpick the way we parent each other's kids, or the way we baby our own…it hasn't! I wish I could say that at times we both don't want to run away and that we are the perfect blended family—we aren't. But the prayer on my knees with my husband was a powerful reminder that God can help us even when we can't see what's worth fighting for.

We are all fighters in one way or another. Some are fighting for their lives; others are fighting for their country. Then there are some of us who are fighting for a cause we don't even know. Sometimes we forget what we are fighting about, and other times will never forget the fight that got us through our battle.

We were born to be fighters. Just like my daughter Bostyn who fought her way into this world, we all have the desire to win and succeed. But what if we are fighting for the wrong cause? What if all the fighting we are doing alone is only getting us further away from what we really want?

ASHLEE BIRK | 177

Every good fight starts with a drive, a powerful force of motivation: Fighting for your little girl in a hospital bed; fighting your own battle with cancer. Some fight their way out of addiction or depression. Some are fighting their way through an imperfect relationship. Sometimes the victor will have to walk away and not look back, and other times the win may come as they have to hold on— even when they can't remember why they are there.

No matter who we are, we will have to fight a good fight. Every good fight ends with love; every bad fight ends with hate. Fighting as a team will get us a lot further than fighting alone.

Sometimes our fight can change the world, and other times our fight will merely save ourselves. There is a battle raging in each one of us, a fight for good and a pull of evil. Not every fight is worth dying for, not every motivation a good cause. Not every fight will be viewed; some battles are never seen with the human eye. We are all warriors from the battles we have won. We are all soldiers when we battle with grace. We all have the power to be our own captain and know when it is time to just let go of a fight that can never be won, or pilot ourselves to a battle worth saving.

Don't lose yourself by fighting a fight of destruction. Some battles only rage because of a fear of losing. If it were easy, it wouldn't make us grow. Life is going to be full of battles, good and bad. Whatever fights you are hanging on to, make sure they will bring you up. Fight for the battles that are worth winning, and let go of the battles that are worth losing. Fight for a cause you will never lose. You are not fighting alone.

CHAPTER TWENTY

# Unclear

**SOMETIMES COMMUNICATION IS HARD. THE INTENTIONS YOU** have when you say something can come out much different than the words that are heard. Communication is a valuable asset that so many of us fail at. When used properly it can help dictate exact information, but when used wrong it can bring a lot of unnecessary heartache.

The day before Emmett's funeral, I got a phone call. It was from the mortuary. The lady on the other end simply said, "I am calling to let you know that your husband's clothes are now ready for you to pick up when ever you want".

I thought maybe it was a prank call. I walked over to the window and stared out at the stale air. "I...um...well, I...are you sure?" I pictured his shirt with bullet holes in the chest and blood that had dripped form his head wound. I stumbled for the words to ask, "Wouldn't you just...I don't understand why I would...Ok, yes, thank you...his clothes...I will send someone to get them."

I hung up the phone, sick that someone actually thought I wanted to pick up Emmett's clothes, and even more sick that maybe someone was pulling a prank on me.

I called the police department to ask the detectives about what I should do. He told me to take a deep breath. I told him the story through my hysteria. He informed me that he had all of Emmett's clothes in his custody, as evidence, and that this had to be a mistake. We hung up the phone so he could go figure out what had gone wrong.

I sat on my kitchen floor gripping my phone—waiting for him to call back. Why had someone done this to me? What part of my pain, did this cruel prankster think was funny? I stewed and stewed until my phone rang.

It turned out that the call had been made by mistake. The office had two calls to make: one to me to let me know someone had dropped off a few letters to them to give to me, and another to a widow who needed to pick up her husband's clothes.

They hadn't called to hurt me; nobody was trying to find pleasure from my pain. It was just a miscommunication, an accident. They hadn't said those words to throw the picture of Emmett's dead body into my mind. They had merely called to contact a wife who had asked to get her husband's belongings back.

A simple misunderstanding—a small mix up—and my world felt like it had turned upside down.

A few days after the alarm was installed, when my kids were in bed, my friend Jenalee offered to have her daughter come sit at my house so we could go to a church activity together. It was a night for moms to get together and learn about new things. I was excited for the chance to go. I was a little nervous to leave my kids; but I knew that it would be good for me to get out and enjoy some time with other moms.

When Savannah walked in with her mom I started talking really fast and telling her how to use the alarm. I rambled on and on about how she needs to keep the house safe and the kids inside their beds. Then I stupidly said, "And if any scary men come to the door—and you feel scared—you can press this button on the alarm and it will call the police for you. They will be here within minutes."

This was one of Savannah's first times ever babysitting. She just sat and stared at me. I said, "Is this a bad idea? Should I just stay home?" She reassured me that she wanted to do this for me, and everything would be ok. I was still nervous, but decided to go.

We stopped by my neighbor Auna's house to see if she wanted a ride; she said she did. She had already told her husband that she was leaving so she grabbed her baby and we headed out. It was fun talking to the two of them as we drove. We didn't talk about anything serious. I was almost relaxed on the drive over—trying hard to enjoy the moment.

We got to the activity and said hello to other friends. We had been there about 45 minutes when Jenalee went over to check her phone in her purse. She had 15 missed calls from Savannah. I grabbed my phone; I also had a bunch of missed calls. We both tried calling her back, but now she wasn't answering.

What was wrong with me? Why would I have left my phone in my purse when we were in such a loud place? Where in my right mind did I think that leaving my house tonight was a good idea?

We ran to the car and drove as fast as we could to my house in silence. We pulled up; the house looked like it had when we left it. No scary guys were at the door. The porch light was on and I couldn't see any evidence that anyone had come to the door.

I ran inside. Savannah was a mess. "A scary guy kept pounding on the door... I was so scared. I kept getting on this stool and looking through the window on the door, but there is no peephole and I couldn't see his face, just the top of his head ... I couldn't tell who it was. He just kept ringing the doorbell and hitting the door with his hand."

I could not breath. *He was here, wasn't he?* Had he come to our house looking for me? My mind was racing a million miles a minute. I assumed the worst. I pictured my babies, all asleep in their beds. What if he had gone through the window when nobody came to the door? What if he was up stairs right now and I was going to lose everyone?

I didn't go to any of the rational thoughts of who could have been at my door. I didn't assume that it could have been anyone else—like my dad coming to check on us, or one of my brothers. In my mind, the only person that it could have been was the man who killed my husband.

We all sat there—going over and over all the facts—trying to figure out what had happened and who had come to the door. Then Auna realized she too had some missed calls. She had been getting calls from her husband on her silenced phone in her purse. She called him back, and all of the sudden the whole night made sense.

Apparently their original plan was that she would leave the baby home with him and their other kids. When we showed up asking her if she wanted a ride, she couldn't find her husband. We would later hear from him that he was in the back yard and she locked the back door when she left. At the last second, she decided to grab the baby and take her with us. So once the husband tried to come inside—he was locked out. He ran to the front yard to get in the garage and the front door was wide open. So: back door is locked, front door is wide open, and the baby was nowhere to be found. Then when Auna wasn't answering her phone—he thought she had left the baby and someone had come in their house and kidnapped her. After she didn't answer her phone time after time, he went looking for someone who he could get a hold of. He came pounding on our door—knowing that someone had to be home—to help him get a hold of me so he could solve the mystery.

It was a scary night for us all—but luckily, one that was all just a misunderstanding.

Misunderstandings rule this world. I would have to say most of our experiences in conversations that are negative, usually begin with someone's words being taken for what they were not intended to be. Auna didn't mean to leave her husband worried about the safety of her baby; she had taken the baby to give him a break and have one less child to worry about. Savannah didn't realize that the man at the door was just looking for his baby; she misunderstood his apparent frantic pounds on the door to be someone who wanted to cause harm.

I should have never set Savannah up to be filled with so much fear if someone were to come to the door; my obsessive fears drove my miscommunication about how to handle a knock at the door.

This whole night was a classic example of how a few words—taken out of context or blown up to something bigger than they actually were—can cause real anxiety and lack of security.

I remember a child game I used to love to play called telephone. You start out with one person whispering in an ear and go down the line until everyone has heard the message. What starts out as simple sentence, can turn into a crazy babble of jumbled words. That is how communication works. We are given information from one source; unaware of if that source knows the actual truth. We take that information for how it is said to us—not necessarily how it was originally intended to be.

Before Emmett died, he was telling lots of versions of what was going on in his life. I knew one version, his family knew a different version, and the people he worked with obviously knew an entirely different version of his story.

On the night that he died, and all the versions of the story tried to come together—it made for a lot of miscommunication. Some of the miscommunications became very hurtful and painful for all the parties involved. Much of the answers to these stories were left unsettled until we all had to sit through a month long murder trial years later.

Sometimes we use communication to manipulate the information that we want others to have about us. Sometimes we lie to try to be something we are not; or we leave out important truths that would allow someone to make a judgment on us— or withhold parts of our life we do not wish for them to know.

Miscommunication can be a result of a truth being changed, manipulated, or diluted—but miscommunication can also come from the lack of clear knowledge. Sometimes someone is saying or doing something out of love—but our ability to see their pure intentions is lacking.

It can be in something as simple as a husband volunteering to stay home with the sick kid from the violin performance. Maybe that wife knows the husband has a favorite football team playing that night, and she turns his trying to do a favor for her into him just being selfish and wanting to watch his game. Maybe he did have an extra motive in his willingness to stay home and take care of the sick baby... or maybe he just really wanted to help her out on a busy night.

It is when we can look for the good that someone is TRYING to say or do, when communication can become what it is intended to be—a way to get information from one source to another.

Not everyone is out to get you. Not everyone is trying to be hurtful or use you. Some of us just truly are trying to be there for you—we just don't know how to show you the way that it is rolling around in our head.

In the months before he died, Emmett would get so frustrated if I would ask him if he was ok, or if something was wrong, when he would answer his phone and leave the room. I wasn't trying to be an annoying wife; I truly just wanted to be part of his life. I wanted to help him if he had problems; I wanted to be a listening ear if he was stressed at work. My intentions were pure; but my ability to communicate them, at times, probably felt smothering and insecure.

It is hard not to look back and think that maybe if I would have just left him alone and not tried to push my love so hard on him—when he was going through his tough patches— maybe he wouldn't have turned to her. And then another part of me thinks, well maybe he wasn't allowing me to be part BECAUSE of his relationship with her.

I will never have the answer for that—but this I do know—my intentions and my desires were of a loving nature. Why would I share these insecurities?... to remind others about looking for the true intentions of another's heart. Maybe what seemed as Emmett's lack of interaction and love for me was merely his internal battle inside himself. I had one interpretation of his communication, but his true intentions I will never know.

Recently, I was sitting in the airport waiting for a flight. To the right of me were about 20 adults who were sitting quietly, much of them on some sort of electronic devices. They were so enthralled in their media they had no idea what was going on around them. To the left of me was a young family with two little boys. At one point they were informed that their flight had been delayed. They made it no secret that they were very angry about this new information. The dad kept getting on the phone and swearing about the situation to everyone he talked to. The mother was doing this bipolar dance of ignoring her screaming sons, and then yelling at them. She was doing nothing to silence their cries, except for the frequent yells at them to "shut up".

Why is it when we, as parents, are worried or struggling with something, do we forget the needs of our children?

It was not those little kids fault that mistakes were made and they were bumped off their flight, and then had to call all the airlines to figure out how they were going to get home—yet this mother was taking all her frustrations out on her little boys.

It was 6:00am. The possibilities of so many factors were playing into those little boys shouts. Their bodies wanted to be asleep; they were probably starving; and they seemed very bored with nothing to do but wait. But as I watched them, I think the main thing they were struggling with was that their parents were completely stressed out.

Kids can feel our emotions even without us telling them what is really wrong. They can sense, just as we can for them, when we are off. They are wired with instincts that allow them to feel the stress, even without any information.

When we are stressed, on top of embarrassed in a large group of people, it is easy to get angry about the annoyance that is right there in front of us. But what if we were to take a step back and look for what was really annoying us? It usually isn't the target that our frustrations are pointing us at that we are really struggling with. It is usually the deeper frustrations that are weighing on us to cause us to get angry at the little naggings, or small annoyances.

As families we do a chase. We go through a cycle of behaviors and fears. It is like a constant dance followed by the same pattern of behaviors, resulting in no change whatsoever. I have heard it been called the crazy cycle—the chase of wanting to feel loved, but needing control. It is apparent in all of us to some degree. We fear we are not loved, so we try to control something. Control doesn't bring about more love, and loving doesn't always give us more control. But as humans we continuously cycle through these emotions of needing to feel the love we desire while maintaining the control we need to feel safe.

At the beginning of our blended family we had many moments when we would do this dance. We would get so worked up about things that our stress would become a family event. I would feel the need to feel more of Shawn's love and I would try to control something he was doing—almost a smothering forced kind of love. He would feel the need to have the power of his freedom, and would therefore withhold some of his love from me. And the pattern would go on and on. My insecurities would play into his and we would end up doing a game of cat and mouse. I would chase him, he would run from me—and both of us continued feeling a large void in our relationship. The balance of power and control, and fears and emotions were like a vicious cycle that would never really get us anywhere at all. The turmoil that our crazy cycle would stir up didn't just affect our marriage—it seemed to disrupt our entire family and each individual in our home.

So how can we help our little ones when we are going through a stressful time? So many times we as adults think we can hide our emotions from our family—we think that our nonverbal communication cannot be read as easily as our words. It would be surprising to really sit down and talk with our kids and come to learn how much they really do know. They are a lot smarter then they let on. They can—not only hear the underlying emotions that are spoken in conversation—they can feel the spirit of contention, or the heaviness of fear.

Every thing a family goes through in this life will leave an impact on each person. Death, divorce, and loss are not just a one time event—they are a trauma that will stay with an individual through out their life. This does not mean that we cannot move forward from these trials, but the impact they have on our beings will be more than we can see with our eyes.

Every moment is important. Every day can teach us so much. We can be so much more than a rolling ball of chaos when troubled times come to us. We can be active instead of reactive. We can stand tall even when the winds seem to get too strong, and the storms of life try to blow us around.

So much of what we do is defined by who we think we are, and who we want to become. But so much of what we find ourselves doing is based more upon what we don't know, and what we can't see in ourselves and in our world.

The only way to stop this cycle is to end the patterns that make it up. Since Shawn and I have learned this valuable lesson in our marriage, we have been able to better look at each other—even in our mistakes and imperfections—and still see love. I wish we could say that we have been perfect at it—not even a little bit—but with the knowledge of our patterns, we have changed the course of some of the struggles that present themselves in our marriage.

It is ok for him to wash the car, even on a night when I just wanted him to stare into my eyes. It is ok for me to be on my computer or clean the house even though he had planned on me watching a car show with him. We have been able to learn we can still be loved, even when we aren't getting our way.

Love doesn't need to be a chase; it can be a partnership. Communication doesn't have to be a fight; it can be a dance.

*"Recognizing certainty biases in our self and others paves the way to better relationships. Understanding that we are all*

*biased with bias-induced fears can help us not be easily offended.*
*We have reason to give people a break instead of harshly judging*
*their seeming irrationality. Our empathy deepens. We can*
*learn to understand people's fears and appropriately help them*
*deconstruct their beliefs about the risks feeding their biases. We*
*can better deal with our own biases about who we think we are or*
*have to be."*

—*Decide now, the good life or the best life* pg. 179 L. Jay Mitchell

So, maybe you have a husband who is so insecure it drives you insane. He is always calling and texting and will never just leave you alone. You see it as a lack of trust for you or a bothersome annoyance; but maybe it is just his own struggle and he is striving to know his worth. Maybe his verbal and nonverbal communication is not a lack of trust for you— but a plea for you to take his hand and see that he is communicating something to you. He wants to be part... because he loves you. He wants to know he is enough... because he needs you.

Does your boss really hate you and the work you do—or is he having problems at home and taking them out on you? Is your daughter very disrespectful and sassing her mouth off at you because she doesn't care about you; or is she having a hard time with the fact that she sits alone every day at lunch? Is your Dad really set against you getting married be-cause he doesn't believe you are old enough to make good decisions—or is there more to his fears about his own insecurities in letting you go?

There is a deeper communication that goes on; it is greater than just the look in our eyes and the words that are coming out of our mouth. Every sentence that is spoken, and every word that is written—comes out because of an emotion.

What words are being said to you that seem to tear you down? What emotions are you not hearing when someone seems to be miscommuni-cating? Maybe there is more to those words than meets your eye and goes into your ear.

Communication is about love. It is about listening with an open mind, and speaking with an open heart. In marriage—and all of our relationships, if we can let go of pride, it is then that we begin to hear each other and the messages that were intended.

Not all intentions are pure, but for those that come with love—let us hear them as the messages they were given as. Communicate with love.

CHAPTER TWENTY-ONE

# Take upon Me

**ONE FRIDAY AFTERNOON, BAILEY AND BOSTYN PICKED**
out some cookbooks at the public library. They spent most of the day
making menus of the things they wanted to cook. All day on Saturday,
they anxiously asked if I could help them make some of the recipes on
their lists. I finally agreed.

Saturday evening, the two were eagerly cooking away. They were acting like such big girls and were having the time of their lives. I was trying to let them take the lead and do all of the things they could do on
their own. They were chopping up vegetables, making salsa, browning
meat, and measuring out rice. Each step was carefully organized and they
worked together to determine what to do next. It was fun seeing them
team up in the kitchen and act so grown-up.

At one point, Bailey took off the lid of our small food processor. However, instead of just unhooking the power button unit, she pulled up the
entire lid, power top, and blades. Since the lid and blades were still engaged with the power source, the machine responded as if it was still connected to the base. When she went to put the lid down, the power button
hit the countertop and the blades powered up in full force—shredding
both of her hands.

It was like a crime scene from a movie. Blood was literally shooting
out all over the white cabinets and floor. Each child in our house was
screaming at the top of his or her lungs. Bailey lost a lot a blood, most of

which was all over the dinner the girls had been working on. The blood was also spattered over the hardwood floor extending from the front door to the back bedroom.

The only thing I remember before going into a state of shock was looking down at her hands and seeing half of one of her fingers hanging by the skin. I could also see the palms of her hands through all the blood. They resembled a piece of uncooked steak. Shawn grabbed some towels, wrapped them around her hands, and within seconds he and Bailey were out the door. He rushed her to the hospital while the other kids and I stared all around us in shock at the bloodstained kitchen.

Five seconds. Literally in the blink of an eye, our house had gone from a peaceful, sweet, safe haven of imagination—to a traumatic war zone none of us will ever forget. As Teage, Bostyn and I wiped our tears and scrubbed Bailey's blood off of the walls and floor, I felt a huge wave of humility rush through me. Somewhere along my journey of writing about the pain of the past, I think I secretly hoped that all our pain was behind us. We had already lived through all the rough patches, hadn't we? We shouldn't have to go through any more pain, or any more physical anguish. I had started journaling our story to document the painful stories of the past perhaps in the hope that all the hard times were behind us.

Well, I can humbly report—they are not. We have not been exempt from cuts and bruises, and even broken hearts. Bailey ended up needing a total of 45 stitches on her hands. Both palms were ripped open. A tendon and vein on her left pointer finger were sliced through—hence the spewing of blood everywhere—and her right thumb was also badly cut.

Her hands were so wrapped up in bandages that she could not feed herself or do any of the usual things she has always been able to do on her own. For the first few days, every time we changed the bandages, everyone would burst into tears—staring at the wounds on her hands and the pain in her eyes. That Sunday, she spent all day in mourning for a life she felt she had lost. Understandably, she was very emotional and in a great deal of pain.

A few days after her accident, I was doing laundry when Bailey walked in with tears in her eyes. I will always remember what she said to me. "Mom…I don't want to be like this. I wish I could run away from it. I don't want to feel this pain anymore…but I've been thinking about some things as I've been sitting on the couch while everyone does everything for me. Remember on Saturday morning when you and I were talking about how all the kids in our family have something they struggle with— like math or reading—and I said I didn't really struggle with any of that. I asked you to tell me what things you've seen me struggle with. You told me that because everything comes so easily for me…you felt that maybe I didn't know how to feel empathy for others who struggled. I think I understand now what you meant. Before this happened to me, I didn't know how to see how others felt, because I'd never felt those things. I've never understood Tytus's food allergies, or Teage's challenge with reading because those things haven't been hard for ME. Not being able to use my hands these last few days has given me a chance to think a lot about what others go through. I've thought about people in wheelchairs, and those who are blind. This has been really hard, but I think I'm starting to understand what you were talking about when you said I needed to feel more empathy for others. Bostyn has done everything for me. She has cared about me more than she has for herself. She has brushed my teeth, and fed me food, and really cared about my pain. She told me that while you were driving to the hospital, you guys listened to *When You Believe*, and you both cried for me. Never before in my life have I felt so close to seeing how others feel in their struggles. I think I even know a little bit more about what Jesus went through when they put the nails through His hands…and I hurt for Him. Just like I didn't deserve this pain in *my* hands, neither did He. But because He felt that pain, He knows exactly what I'm feeling right now."

*That moment when you see before your eyes the pure tender truths that only a daughter of God can teach you.*

Empathy. We know Jesus Christ has it for us...but how many of us have been given the opportunity to feel it for Him? I don't think I will ever look at the scars on my little girl's hands without thinking about a Savior who took on similar scars for me.

We are not alone in our struggles, and that week I didn't just write about a past pain when I felt alone—I watched my daughter live through current pain. It was a trial I couldn't take from her in any way. I am starting to wonder if after our conversation on Saturday morning, she went up to her room and prayed to receive more empathy for others, a lesson not easily learned just by watching another suffer.

Not all of us will receive scars in our palms to help us remember the sacrifice that Jesus Christ has made for us personally, but we will all be given trials. Each person on the earth will go through pain—maybe not always physical, but we will all go through some sort of suffering.

The grace of God can't be fully comprehended until we are able to use it to help us overcome our trials, and find peace in our pain. We can read about another person's experience and feel empathy for the suffering of others—even for the pain Jesus suffered as they nailed him to the cross—but it isn't until we suffer ourselves that we fully comprehend the magnificence of His sacrifice. It is through our own physical and emotional pain that we can come to have empathy for our Elder Brother, who willingly suffered for us.

Jesus Christ chose to take upon Himself *all* of our pain. He did it willingly because he wanted to know exactly what we were going through. I know that with that empathy, He is much more equipped to kneel at God's feet and plead for the forgiveness we need. He has felt each pain and therefore knows of our suffering when our actions fail us.

I can almost picture Him—on the dark days when I have failed as a parent—begging God to forgive me. I can hear Him telling of the pain that was in my heart on a day, just weeks after Emmett was shot, when the kids were trying to let Tiffanie and me sleep in. They went into the pantry and got out their own cereal, only to drop a bowl and set off the security alarm. I imagine Christ telling Heavenly Father of the fear coursing through my veins as I ran out to the kitchen thinking I was going to find Rob in my house. Even though that wasn't the case, my panic caused me to yell at my kids and their spilled milk. The fear in my screams wasn't about the dropped bowl, or the piercing sound of the alarm—it was about everything that alarm *could* have meant. It was about a fear much greater than a spilled bowl of cereal.

I can almost see Christ as He knelt at the feet of our Father explaining my mistake—with tears in his eyes—pleading for God to forgive me. And just as Jesus had empathy for those who drove the nails into His hands, I know He feels the same for us as He pleas, "Father, forgive them ... for they know not what they do."

I know that because Jesus chose to feel our pains—instead of receiving revelations about them—*He* is our greatest advocate. Without feeling my pain, Christ could never describe my actions so perfectly. Without knowing my fear, He too would only want to condemn me for my mistakes.

I pray that each of us may take advantage of the little moments—the times when we want to scream *WHY ME?*—to better understand the sufferings of others. And in so doing, may we find empathy for the One who has felt them all, and be a little more grateful for all of the blessings He has given to us. And as He takes upon Himself our pains, let us try to understand the great sacrifice it was, even for such as Him. He didn't do it because it was easy. He took upon himself our pains because He knew that He would be able to save us when we alone could not pay the ransom for our sins.

His suffering was not in vain ... and our pain doesn't have to be either. Turn to Him when the load you are carrying gets to be too much to bear. He will take upon Himself the scars that you may never see.

The scars of my pains will forever be a reminder of what He suffered for me. As I take His name upon me, my suffering will always bring me closer to the eternal being He is helping me to become.

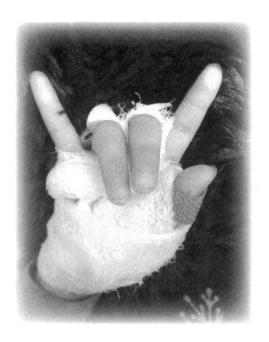

# CHAPTER TWENTY-TWO

# Crack the Walls

**ON THE SECOND WEEK, WHEN BOSTYN WAS** in the hospital
with her eye infection, they moved us to a different floor than we had
been the previous week. I began to notice that no matter what time of day
or night—every time I would walk through the hall to go see her, I would
hear a baby screaming in a near by room. After a few days I decided to go
and ask the nurses if there was anything I could do for the crying baby.

At first the nurse was very resistant to even talk about the crying child
on the other side of the door, but after a few minutes of my persistence
she opened up, "You know, that poor little baby is dying. I can't tell you
any details about her condition ... but it has been the saddest thing I have
ever had to watch as a nurse. Her parents are mad at God. They don't understand why they are being punished and they are losing their little girl,
so they hardly come here anymore. There is only so much time we can
spend with her, but she cries for them all day and night."

As I walked to Bostyn's room I pondered on how a parent could get
to that point. How could you remove yourself so far from your suffering child to let the importance of their emotions fall below your own?
I decided they had to be surrounded by walls, or some sort of barrier
that somehow shielded them from seeing their child's needs. Somewhere
in their journey they built an imaginary protection to shield themselves
from their own pain of losing her. Walls of fear or hate. Even at a time
when their little baby needed them the most, they let their emotions or

pride keep them from her. It seemed that somewhere inside of them they truly believed that they were punishing God for their trial—but the only one suffering was their already terminal baby girl.

Each person that has ever lived has had a completely different experience in life. Some have found to trust their world, and others have been given every reason to never let anyone in. In my experiences with pain—I learned to build walls: walls of protection to keep myself safe, walls of hate to keep my heart from getting broken again, and walls of fear to keep all the scary parts of the world out.

The building of a person's walls begins anytime a negative experience teaches them to fear or hate the world. Our physical bodies, mental cognition, and emotional capabilities all play into the building of our "walls". In a state of crisis our physical bodies snap into a "fight or flight" mode. Our mental state is heightened and everything that we feel or see is expounded. Every emotion is more powerful, and every pain is more excruciating. In that split second where all of the powers that make up our existence are on over load, our brains work together with our emotions to build walls of protection to ensure that this experience is never duplicated. Whatever steps came to be, to lead up to that pivotal moment, our beings want to shut us out from ever taking them again.

It is in those experiences—of our emotional, mental, and physical being coming together to build our walls to shield us from future pain—that we learn to block things out. We learn to shut things down, or run from the present to ensure the past is not duplicating itself. We fight … or flight.

And that is where our triggers come into play. If we have had an experience that has caused us to build a wall, and something comes seeming to threaten to duplicate that past experience—triggers fire and our minds begin taking us back to the fight or flight feeling that happened when the original pain took place. Sometimes it is obvious where these walls were built, and other times we have no clue why we structured them in the first place.

For me, at this time of trying to build a new family, and waiting for a murder trial it seemed I was surrounded by an imaginary structure of walls. Some of them were very obvious, and others I don't know that I will ever know for sure why they were built.

One thing is for sure—for every reason I found to dig my deep hole of despair and build my mountains of walls, my family would give me a reason to climb my way out of it, and break them down. It seemed that for all the days we had our blended family misunderstandings— we built new walls around ourselves. But for every dark day, we began to have moments that would help us remember the simplicity of love and hope that would help us break them down.

Just when I would think I had it all figured out, it seemed I would get thrown a curve ball, or would be given a new fact from the case that would drill a new spot inside of me and open a different pain. From where I stood … my life looked complete, and yet—I did not feel whole. But despite my walls of protection, Shawn continued to pull me up on the really dark days.

One afternoon after I received a rough phone call from the detectives telling me about a piece of information they had found on Emmett's computer, I was struggling really bad. Walls of fear were shooting up all around me, and as the afternoon continued I could feel the darkness of the truths I had been told surround me. Receiving new information about Emmett's past didn't change anything—but it challenged my ability to move toward the future with faith.

Shawn came home early from work and told us all to pile in the car. The thought crossed my mind to go get in bed and send everyone else with him, but I buckled in my seat. Nobody knew where we were going. The kids laughed and joked as we drove. I sat quiet in the front seat still surrounded by my gloom. I could hear the kids begging him to tell them where we were headed, but he held strong in keeping his surprise a secret. I remained pretty quiet rehearsing the past in my mind and trying to see where in it everything went wrong, in an effort to prevent it in the future.

Soon the car came to a halt as we pulled up to the most ghetto little bowling alley I had ever seen. Shawn looked over at me, "Here we are! This is what we ALL need today."

It didn't look very promising, but out of the car we went. Shawn grabbed Ty's car seat out of the car and I threw Kaleeya on my hip. The big kids marched hand in hand inside. They bowled their little hearts out; and laughed their heads off. It was like we were in Disneyland with how excited the kids were to just be together playing as a family.

At one point I sat on the little bench and just watched. The smiles on their faces and the spirit in their giggles began to brake down the wall of fear that had spent the day building up around me. The phone conversation that had taken place earlier began to fade out of my mind, as I saw my family smile in their joy. In that moment tears fell down my face, but they were tears of gratitude. I smiled as I saw my crew come together and laugh. I was grateful for a husband who knew how to play, even when everything around me told me to run…or fight. He knew how to smile and help us step away from the heavy parts of our life. He helped me see that even though I was surrounded by walls, we could break them down together.

*For every hole that had been made in my heart, I had to find new ways to keep it beating—and sometimes the best medicine was laughter and love.*

Despite my irrational internal desire to wait around for the trial for our life to start, Shawn was determined to start new traditions. I remember our first New Years Eve together like it was yesterday. He had all these grand ideas of what the night would look like. He carried each child's mattress down the stairs and pulled ours off of our bed. He positioned each one on the living room floor in a "camp out". At first it just seemed like a ridiculous amount of work and a great big mess, but as the night went on—I began to see the purpose of his plan. We laughed until midnight while the New Year began.

I remember holding his hand under our blanket and feeling a glimpse of being whole. I remember kissing each child on his or her cheek that night praying with all my heart that the mark of the New Year would bring us peace. My only New Year's Resolution was to not have any more change. I hoped for a normal time to come my way, one where the only cares I had were what to make for lunch and what movie to go to on date night. I hoped for a year of pure, sweet tender moments that could remind me over and over again what I was fighting so hard for.

And boy did I fight. I fought every day to see myself. I prayed every hour to not hate. I cried every night for the answers I still yearned to hear. But more and more, I prayed for the ability to laugh. I yearned for the desire to smile. I fought for the desire that once came naturally—to love. I begged God for the sparkle that once shined in my eye to one day shine brighter than it ever had. I begged every night that I would one day feel whole, and that the walls that had come to block my view would one day crumble.

Although the fighting for these blessings seemed to never cease, I began to see more of the little glimmers of sunshine as they came into my view. I tried hard to let the fun parts of life into my heart. I searched for reasons to smile even when my heart was breaking.

Walls, each of us has built one—but that is not the hard part. The challenge comes when we must break them down. A country is built one city at a time; a city is built street by street; a street is built one house at a time; a house has to be built wall by wall. Just like a house is built with walls to protect what is inside, we too build walls around us. Walls of fear, walls of hate, and walls of protection. Some of these walls are necessary for us to progress in life, and yet ... most of them hold us back from where we really want to be.

In all the days of our lives, we will either be building or breaking down these imaginary—and yet very real barriers. It will be a constant cycle of progression. Some days pieces of the bricks will fall, and other days new bricks will form.

Walls are a protective mechanism to help our souls feel safe, but they can also stop us from really giving and receiving love. Whatever emotion has been the foundation of our walls, love can crack each brick: loving those around you, loving those who have hurt you, and most importantly loving yourself. As those walls get broken down, piece by piece, you will begin to feel the love of those who believe in you. You will begin to see your worth in this world, and you will be able to feel the love that God has for you. Every day of your life you can have the gift to see your worth.

I have always wondered what it will be like to grow old and look back on my life. What bricks will I have willingly built around myself, and what walls will I have fought my way through? What will I wish I did differently, and what will I be glad I didn't forget?

If you were lying in a hospital bed at this very moment what would you regret? I don't think there are many who are going to lie on their dying bed, wishing they had spent more time at work. Most will probably never wish they went on another trip, or had more money to buy another car. I doubt our last words will be about a bigger house we wished we had built, or the boat we never had.

I think most of our regrets will be about our relationships. We will remember the times that we failed our loved ones. Failed to teach them truth. Failed to be there when they needed us. Failed to show them that they played a part in helping us through some of our hard times, and failed to forgive them for any pains they had caused us—but I think even more, we will regret the time we forgot, or refused, to say we were sorry. The moments they needed us, but we did not let them in. The times when the walls that we had built around ourselves prevented us from being the person we wanted to be. It is the relationships in our lives that we will look back and wish we could do over—not the "stuff". We will wish we would have let our loved ones in, and not pushed others away.

We build walls to keep ourselves safe. Abuse or neglect give many people a foundation to build a wall to never let anyone else get close to them ever again. Physical pain, and emotional abuse spring forth barriers that stick with a victim as they try to find a life capable of living with their shield up to block out the world. With these walls surrounding us—we are not able to fully live life to the fullest.

Fear doesn't have to shut us down. When we have those moments, where the walls we have built seem to shut everyone else out—pray to your God that He can help you break them down. Ask for His hand to guide you to the freedom you seek from your past.

Forgiveness is the answer to broken hearts. Love is the power that can break down our walls of darkness. Maybe love doesn't change your son's negative behaviors, but at least he still knows who cares. Maybe finding happiness won't mean your husband comes back to life, or leaves his mistress to come home. Maybe your mom never returns from the selfish ways that made her let you go. Maybe forgiveness doesn't save your marriage, but it can save your soul. Maybe hope doesn't save your baby dying in a hospital bed, but at least her last breaths were spent in your arms.

Sometimes our relationships are part of our test. A loved one's loss, and their pain bring us times of doubt in ourselves and in God. I believe it is all part of our test—to see where our hearts belong. Is your love for God only apparent when you can see perfection in your life, or is your faith in Him much more than where you are or what you are given?

We don't have to shut each other out. We don't have to run or fight our way out of our pain. There is a gift given to all of us that can break down those walls. Love, hope, and faith are the foundations that our lives can be built upon. Through the grace of God, all wrongs can be made right. All of our relationships can grow, and all of our walls of fear and hate can erode.

Not all days will be bright, but there is light in each one. Before you build a wall to keep the darkness out, make sure it won't block you from the light. Break the bricks that are building around you; crumble the towers that are keeping everyone out; and crack the walls of fear that stop you from smiling. Yesterday might have taught you to shut it out; but today is the day to break through.

# CHAPTER TWENTY-THREE

# Patterns in our Soles

**ONE DAY KALEEYA, TYTUS AND I WERE** at the pool. The big kids were at school. We were having fun playing in the water and enjoying some one on one time. The pool was empty for a while until another little family showed up. The parents had two young girls and an uncle and grandma with them. Their kids and mine started to talk to each other. The family was visiting from another state and the girls were six and four. The dad and uncle were in the water with the kids, while the mom and grandma stayed in the shade. Kaleeya and Tytus got out a few toys to share and they began to play some games together.

Soon Tytus was getting cold and wanted me to come sit on the lounge chairs with him. I left Kaleeya in the shallow end to play with the two sisters. I watched from my chair with Tytus snuggled up close to me.

At one point Kaleeya came over and whispered into my ear, "That dad is very kind." Then she headed back into the water. For a second I almost took her comment personal—as if she had just told me that I was not nice. So I became intent with my watching to try to figure out what made him so great.

As I watched, I began to see what made this dad so kind. He was a doormat! His daughters were very bossy and ungrateful for everything he did. He was hopping around like a circus clown trying to make them happy. He was bending over backwards and doing anything they demanded and everything they wanted. "Kind" was an understatement for the patience this man had with his very demanding and degrading daughters.

I could tell Kaleeya was getting sick of being told what to do, and was not impressed with the bossy duo. Soon she found her way onto my lap. Not long after she sat down, Tytus decided he would take his turn in the ringer—he headed over to play with the girls. I knew he could hold his own, but I started to get a little nervous for him to go into the game of ingratitude that was taking over the pool. This time Kaleeya and I watched from our seat.

I noticed that every time one of the girls would begin to get upset, the mom or the grandma would yell something at the dad, saying things like, "Just let her do it!", "She is talking to you!", "Listen to her!" As if the dad had no voice, he would just do exactly what the four year old, his mother in law, or his wife was getting mad at him for.

My mind raced back to all the lessons in college psychology classes and books I have read—learning about patterns in a family's background. I started to overanalyze this young family and the example the grandma and mom had obviously been to these young girls. They had taught them to nitpick and never be grateful for all of the things this father was obviously trying so hard to do for them. It was like the more he tried to show his love—the worse he was treated. I had the diagnosis all mapped out in my mind of all the things they were doing wrong in this scenario. I wanted to sit them down and share my knowledge on how to help their family break the patterns they had passed down from generation to generation, and show them why they needed to change.

Soon the youngest sister was throwing a fit and yelling at Tytus, her uncle, and her dad. She was telling them that they were not passing the ball in the direction that she wanted it passed in their game. The dad and uncle began to apologize to the little four year old, and threw the ball around the circle in the other direction. Soon the ball came to Tytus. He tilted his head to the side, glanced at the four year old, looked over in the opposite direction and threw the ball as hard as he could in the direction she had demanded it could not go.

At first I was proud of my little guy for standing his own with this snotty little ungrateful girl—she had a pattern in her family that obviously needed to be changed. He was showing her exactly what she needed to see. She didn't rule the world! Not everyone was going to roll over and allow her to be the queen! Somebody was going to have to show her how to break the patterns her mom and grandma had passed down.

And then it hit me like a ton of bricks—Tytus' response was learned from the patterns of the bull headed stubburness that were potent in my own family.

My thoughts turned from this imperfect group of people—to my own imperfect crew. I began to think of the many patterns that had streamed through the generations, past and present, and the role that these patterns had played in our own lives.

I sat on that lounge chair with Kaleeya on my lap thinking back over the patterns of my past. Some of my strengths were the qualities that pulled me through some very hard times, but other times those same strengths have been my weaknesses.

I pictured my strong internal drive to have everything pulled together. I have to admit I am a bit of a control freak—but I am not alone in this intense behavior. I come from a long line of control freaks. We like to make sure we know exactly what is going on with each of the eggs in our baskets. We like things to be done the way we like them. We have an opinion about the little things others are doing, and have a tendency to think our way is the easy one. We like to see ourselves as pretty with it, and on top of things.

So obviously we also have a bad case of denial as well—because when you like to have control over everything—you usually don't feel like you have control over anything.

One problem with thinking you are the glue that holds everything together—when your world crumbles...you will spend a lot of time trying to figure out what it was that you did wrong. It is hard to give up the power, even when things happen out of your control.

I remember at those beginning stages of my marriage to Shawn being plagued with this strength and weakness of wanting power. I truly believed that if Shawn's attention wasn't fully on me, or the things that I thought he should be focusing on—he didn't love me. If he didn't do the thing I suggested he do, he didn't value me as a person. If he didn't ask my opinion...then he didn't care about me as a partner. If he was spending his Saturday washing all of our cars, when I had the expectation that we all went to the park—he must not love me enough to know what I wanted. I felt that he should value my opinion—because in my mind, my ideas were the best. He should read my mind, because if he loved me...I wouldn't have to ask. If he cared enough about me, he would just know what he was supposed to do. And since I was so good at pretending that I had it all put together, he should value my very wise opinion.

Then Shawn had this pattern of believing that if he didn't give Jordyn his unconditional, undivided attention when she was at our house—she wouldn't know that she was loved.

At this point in our marriage, we were still far from realizing this pattern of "chase" we would play, and we were too overwhelmed with all that lay ahead to even know where to begin to address it—so we spent a lot of time darting around it and avoiding each other because of it.

In turn, the control freak inside of me began to lose it. I remember one afternoon, after receiving another one of our many "the trial has been postponed again" calls, I was taking Tytus into the doctor for a well check appointment. My pattern of wanting control was at an all time high. The trial date—that had been written in permant marker on my calendar, was not going to happen again; Shawn had spent a whole weekend ignoring me to caress his need to make Jordyn feel like his number one, so he didn't fear her feeling unloved; and Tytus was having problems with his emotional health and allergic reactions.

My control barometer was in the red zone. I sat in the doctor's office waiting for our turn, the whole time on the verge of tears. Soon the nurse called us back. We sat quietly in the check up room—my face was on fire from holding back all of my emotions. Just like many in my family who had gone before me, I tried hard to sweep my emotions under the rug to keep up my perfect front.

The doctor finally walked into the room. He asked a few questions about Tytus, and did the usual checks. We discussed a few things that we could try for the little guy's reactions and the doctor was about to leave the room. As he reached for the door he turned around, "Ashlee... are you... are you ok?"

With that permission to share... the storm began, I could not keep my tears in any longer, "I ... I just can't do it anymore. They called and changed the date of the trial again, and everything is just so hard... I just... I think they picked the wrong girl for all of this; I am not strong, not even a little bit. I can't keep doing this. I feel like I am going crazy. I miss my normal life, where I could just be a mom... and do the normal things I once thought I was good at... and I just can't take much more. I try to look like I am strong... but I need some help. I don't know who to ask, or where to turn... it is like everyone thinks I am just fine now that I got married... like all the sudden I am not broken... and I just don't know how to let go of all the control that I have lost, and I don't know what I have control over. Everything is just... everywhere... and I don't have control over any of it. I couldn't control Emmett dying, or if he loved me. I can't control if the trial will ever end... or begin for that matter. I am trying to be a wife and mother, but I am just so fractured... and I... I ... I am losing it."

I am sure he wasn't expecting all of that when he asked if I was ok. He looked startled and resumed his position in his little rotating seat in front of us—this time I was the patient. "Ashlee, you are doing an amazing job. I know so many people who have been watching you through everything and they tell me about how strong you are, and what a great mom you have been. I can't imagine all of the stress that is constantly on you through all of this, and the wait … I can bet is excruciating. Would it be ok if we had an appointment just for you to see if maybe we can do something to help you through some of this stress?"

Wall of pride … *NO way, you can't possibly take medication … you have made it this far on your own, you don't need this. You need to be strong, you need to fight through it. You have control of yourself. You don't need help. Medication is for the weak, who need help. You are strong … you don't need help … you have got this.* The thoughts in my mind tried to talk me out of it, but the peace in my heart knew that he was right. I was going to lose it, and it was ok to get some help.

Within a few days he had prescribed some anti anxiety pills. I only had to stay on them for a few months, but I don't know what I would have done without them. That pattern of bull headed "I can do anything on my own" attitude maybe got me through a lot of hard things, but it also hurt me. So many times that I needed help, my stubbornness held me back from getting it.

Even last summer, I had a sore tooth for months. Instead of just going to the dentist and letting them fix it, I tried to tough it out. Where did that get me—absolutely nowhere! My tooth was still killing me, and I didn't gain anything from waiting, except a summer full of toothaches.

Why are we so set in our ways? Why do so many of the enticements our ancestors struggled with, do we carry on in ourselves? How many times do we get frustrated with our loved ones for a characteristic they portray—when we ourselves do the same thing?

I laughed the other day at the park when Tytus was ticked off about me letting Kaleeya ride her bike around the whole pond. He dragged his feet and whined the whole way because he wanted to run up and down the hill instead of ride around the trail like we had planned. Where did he get such a stubborn control freak arrogance? … well he got it from me!

So I am learning to laugh when my kids do something that I probably did a million times to my own mother. They come in their own package, but some of the things our children do that we see as weak—are just some of the strengths we have passed on. Someday those strengths may pull them through something hard; and other times these weaknesses may hold them back.

Every family has patterns that have been set and carried on for years. Some of these traits are priceless treasures and amazing characteristics, but many are dark emotionally driven fears. What patterns have your family passed down that are not worth carrying on? I made a list last night of all the patterns I don't want in my family anymore. Some I saw in my husband or our children—but most of them I found within myself.

Every family is unique and different. Some families are excellent sweepers. Everything is swept under a rug, where they feel it is safe and will never be revealed. Some families are fakers, they pretend everything is perfect on the outside, and then behind closed doors everything explodes. Some families struggle with addictions. Some families struggle with arrogance and pride. Some become doormats and let others walk all over them. Some families have histories of affairs, or gambling or pornography addictions. Some families are sleeve wearers—they tell everyone everything that is going on in their life and in their mind; and then others hold everything inside.

Now I am making the human race sound like a bunch of sheep—like we are all just followers. I know that not all people follow the patterns of their heritage's past…but I believe that is because somewhere the patterns were broken. I think we all have weaknesses that can be passed or carried on in our beliefs and behaviors, but many have learned to overcome or break these patterns.

Our history is not our destiny.

Just because your dad, your grandpa, and your great grandpa died of an alcohol addiction—it doesn't mean you will. *I believe we have a choice.*

If alcoholism is in your blood—don't take a sip. If you have already been sucked in by that addiction—get help out. Maybe your mother beat you every day of your childhood—that doesn't mean you have to become the same kind of abusive parent. Maybe your dad was a yeller—and you hate that you have followed his lead. You can stop that pattern in yourself! We are never destined for anything. We may feel that the weaknesses passed on from our parents tempt us to join them—but the only way they win... is if we lose.

We can chose to follow in footsteps, or we can pattern our own course.

Every trail that has ever been trod had to begin with one person. Some have called these pioneers—the first to adventure from the normal life they once knew, creating a new path. Being a pioneer doesn't always take a wagon and some oxen. Being the pioneer of your life can mean breaking patterns that were once followed blindly.

Stop chasing the patterns of crazy that came from generations back. You will never have all the control of the things around you, and you will not always feel like the #1. You may never feel like you have it all pulled together, but you can find hope in yourself as you center your desires on making yourself the best you can be. You may not be able to change anyone else, but you can always make a difference inside of yourself. Sometimes that means asking for help, and other times it means figuring it out on your own. Fighting to change a pattern doesn't always have to be done alone, but sometimes it is when you make shifts on your own that you will find a true change of heart.

One thing is for sure—patterns of behavior were not all intended to be carried on. They may be the tool that is holding you back from the life you want to have. Just like the walls of the past that get triggered to be built, patterns of the past can be broken and changed.

Examine who you want to become, and what behaviors or patterns are keeping you from those goals. And then make a change. Seek for a power much greater than your own to help you find the answers to change the parts of you that are holding *YOU* back. It is inside of ourselves that we will find the answers to our role in the world.

> *"If you really want to understand the social world, if you really want to understand yourself and others, and, beyond that, if you really want to overcome many of the obstacles that prevent you from living your fullest, richest life, you need to understand the influence of the subliminal world that is hidden within each of us."* (pg.189)
>
> —Decide Now: The Good Life or The Best Life L. Jay Mitchell

Maybe your walls were built with the patterns from the examples before you, but you can be the pioneer to a new pattern of life. Our heritage of weakness doesn't have to be what we become. Turn to God to make those weaknesses become strong. He has promised that his grace can heal even our weaknesses, and they can become our strengths.

Believe in Him as your soles find new paths from the ones you once followed before. Take His hand, and let Him help you remember the worth of your soul... for you are great in the sight of God, and even your path matters to Him.

CHAPTER TWENTY-FOUR

# *Perfectly Imperfect*

**AFTER EMMETT DIED, AND EVEN AFTER I** married Shawn, I remember spending hours trying to change myself. I didn't feel good enough to leave my room without my make-up on, or my hair done. I didn't like to look people in the eyes, for fear they would see all the broken pieces I had inside of me. I wore high heels everywhere I went. Even on a morning adventure to the park with all the kids, I would get dressed up and waddle around in my fancy shoes.

Why? I didn't know it at the time, but looking back it is all so simple. I was scared to be me. I was frightened that the minute I relaxed and walked around as *me*, people would see why Emmett chose *her.*

I wasn't enough for Emmett then, I was scared to not be enough for Shawn, and I had come to not be enough for myself. My fear of inadequacy in my marriage didn't just build a wall of protection around me; it gave me a false sense of who I felt I was supposed to be.

Shawn spent many days begging me to just stick on some jeans, tennis shoes and a t-shirt—but I could not do it. I didn't want to feel inadequate in anyway. I didn't want to give anyone a reason to talk about why I wasn't enough, and I especially didn't want to be put in a situation where I felt like I didn't measure up.

It was like I lived in this imaginary world—where everyone was looking down on me and laughing at all of my imperfections. The accusations that had been sent my way didn't just flash across my computer screen, or enter in my ear—they pierced my heart. I read them over and over, and recited them to myself as if they were gospel. *If you had been a better wife... Emmett would still be here. If you would have given him all that he needed, he wouldn't have gone looking for it somewhere else. If you were enough for him, he wouldn't have turned to her. It is your fault Emmett died.*

Though I had the perfect knowledge that I was not there when he died, and I did not pull that trigger, those lies posed as truths inside of me—and they burned holes in my soul. I spent much time pretending that they did not hurt, but the more they lay hidden...the deeper they reached.

Instead of working on digging up my own pain, I spent much of my time trying to help my children heal. One afternoon on a quest to find a grief therapy group for the kids—I came across one for me. After I hung up the phone I almost laughed at the thought. *What would a grief therapy group do for me? I don't need anyone else to tell me how hard death is to face in reality. I have already faced the fact that Emmett had died, and he was gone. I was beyond the need to talk about my grief.* I quickly forgot about the grief group and carried on with my day.

A few days passed and the grief group kept popping into my mind. One night before turning out the lights for bed, Shawn said, "Hey, you ok? You seem very deep in thought."

I finally shared my thoughts. I said, "So I have been looking for a grief group for the kids to go to—I think it will help them work through some more of the stuff that counseling hasn't done—and I...I didn't find them a group, but the number I called was...it's a grief group for adults. It is a six-week course, and it starts tomorrow. I don't want to talk about my stuff, and I don't want to go...but I can't stop thinking about it. Maybe I should go...so I can help people in the group. "

Shawn grabbed my hand. "You should go, Ash. What do you have to lose? I mean, just because we are married doesn't mean that it has just gone away. You walk around like everything is perfect, but I can see sometimes that you are still hurting inside. If you want to go, I support you. I think you could help people in the group… but I think it might be good for *you*."

When morning came the next day I was so nervous my stomach was churning. I said goodbye to my family and got in the car. As I drove I could feel my tears on the verge of breaking. My first thought was that I didn't want to mess up my mascara. I didn't want to ruin this group's first impression of me. No! I was going to drive alone in the car without my pain. I didn't want to think about Emmett's death. I wasn't going to ponder what I was going to have to say at the trial; I wasn't going to rehearse what I would say if I walked into the grief group and Kandi was there. I was going to be strong and not show any of these emotions.

I was afraid to cry in fear that it would mess up my makeup, but most importantly I didn't want to let anyone in. I decided as I drove that I was going to be stronger than ever. The past was in the past. I was a warrior, and I was going to this grief group so I could help all the sad people in it who were not as strong as me.

I pulled up to the address the woman had given me over the phone. As I stepped out of the car a wave of the past rushed over me. I knew this place well. Emmett's step mom Denise—who had died a few weeks before Teage was born—had her funeral here. *A funeral home? Really? My new grief group was going to take place every week in a funeral home? Why did it have to be a memory from my past? How was I going to be able to help people if I was busy thinking about my own pain?*

I tried hard to push that hard memory out of my mind as I pushed down the even larger lump in my throat. *I was not here to cry, I was here to help others.* Just like the many other times I had tried to lie to myself about my emotions, my face burned with all of those I was trying to hide.

I sat down with my arms folded. I glanced around the room. It was filled with sad faces, many who had been on the earth many more years than I had. Each person had a story, and you could see it written all over his or her face. My heart raced as my soul could feel all of the pain that filled the room.

The session began. The discussion leader asked us to go around the room and introduce ourselves and tell a little about why we were there. As each person spoke and the spotlight got closer and closer to me I began to rehearse in my mind what I was willing to share.

And then my turn came. I began. "My name is Ashlee. I…I was made a widow last year in March and I have five kids. I am remarried now and have a new daughter." I bent my knees to take my seat.

Then my heart took over. "I…My husband was killed…because he was cheating on me. I…my heart still hurts. I try to pretend that everything is perfect. I try to tell myself that it didn't break me, but I am drowning. I…just want to feel normal again. I want to remember how to feel, and how to love. I…just…I am trying to figure out how to make my life right, but it is just so hard. The trial hasn't even begun and…some days it is all I can think about. I just don't understand any of it. Why…did …why did he have to die? Why did that gun have to fire? I…just don't understand. I am here, because I don't know what I am doing. I am trying to figure out how to be enough for a man again, but really I just want to know how to be enough for myself. My husband wasn't just killed… he was murdered by a mistresses angry husband. He didn't want me. He was choosing someone else. But what hurts the most is the fact that I still wanted *him*. I still wanted our life. He wasn't the perfect husband. He wasn't always the perfect father, and he was making a really big mistake. But he was OURS. He was the man who I devoted my life to, and he was taken from me before I got to do that. I had a perfect plan…and it was going to be…perfect. So now I just want to know how to let that go, so hopefully someday I can breath again. I want to perfectly love again. I want to be the girl I was before he died, but I don't know how. I miss him, I miss the perfect life I had…but most importantly I miss me."

And there it was. I was not perfect. For the first time since Emmett died I was standing in front of a group of strangers telling them how imperfect my life was. I wasn't pretending to be something or someone else. I was just me.

What is perfection? My view of this word has changed in the last few years. It started as a glimpse of a life I thought I had. Then it changed to an image I thought I must be. That week I came to see perfection in a whole new way.

Once my heart poured itself out to this group of strangers I knew I wasn't just there to teach—I was there to learn.

Perfection is sitting for hours in a room full of elderly widows learning about love. They poured their souls about a life they once had. They cried tears for the perfect days they shared and the imperfect partner they had loved; they opened up their hearts about the dreams they had watched come true.

As I sat in that perfect moment, in that perfect room, I felt a glimpse of hope. I had so much that had been taken from me, but all of my dreams could still come true. Though my life with Emmett was over, my story was not complete. Though my perfect dreams had once felt shattered, I could still learn to live a new one.

Perfection feels like the only dream we should want to obtain. But what if perfection is happening right now? What if—even through the imperfect past and the imperfect days we now live—we are living the perfect life we were always meant to?

Our days will be hard. They will not be perfect. Our makeup may smudge with the tears of our pain; some days we might not ever make it out of our pajamas … but life is so much more than what we once thought would make it perfect.

Life is about love. Love is about family. And families are not perfect. Some days we may lose; others we may win—but in the end all that will remain are all the things that make us imperfect. High heels are not what make us whole; and makeup doesn't change who we are. To truly find your worth you have to search for it *inside*.

You will find it when you least expect it. Your worth in God's eyes will not be found in a box; it will not carry a price tag. It will be a radiant light that permeates from inside of you.

It hurts to feel that you do not measure up, it is scary to wonder if you are enough. Before you wait around for someone else to build your sense of who you are—Find it in yourself.

There is One who has always seen your perfection through your flaws. God's grace can be found in the little moments that are there to remind you that even though you are not perfect, and even though your path has been rocky—you are perfect to *Him*.

You are perfectly imperfect, just the way you are.

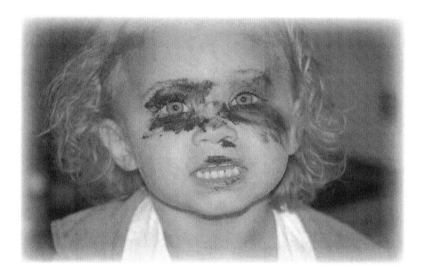

# CHAPTER TWENTY-FIVE

## The Tempting Road

**CHRISTMAS 2011 WAS ON A SUNDAY. MY** Bishop called a few days before Christmas and asked me to bear my testimony—get up and share what I believed—at the end of the sacrament meeting. I agreed I would—but after I hung up the phone I didn't think twice about it and carried on with my preparations for Christmas.

Christmas morning came. When the Bishop announced I would be coming up to speak I started to get butterflies in my stomach. I wasn't a huge fan of public speaking, and hadn't done much of it since Emmett had been killed. I walked slowly up to the pulpit very unsure of what I was going to say.

Every eye in the room was on me—I began to feel not only inadequate in bearing my testimony in front of all of them, but claustrophobic that they were all staring at me.

I got close to the microphone—still with no idea of what I was going to talk about. The minute my mouth opened I felt Emmett's presence. I was overwhelmed with peace and strength.

I bore my testimony about my faith. I poured out my heart with all the truths I had learned. I thanked Jesus Christ for the power He had sent me in that year—but then I felt the need to share some of Emmett's down fall... and then challenge everyone in that room to make right any wrong doings they had done in their lives. I begged them to put their families first. I challenged that entire room to change the sins that were tempting them to fall.

When I finished my testimony, I went back and sat down with my family. I felt a little overwhelmed with all I had just felt I needed to share—but almost embarrassed of the cry to repentance I had just showered over a room full of faithful people.

That night I received a phone call I will never forget. The woman on the other line was in tears, "Ashlee… I just… I just needed to say thank you for the courage you had today to say the words my husband needed to hear. He has been struggling in similar ways to Emmett, and the things that you said today… changed him. He finally opened up to me—and has asked for forgiveness. He has been struggling with so many temptations and has not let me be part of his struggles… but for the first time in 13 years—he has felt the need to change. I just… I wanted you to know… everything you said today—was for us. Thank you for being willing to speak from your heart about the truths we needed to hear. I am sorry for everything you have been through… but… you… I think you have saved my marriage. Thank you for following the spirit and being that voice. The greatest gift I could have received today… Merry Christmas Ashlee. "

I didn't know back then I was ever going to share even parts of my story ever again… but doing so has brought many more experiences such as this.

In October 2014 I was privileged to share my story at The Togetherness Project, a biannual conference for women whose spouses are struggling with pornography addiction or infidelity. A few weeks before the conference, I was given two tickets to give away on my blog. As candidates sent in their requests, I had the unique experience of hearing hundreds of personal stories of heartbreak and pain. I can tell you one thing—I have never felt so surrounded by support of those who have been where I have—but I also have never felt such a heavy heart for so many people I have never met. A cloud of gloom surrounded me as I stepped into the shoes of each and every woman and man who told me their story.

I had an overwhelming amount of empathy for all the victims who have suffered because of the actions of another person—but for the first time in my life I had an outpouring of empathy for the victims who are suffering because of their own mistakes.

One email I received I will never forget. It started out like this—"I am like Emmett. I have done everything wrong. I have lost everything—and for what? My selfishness has destroyed my family and I hate myself for it. It is too late for me, just like it is for Emmett. There are no apologies that will take away the pain that my choices have caused."

As I continued to read this heart felt email from a man in pain—my heart hurt for *him*. Tears fell down my face as I thought of all the men and women who have stood at the crossroads where Emmett once fought with that powerful temptation to walk down a dark road for "just a minute".

I don't think I have ever viewed the world with such a somber heart as I have come to terms with this truth—we are all victims. At times we have all been wronged against a life we set out to live. We have all been down a road we never intended on traveling—yet so many of these diversions in our path have come because of pain we have caused ourselves.

Infidelity is not something anyone plans—yet so many relationships will experience it. So my heart goes out to all of the victims who have suffered watching someone they love give into that temptation … but that day my heart went out to all who have become a victim of their own mind—a puppet in the enticement that was orchestrated to make *them* fall.

No one plans for their life to be one that hurts others. None of us want to fall into the temptations that have plagued our thoughts. We don't always remember that Satan has a plan of his own—and he will do everything he can to make us believe his lies.

Not one of us is exempt. That moment when our eye catches someone's gaze or we sense that someone is trying to be flirty. That moment … that one moment—is ours. In that very second our mind stops us to question how we will handle our thoughts, and it is there that we must take the power. It is at that crossroad where we decide if we win—or if Satan does.

He wants us to think that because a temptation has entered our mind—
we have already failed—and we are not worthy. It isn't about our worthi-
ness. Every single person will be tempted at some time—with something.

Just because an unhealthy enticement comes to your mind... that
doesn't make you a bad person. It is what you do with your thoughts that
will determine what road you will take. Carnal desires come naturally. They
do not mean that something is wrong with you. We all have desires to know
we are: successful, valued, appreciated, attractive, glamorous, sexy, wanted,
and enough. Being accepted and seeking approval is basic human nature. It
is where we turn to fill those desires that can lead us astray.

There are so many healthy desires that can, and should, be kept in the
relationships they were promised to. Your spouse can meet those crav-
ings and needs your body yearns for. Realistically the excitement and butterflies may not last, but they can be replaced by commitment and respect
that can help your love last forever.

If you have felt the temptations of the world—you are not alone. That
is part of our mortal test. We will be tried and tempted—just as Christ
was. It is through our resistance to these temptations that we will learn
true obedience. We will gain greater faith, empathy, and compassion for
those who struggle. We will have a greater perspective when we step in
another's shoes and feel the pain they have felt, as they have been plagued
with temptation.

Robert D. Hales taught of Christ's resistance to temptations when he
said, "Then Jesus expressed His commitment to obey, saying, 'Father, thy
will be done, and the glory be thine forever.' Throughout His ministry,
'He suffered temptations but gave them no heed.' Indeed, He learned
obedience by the things which He suffered.'"

*Jesus chose to feel all our pain—including those put upon us by our own
choices.*

He has been where we have been—even in our strongest temptation. He has felt those deep dark secrets that bring sorrow to our souls.

He has felt the temptations that each of us has battled, and He has given us a perfect example of how to resist them. He gave them no heed. That doesn't mean it was easy—but He knew the resistance to these temptations would be worth it.

He didn't just know of our personal demons, and deepest temptations—He felt them in his soul. It is His sacrifice that makes it possible for Him to kneel at God's feet and be our number one advocate. He knows how hard these battles are to overcome—*because He has.*

I don't think I truly understood the magnitude of His sacrifices, until I was in a position that I too had to overcome my own difficult battles. I can't imagine the torment Christ felt enduring our sins and failures. Just as He was tempted—and overcame—we too can follow His example, leaning on His strength to pull us out of the deepest trenches.

No temptation is too great, no darkness too bleak, for us to call upon His help. Those feelings that our mortal bodies crave can be used for good. Cherish the relationships that they were meant for—and those desires will bring you closer to God. We can be stronger than the negative thoughts that pop into our minds. We can overcome any temptation that is leading us away from our true selves.

We are going to be tempted—not just in our fidelity to each other—but also in everything we are…and everything we do. Our temptations might be as simple as having hate in our hearts. Some might be tempted to forgo forgiveness. Some struggle with: addiction, fear, anger, resentment, entitlement, abuse, and deceit.

Temptations are enticements—when put into action they keep us away from our goals. I believe that Satan is the author of all temptations, for he knows if he can get us to sway on the simple things—he might be able to get us to fall for anything. However, I believe that God allows us to feel those enticements because they are the tools we need to gain greater faith in obedience. When we battle our enticements with God by our side—we learn of our need for Him to help us overcome; but when we lose to our temptations—we are given the opportunity to return to Him and seek true repentance for our sins. Either way, though hard to bear, the enticements serve a great purpose for us in developing our faith in our Creator.

Sometimes it is our reactions to another person's struggle that can help them remember who they are. One morning I walked into Teage's room to see he had taken snacks from the pantry in the middle of the night and had an all night party. I wanted to scream and yell at him. I wanted to tell him what a stupid decision he had made. I was tempted to swat his butt and make him stay in his room for the rest of the day. I didn't understand the irrational thoughts he must have had to make him steal food and hide it from me. I was totally out of my mind frustrated.

I stepped outside of his room and said a small prayer that I could know how to handle the situation and stay centered on my goal to help my son learn from this mistake.

As I walked back into his room these were the words that came out of my mouth, "Teage, there is nothing you could ever do that would make me stop loving you." Now this doesn't mean we didn't talk about the consequences and the choices he was expected to make in the future. All that statement meant, to me, was he needed to know that no matter what choices were made—he was loved.

Separating actions from the love we have for someone else is not easy to do, but it is what Heavenly Father does for us. No matter what we have done—the mistakes we have made do not change the love God has for us.

My temptations have never involved a gun. I have not felt the need to seek another person outside of my marriage—but I have been tempted to be less than I am. I fight the enticement to hate those who have hurt me; I struggle to see my own worth. I have doubted my story and feared my chance for happiness was taken from me. I have questioned the good-ness of others, and I have forgotten myself. There has even been a day when I have been tempted to smile back when an inappropriate glance has been sent my way; I have been enticed to spend too much time in front of the mirror—or my phone. Some days I have been tempted to just stay in bed; some times I have battled the feeling to hate myself. I have been annoyed with my children; I have been angry with my spouse. In all of these temptations, I have grown closer to God as I have fought my way through them—some successful, some less so.

I have felt the darkness of the world in those moments when my thoughts have wandered from my goals. I have been reassured that there is light—when I steer my thoughts back to Him. In those dark moments when Satan wants my mind and my heart to believe the lies of the world, I have found that I can be stronger than him. I can get on my knees and pray to God that He sends me the help I need to overcome my enticements and not give into Satan's temptations.

The world can only win if we give temptations a second glance or allow ourselves to be attracted by them. It is not our enticing thoughts that will define who we become. It is the strength we use to control them that will empower us to stand, to show Satan who wears the pants in our relationship with him. He isn't waiting for us to give him permission—he steps in any time he sees a crack in our armor. He tries to make us believe that those negative thoughts—are just who we are. If he can get us to doubt ourselves because of the thoughts that have entered our mind—he knows that our fall will come naturally.

Enticements are just thoughts; but when we follow these thoughts and put them into action we give into temptation. We do not have to be perfect—but I can promise you … as you take control of your thoughts … you will have better control over the decisions you will make.

So to all the "Emmetts" who feel they have lost their chance to right their wrongs—your time is not done. You have not lost your chance—just as I believe Emmett still has the opportunity where he is now—to right the wrongs of your imperfections. Every day is a fresh start, an opportunity to be better…to do better…to be more. It is not too late for any of us.

ASHLEE BIRK | 225

Even if you feel like you have gone too far down the wrong path—it is not too late. Turn to Him even in the pain that you have inflicted upon yourself. Those temptations were real—and the decision to make them was tragic—but those choices do not revoke the love God still has for YOU. I know that God lives, and as His sons and daughters He sees our worth no matter what mistakes we have made. He believes in our dreams and He will do all that He can to bring us back to the light our hearts still long to find.

To all the imperfect sinners of the world—so to every single one of us—we are not alone. We can overcome this world. Because of Him— even we can find a higher road when we are tempted to settle for the dirt. Because of Him—we can walk away from the deceiving powers of Satan. Because of Him—even on the road to temptation we can find strength to help us overcome. His grace can make us whole.

CHAPTER TWENTY-SIX

# Ship of Dreams

**EVERY SHIP THAT HAS EVER SAILED HAS** a captain at the helm. The captain's first job is to believe in his vessel. He may know of the imperfections it holds, but encourages and finds the beauty in his ship. He knows the job isn't perfect, but he feels blessed to be given the opportunity to steer such a magnificent unit in the direction it is intended for. Every captain begins their journey with a plan—a map of the course they want their ship to carry them. They continue with faith that the mapped course will be well, wonderful, and as close to their plan as possible. I can imagine the first time a captain lays eyes on the ship— their heart skips a beat. They are so excited to see in person…the vision from their dreams.

I was that captain.

I remember the first time I saw it in person. I had studied the pictures online, but in real life it was even more magnificent. As I stepped out of the car it was almost like I heard angels singing Halleluiahs. Their chorus carried on as I walked up the front walkway.

It was the week of Thanksgiving 2009. We had just pulled into town— me with our four kids piled in our minivan, and Emmett in a U-Haul full of our belongings. The minute we pulled up to our new house, my heart skipped a beat. We had made it. The house of my dreams—and it was going to be ours.

For the first time in our marriage we were going to be out of school and making our own money. Emmett had been given the opportunity to spend his last semester doing an Externship for the public defender's office while he began his career in Bankruptcy Law. We had four amazing kids, and we had each other—and now to top off all of our blessings—we were getting our dream house. All of the goals we had planned for our young family were being checked off of our list...one after another.

The closing for our house didn't come the next day as we thought it would. Luckily my brother Jeff and his family were out of town for the week spending Thanksgiving with Dani's family. So we bunked up in their house with our U-Haul parked out front.

As the week progressed, we continued getting our closing date moved out. Thanksgiving came and went, and we still did not have the key in our hands. Finally, on Monday, the call came and the papers were ready for us to sign. We were like giddy little schoolgirls as we drove down to the title company. Our first house—it was like a dream.

We walked out of that office like we had won the lottery. We were so proud of our new adventure, and my mind reeled at all of the perfect days that would take place for our little family in that dream house.

Emmett helped me unpack the truck, and then he headed out to catch his plane. He still had finals to take back at Gonzaga, and our delayed closing date left the kids and me alone in our big empty house to begin unpacking.

He was gone for two weeks for his tests—and everything that could have gone wrong did. We got the stomach flu, and our washer and dryer had not arrived yet. Many days I would load up all four kids in the car and heap puked on sheets into the trunk and cart them across town to Emmett's dad's house to do wash. He was in Mexico but luckily had sent me his garage code.

The kids were having a heck of a time adjusting to being in a new home. Furniture and appliances were yet to be delivered. It was just a rough couple of weeks all together—but I didn't even notice. I was still in awe of all the dreams I was watching unfold. I laughed every time we threw up all over ourselves and I began to make a joke about how many gallons of puke I could carry in my car. I was in a fairy tale. One that was full of dirty diapers, and puked on sheets…but I was living my dreams. I was the luckiest captain alive.

Many people have told me they didn't realize how much work being a parent would be until they were thrown into it. I never saw it like that. I knew exactly what each of those commitments entailed, and I still loved every second of them. Now I was doing them in my dream house—with my dream family—life was close to perfect.

I continued to steer my course. I cleaned up scraped knees in that ship's quarters. I changed diapers and got poop (literally) on my face. (For those of you who witnessed that one I am eternally sorry—some things can't be unseen). In that house I read for hours—chapter books about the adventures of a brother and sister who believe in a magic tree house. I hauled groceries and babies in and out of that front door. I built snowmen in the front yard. I decorated and cleaned and organized. I baked cookies and walked to parks. I taught my babies how to ride their bikes on that street, and to swim in that neighborhood pool. I burned dinners and broke glass cups in the sink…but every night I snuggled up close in its safe walls and I smiled. My dream house was proving to be everything I had mapped out for it to become—a haven for my future, and a keeper of my love.

But somewhere a long the way…that house became everything it never should have been. The darkness that grew in its walls—in just one night—became more black than the night sky. The fear that penetrated my dreams while I tossed and turned in my ship, threatened the peace that it had once promised me. All of the sudden, a house that once seemed to be my "Captain's dream ship" began to be a reminder of all the wrong turns that were taken despite my happiness inside of it.

Shawn had stepped in, and taken a spot in that ship that had already been walked all over. He started to feel as if he were a replacement. He felt threatened by a distant glorified memory of the past. He walked around inside the walls of a dream he wasn't always a part of. We talked many times about starting over somewhere else, but the thought of leaving my ship felt like another abandonment I did not feel prepared to face. So we stayed—many days both of us on autopilot to avoid the feelings of inadequacy we didn't want to acknowledge, or the abandonment we did not want to face.

Almost every night, after Emmett had died, I had horrible dreams. They usually rattled me up, but some nights were more debilitating than others. Each dream was very vivid, and usually always ended in the same way—with someone I loved dead.

One night I had another nightmare, but this time it was a mix of both of the worlds I had tried to cram into one ship. In my dream Shawn and Emmett were both there in our house. They were staring at each other, almost as if they wanted to fight one another. They began talking very angrily and then started screaming at the top of their lungs. All of the sudden there was a gunshot—but this time *they* were shooting *each other*. Rob wasn't the one with the gun...they were. And by the end of the dream, they were both dead on my living room floor.

My eyes jolted open and I was in a state of shock. Panic shook through every part of my body. My heart felt as if I were having a heart attack. I moved my hand toward the other side of the bed. Someone was laying next to me. *Who? Emmett? Did none of that really happen? What was real? Emmett... he... is dead?... That can't be real. Emmett can't be gone. But... what about Shawn, where is Shawn? I need Shawn.* My mind raced through all of the bad dreams—and all of the living nightmares that had played out in that very house.

The panic attack lasted a few hours as I tried to figure out, in the darkness, what parts of my horrors were real—and which parts were just dreams. Many hours passed before any sort of reality could settle in my heart. I never went back to sleep—just stared into the darkness trying to piece together the past.

By the time everyone else in my house woke up, I had a plan. We were getting out of that house! I couldn't wake up from another nightmare in the same place where all the pain had struck me.

That afternoon we drove around to try to find a new place to live. It didn't have to be a dream house—just a house. One where the kids didn't have to change schools, but there were enough bedrooms and a back yard. Just a house—one that didn't hold any memories from our past. A house—that when I woke up from my nightmares—I was somewhere different then the place where they came true.

We turned onto a road I knew well, and there it was—a sign. I had just been visiting there a few days before. I called my friend and said, "Hey, you have a sign in your front yard … you selling your house? Can we come look at it?"

That night we made an offer, and closed a few weeks later. As we packed up our belongings, to move to the new house, I had so much hate in my heart. I whispered to its walls of all the things it didn't do for me. I screamed from the top of my lungs—when I went back alone to clean—of all the HELL that it had put me through. I blamed my house for all the unknowns I still hoped to hear—like it had been hiding the truths from me.

I wasn't sad—I was relieved to leave it behind and move on to a new ship. I didn't need my dream ship to smile, and it had proven it wasn't going to bring the happiness I felt it had promised me. We thought about keeping it as a rental, but I didn't want to step foot inside it ever again. So we threw a *For Sale* sign in the front yard, and walked away.

One day I got a call that an offer had been made and I needed to go into the Title company to sign the house over to the new owner. Again with hate in my heart, I robotically signed all the papers with "good riddance" under my breath, and headed out to the parking lot.

I got in the car to drive home. I was flooded with the memories of the first time I had signed papers on that house. Tears started to well up in my eyes. My heart began to feel heavy the closer and closer I got to my new home. And then the panic hit. *My ship had sunk.* I remember saying a pleading prayer to God that day. "What was so wrong with my plan? What was it in my plan that didn't work? I had it all figured out. Why wasn't the course I mapped out enough? Why couldn't the dreams I had written so long ago... be the ones that I lived?" No answers came to settle my heart.

I felt like the captain of the Titanic that day. I can picture him watching as his dream ship went into the water. I bet he played—in his own mind—all the memories he had leading up to the moment when he was made the Captain of it. His pride and dignity sunk before the ship went under. He knew in that moment that he was not in control. He saw first hand that no matter how much love and honor he put into his dream... it still sunk.

The captain of Titanic didn't get to safety to watch his dream ship sink—he went down with it. He gave up his ability to ever sail again, when the thought of losing his dream was too much to take. He saw that sinking ship as a failure of his own doing—and he didn't allow himself to look to the future for a new dream. He died inside of a sinking ship—his dream ship took his life.

We don't always get to plan for the icebergs in our lives. We don't always get to choose to steer our ship around them. Sometimes it is too dark to see them coming, and other times we have too much light in our eyes to see the dangerous waters for what they really are. Sometimes our dreams are going to hit icebergs. We are going to be slammed into the currents and our ships may even sink, but that doesn't mean we stop being the best damn captain we always wanted to be.

I didn't ever think as I turned that key for the very first time, that I was opening up the door to a sinkable ship that would hit an iceberg. I thought for sure that my voyage was going to continue to be blessed with smooth waters.

Signing over the papers to my dream ship was a big day for me. It was a symbolic reminder of the failure that dream had become, but unlike the captain of the Titanic who went down as his dream sank to the bottom of the ocean floor—I am still sailing. I am still pioneering this thing we all call life. I am still hitting icebergs and catching waves. Sometimes those waves have been a small rollercoaster, and other times I have wiped out. There have even been days when I have questioned why I didn't just sink along with it.

Life isn't about the ships—it is about sailing them through the storms. The captain of the Titanic didn't have to go down just because his dream seemed to be over. Maybe your dream house turns out to be the pinnacle of your fall—or maybe your iceberg was just the turn you needed to find a different course.

The loss of our dreams is not the end of our hope. Find hope in the fact that when God closes a door—He will always open a window. It may be a different view than you had planned—but you still will get to watch as your life unfolds.

Don't go down with your sinking ships. Businesses are going to fail; marriages are going to end; and we are going to lose the people we love— but we don't have to lose ourselves. The dreams that end give us an opportunity to find the next one waiting around the corner. There are no endings in this life that are eternal—only beginnings to new dreams.

You are the captain of your destiny; you hold the wheel...but God steers the course. Don't let your fear of your sinking ship stop you from walking away when it falls. Don't go down without a fight. You are the dream—the ship was just trying to take all the credit. It is *you* that made that ship one out of a dream.

The Titanic was never designed to hit an iceberg—but we came to earth knowing we would. We were never promised that all we would sail were smooth waters—but we still chose to come down as determined Captains piloting ourselves through the waves.

Stand tall in the storms that are trying to take you down. Your life is more important than the seemingly failed dreams. Dreams were never meant to be written—they are made to be lived. If your ships have sunk, and you are wondering why you should continue to sail—just remember that a new ship is waiting for you. You may not be able to see it from the bottom of the ocean, but something great is waiting for you. It might look different than the life that hit an iceberg—it may be far from the map you tried to plan—but you still have the ability to captain a new course.

Stand tall, you are not alone. We are all captains, and each one of us has—or will someday—lose a dream ship. *Don't let your fear of losing your dreams stop you from living them.* There isn't a perfect course—only imperfect captains hoping they will never give up the fight … to keep sailing.

(Thanksgiving 2009)

# CHAPTER TWENTY-SEVEN

# *Thankful*

*The definition of Thanksgiving is: the expression of gratitude, especially to God.*

*Gratitude is defined as: the quality of being thankful; readiness to show appreciation for and to return kindness.*

**I HAVE SO MANY MEMORIES OF THE** Thanksgivings of my past...

I remember cramming sixty or so people into my grandma and grandpas farm house and eating the most delicious food ever. I remember cousins and aunts and uncles, and most of all, my great grandma who lived in a little house next door.

I remember staring at her paralyzed arms that hung by her side, and listening to her stories of Thanksgivings gone by. I would sit in her living room for hours—and watch her little space heater light up and turn off—as she repeated old stories and remembered new ones. I studied her white hair and her wrinkled skin. Every word she spoke to me was filled with life, and so many memories of her past.

I never thought about the memories I was creating—that they would one day be the stories I would sit and tell my great grand daughter some day. I just figured life would always be the way it was. It never crossed my mind that each holiday I spent would one day be a distant snap shot in my mind. I always thought I would be the young carefree child running through pastures and chasing pigs. I had no idea that Thanksgivings would ever be any different—but I soon learned that truth.

When my parents got divorced our traditions changed. Everything that once seemed concrete and secure—was all the sudden different every year. I came to understand my new normal and appreciated the different kinds of memories that were created each year—at the two different houses. My parents both remarried and our families grew. New relationships brought an even broader spectrum to the memories of my holidays gone by.

I remember Thanksgivings at my mom's with our blended family. They were full of people, and full of love. We had so much to be thankful for—and we were.

Every year was a different group of siblings, and different memories created.

Soon I was off to college. I stuck to the rotations of holidays with my little sisters—switching off at our parent's house's each one. A few weeks after Emmett and I started dating I planned to go to my dad's for Thanksgiving—by chance his dad lived in the same town. We decided to go together. We drove a few hours out of our way to pick up my little sisters, and headed to see our fathers.

By the time we were half way there snow had begun to fall—and we were in a full on snowstorm. We could barely see the road and I started to get nervous. Emmett reassured me that everything was going to be ok—that he could see the tracks of the truck in front of him and he would follow them closely.

Way past midnight we rolled into town. We met each other's fathers for the first time the next day. That was our first Thanksgiving together, and the first time Emmett told me he loved me.

The next time Thanksgiving came around we were married. We went down to Arizona with Emmett's mom to visit his stepbrother and their family. We hadn't found out I was pregnant with twins yet—but my belly was huge! Everywhere we went people would ask me when I was due. . .

I was only three months along! A few weeks later, on Christmas Eve, we found out there were two babies—and they were identical girls!!

The next few years of Thanksgiving traditions were filled with babies. We always traveled to see family—switching between our four sets of parents. With so many parents, we always had somewhere fun to go and celebrate. I loved watching our babies with the extended parts of our families that meant so much to us.

Thanksgiving 2009 we moved into our house. The next Thanksgiving, before Emmett died, we went and stayed with my Aunt Diane and Uncle Dave. The house was filled with people. It reminded me of the Thanksgivings from my childhood—filled with cousins and aunts and uncles and grandparents.

So many memories of Thanksgiving bring peace to my heart. It is weird to look back, and hard to not wish to have a piece of those days come to life again. So many family members, in my memories, have passed away. It is strange some times to continue to celebrate without them.

Thanksgiving is a tradition that has always meant a lot to me, but one memory in particular stands out in my mind—the moment I felt in my heart the true meaning of Thanksgiving.

Shawn and I had not been married long when Thanksgiving rolled around. We had no traditions together—and frankly we were both a bit scared to share any traditions from our previous marriages—neither one of us wanted to feel like a replacement in the other person's holiday celebrations.

My brother Josh invited us over for dinner. My sisters, and dad were all getting together there, so we decided to go and take Shawn's parents with us.

Walking in I was a little bit nervous. It was our first real family event all together. I didn't know how everyone was going to respond to each other. Everything was so new. I didn't want any awkward conversations that made any of the parties' feel uncomfortable—or not part of the family. I hoped no one would bring up Emmett, or things from the past we used to do with him. I worried Shawn would feel like a replacement if anyone was to say how they missed Emmett.

Then on the other hand, I didn't want anyone to feel like they had to pretend they didn't miss Emmett. There was a whole in our family from his death. He had brought many of them together and had been the glue to so many of the relationships in our family. I wanted to be able to honor their grief... but I was so scared it would push Shawn or his family away.

I became so worried about what others were saying and doing... I was hardly enjoying the day.

Dinner was great. The food was amazing. Everyone was kind. Nobody brought up Emmett, or said anything to make things uncomfortable. After dinner we were all sitting around and each person began to say something they were thankful for.

When my turn came I stood up. I did not know where to begin. I felt a lump in my throat as I pictured memories of Thanksgiving past. I stared around the room. Gratitude filled my heart as I looked at each face in front of me. Tears came to my eyes as I fumbled for the words to express the thankfulness that was in my heart. I said, "This has been a very hard year for us... As I look around this room I am overwhelmed with so much emotion. When Emmett died... we were broken—we were lost. That was really hard, trying to be everything for everyone—and wondering how we were going to make it through. Because of everyone in this room, we didn't do it alone. I am thankful for each one of you. We have been blessed with so many blessings. One in particular—we were given a miracle. This amazing man who swept us up and gave us a reason to find good in this world. Shawn, you didn't come to replace Emmett—you were sent as an angel to give us hope. You believed in us in a moment anyone else would have walked away." I looked over at his parents, "Your son is what I am thankful for this holiday—and I am thankful for both of you for raising a noble man who was worthy to be such an angel. Life has not been what I thought it would be—but I have so much to be thankful for. Thank you to everyone in this room for being there for us—and giving us a reason to remember all that we still DO have. I am thankful for this amazing family and the many blessings Heavenly Father has sent us ... each one of you."

I hadn't planned a single word—but once they hit the air, my fear of anyone else making everyone uncomfortable by mentioning the past... was gone. I was so afraid that the past was going to ruin the moment—but it was in that moment that I realized ... it was the past that had brought us all there.

Every Thanksgiving I had ever celebrated made up my memories— but the things that were in front of me that day—were going to help make up the future. And I was thankful for them all.

Thanksgiving—a time to give thanks. There will be memories of the years gone by; there will always be hopes for the years ahead ... but really all we have besides a snap shot and a hope—is today.

Wherever you are this Thanksgiving—or any holiday—make it count. Find the beauty in the room with you. Don't worry about the memories you are missing, or the ones gone by—focus on the memories you are making. Live in the moment. Put away your phones and your computers—and live for today. Make a memory you can tell to your great grand daughter someday as she sits on your couch ... not knowing all the memories her life will bring.

Life is not going to be the same every year. People will come, and others will go. Traditions of the past are fun—but they do not make a holiday. Holidays are for relationships—strengthening the bonds of the people we love. Don't let your fear of losing traditions stop you from cre- ating new ones. Embrace the imperfect things you are thankful for just as they are. No year will ever be just like this one—so that makes today pretty dang special.

Thank you for finding hope, for seeking faith, and for embracing your story.

The ideals of our pasts and the hopes for our future are only a little part of our lives. Thanksgiving is giving thanks for what we have right now. I am thankful for grandparents who have given me so many memories. I am thankful for parents who teach us so much and give us life. I am thankful for Emmett and the love I shared with him that brought me five of my babies. I am thankful for my healthy body that made it possible for me to bear each one. I am thankful for my children and the different gifts they have brought into my life. I am thankful for Shawn and his willingness to see past the fractured parts of me—and find the good. I am thankful for Jordyn who came to complete my motherhood. I am thankful for our very imperfect family that continually teaches me about patience, hope, and hard work.

I am thankful for the broken road…that has lead me to today—because without it…I am not.

Here is to new traditions—living the stories that will one day just be a faded memory of the past.

God has given us a lot to be thankful for…the hope that all of these memories can last forever. The grace of His Son—Eternal families—Life that does not end. And for that, this day—I am so thankful.

May your days be filled with gratitude—and your heart be filled with love, for the memories of holidays past, for the hope of holidays to come…but mainly for what we have to be thankful for today.

CHAPTER TWENTY-EIGHT

# *Changed*

**I DON'T THINK WE WILL EVER FULLY** comprehend the impact someone will have on our lives until they are gone. It has been said that no one really hears your voice until you no longer have one. Many artists don't sell their masterpieces until after they have passed away; many noblemen are not considered smart in the flesh. I think that this is partly due to our human imperfections. When a person dies, most of the time they are remembered for the good that they brought to this world. Why is this true? Why do we wait until someone is gone before we see him or her for who they were?

I believe the day-to-day tasks we all carry, in some ways block our views of each other. It is hard to see the little things we do right for one another, when the things that are done wrong seem so huge. We remember the past sins and imperfections when looking into someone's eye. We remember any pain they have caused us, and we fester the hate that has boiled for them in a moment of a heated battle.

When a person is no longer there to look us in the eye, it seems it is then we start to remember the things that were much more deep than face value. When we are left in our despair—when someone passes away or walks away—that is when we have to face the parts of them we could not see.

I had been through the loss of my first marriage, with the pain of losing the good times—but even worse…with a knowledge of all of the bad. I was constantly fighting to remember the wonderful parts of life through the hate that had become the center of my gravity.

For me, my second marriage—full of walls and triggers—was a tangible circumstance that gave me the opportunity to try to look for the good in the moment. It was easy to see what was hard, and overwhelming to feel the weight of our challenges. With the fear of the past, I was often blinded by it in finding hope in the future. It was a lot easier to see the fault in my situation than to look for the good.

One weekend my extended family had a reunion. Shawn still had not met many of my cousins, so I was excited to take him for the first time. For weeks we talked about it and anticipated getting out of dodge. We left as the sun came up. It was our first real trip as our new family.

Shawn and I couldn't stop talking the whole way there. While the kids focused on their movies and snacks—we focused on each other. We laughed about the funny things the kids were doing and marveled how much they had already grown. We cried as we reminisced about the roads that led us to become the family we now knew.

Shawn had such a light in his eyes, one I didn't always notice when I was surrounded by the mundane tasks of parenting and housework. I just watched him as we laughed and drove. I remember a few times tearing up for the amazing amount of love I felt for him. It wasn't just the marital connection that I could feel that day—it was as if I could feel our souls starting to see each other in a way they never had before.

When we pulled up to the reunion my heart was racing as I anticipated introducing Shawn to some of the amazing family members he had never met. I could tell he was nervous and a little overwhelmed with the huge amount of extended family surrounding him. He was welcoming and loving as everyone surrounded him and stared at the new man in our family.

A few weeks before the reunion my mom asked my girls and me to sing with my little sister Abbey and my cousin Tiffanie. We had practiced many times and I felt confident that I could keep my emotions at bay while we sang.

After pictures and dinner the program began; our song was at the end of everything. The minute the music began, my thoughts fell back in time—Taylor, Grandma, and Tiffanie and I were at *Wicked*—hearing the song *For Good*, and for the first time since Emmett was killed I was remembering him and the good times we had. In that moment, I thought I was singing the song for him. The *whys* began to race through me and I could feel the past pulling me back. My whole body hurt with each note I sang. Why did he have to die? Why didn't I get to finish that part of my story? I began to feel my panic attacking.

I looked out in the audience to find my babies—all I could see were two blue eyes looking back at me. Shawn was smiling from ear to ear. A wave of peace filled my soul—I wasn't here to sing this song for Emmett … these words were for Shawn.

My heart felt full as I sang the words that had once given me hope for my past, in a time when I had none. Emmett had come into my life and changed me, but Shawn was the owner of the blue eyes that were watching me. He was there as I was figuring out what parts of me were still worth living for. He was holding my hand through all of the heartache I was still fighting to overcome. He was the one I was waking up to every morning—not Emmett. We were not replacements of a void that was lost … we loved each other. In that moment as tears rolled down my cheeks—with my heart open for all to see—I knew that one day I was going to figure out how to give Shawn all of me. One day, I would not be a broken version of myself and I could be everything he deserved. I knew it was going to take time … but he was worth it. I did not know what life held for us, but I knew without a doubt—*because I knew Shawn … I had been changed for good.*

As my thoughts shifted to Shawn, that song became one of hope for the future. I was no longer singing the lonely duet of time gone by—I was professing my love to the man who was standing by my side and loving me … for me.

Sometimes we look back—and other days we look ahead. That weekend I had so many moments that I knew I was right where I belonged. It

didn't have to make sense; I didn't have to have all the answers of the past…
because I was surrounded by the future—I was surrounded by love.

Life is hard. Period. It was hard losing Emmett, and a life I thought I
could control. It was hard being a widowed single mother, left by a man
who was murdered for sleeping with his paralegal. It was hard being new-
ly remarried and trying to navigate through all my pain to find trust and
love again. It is hard being a parent, and some days I question my worthi-
ness to do the job right. It is hard reliving the past, on a journey I would
have never chosen for myself… but it is right where I am supposed to be.

I never knew I could be married to my best friend. I never knew that
teamwork was possible even through rocky roads. Shawn and I have seen
our fair share of mistakes and heartache, but we have been blessed to stand a
little taller despite them. He has shown me that repentance and forgiveness
are possible in marriage. We have learned a lot about unconditional love.

Shawn has showed me great faith as I have asked him step in as my
husband and the father of our household. Even just living in the house
where Emmett once slept, and taking a shower in his bathroom have been
moments where he felt as a replacement.

I have asked him to go back to my parent's ranch—where Emmett and
I lived during law school. I remember the first time I walked Shawn into
that house—missing Emmett so bad it hurt. Shawn knew it, and I knew
it—it was strange. I spent the week trying to take Shawn to all the good
memory spots I had spent with Emmett. I wasn't living life—I was trying
to recreate the past. It didn't make for a creation of new memories—all it
created was a feeling in Shawn that he was a replacement.

I finally learned this valuable lesson: creating a new family doesn't happen by living old memories over again—it happens by living new ones. It
hasn't been easy for either one of us. The first few visits we spent at that
house were rough… but eventually the old memories of the past faded,
and the new life of memories we were creating took their place. Now we
don't go on vacation to remember the past—we go to create the future.

We make sacrifices for those that we love. We change each other.

Look around you. Everyone you meet is going to change you for good... some for the better. Don't forget to see the little glimpses of hope that are sent to remind you to keep putting one foot in front of the other. It will be hard. It will not always make sense... but life—life will change you. Some things we will never know WHY, but as we let go of our fears and make room for faith—we will be shown HOW.

Maybe most of what we say won't be remembered until we are gone, but that doesn't mean we stop trying. Be that friend; be that wife and mother; be that husband and father... that will change people for good. What they will remember is that you lived, you loved, and you made every day count. Tomorrow might seem far away, but once today is over... it is all we have got. Not all yesterdays are worth remembering, so make today one you will never forget.

# CHAPTER TWENTY-NINE

## Our very last day

**ONE NIGHT WE WERE ALL SITTING AROUND** on the floor building a large castle out of lego blocks. When it was complete someone decided we needed to test out its durability. So the idea was thrown out that we all throw a block at it to make sure it could withstand outside sources. Well like most lego block towers—ours fell over. Everyone was laughing… everyone that is but Bostyn. She burst into tears. She was so angry she started yelling at everyone in the room. She was so emotional about the knocked down block tower, Shawn finally suggested I take her into a nearby room to help her calm down.

At first she was still very angry. I kept asking questions about the block tower and what about it falling had made her upset—we didn't seem to be getting anywhere. Finally I got the thought to pick her up and put her on my lap. She continued to cry in her frustration. I finally said, "Hey… Bos… what is really going on? I understand you are frustrated that the blocks fell over, but is this about anything more than that?"

She buried her face into my shoulder and her angry sobs turned tender. She tried to speak through her tears, "Mom… my life has been really hard." She started shaking and squeezed me closer. "Everything I care about gets ruined. All the pets we have had… all the things that are important to me… Daddy Emmett. Everything I try to work hard on… and are important to me just… get ruined. One day I am going to lose all of you… because that is what I do… I care about stuff… and then it gets destroyed."

By this time tears were falling down my face. I had little left I needed to say about the blocks. I totally understood where she was coming from—for I too had been there many times.

Not long after we moved into our new home, I got a phone call early in the morning. I reached for my phone—assuming it was a detective or attorney calling about something to do with the trial— surprisingly it was a number I knew well. I answered with a smile—knowing it was just my mom. She said, "Ash?" There was a quiver in her voice, "Ash...Uncle Dave is in the hospital. They are thinking he had a stroke, and don't have a lot of answers. It seems like everything should be ok, doctors are talking about putting him on a helicopter and bringing him to a hospital close to you guys for a surgery so you might be able to go see him later today... but for now I just really need you to put him in your prayers."

My Uncle Dave was more than an uncle to me. He was like another father. He had been there for me so many times in my life. I had always been able to count on him. My heart hurt to think he was sitting in a hospital bed in pain.

I thought about the year we lived in their house with them after my parent's divorce. I was such a snotty, ungrateful little fourth grader, but Dave was always patient with me. I thought back to all the years following when we lived up the street from them. My mother was a single mom with five kids. He gave her a job as a receptionist at his office so she could afford to live on her own. I pictured the time he took me to a Daddy Daughter luncheon. We were both dressed in country western clothes. At the time I was so ungrateful to him, but I had cherished his willingness to be there for me. I pictured Kaleeya's blessing day. Emmett and I wanted her to be surrounded by family—like the twins and Teage had been at their own blessings in Logan—so we drove down from Gonzaga to bless her in my Aunt Diane and Uncle Dave's ward.

My mind snapped back to reality where my mom was still on the line telling me all she knew about Dave's condition. My emotions were at the surface and I wanted nothing more than to hang up the phone so I could try to figure them out. I could barely speak. I said, "Mom, I...I better go." *NO! Not Uncle Dave.*

I hung up the phone and fell to my knees. I offered a silent prayer, "Heavenly Father, Why? Please...please help my Uncle Dave. He is such a good man who means so much to this family. Please help him that he can be watched over today as they figure out what is going on with him. He is going to be ok, right? He will be blessed...he deserves to be healed...everything is...is going to...be ok...right?"

An incredible peace came over me and I got chills all over my body. At first it felt as though it was the reassurance I was looking for—that all would be well. Then inside my mind I heard these words—*It is his time*—my heart began to pound out of my chest. I screamed out loud, "NO! NO it can't be his time. He is doing everything right. He needs to be blessed with good health. He needs to stay here for his family. Aunt Diane—she can't possibly be alone. She needs him. They love each other. Please no. Our family cannot handle another loss right now. NO! Please. He is a good man. Save him. Please...please...don't let him die. We need him here. It can't be his time. I am begging...please save him."

Tears were running down my face and I was begging God to send us a miracle—but the feeling did not leave as I continued to be overwhelmed with the thought that my uncle was going to die.

My heart felt heavy. *Why? Why my family? Wasn't it another family's turn?* We had already lost so many people in the previous few years. Since the twins were born we had lost at least one family member every year. I had said goodbye to: an aunt; a great grandma; two grandpas; Emmett's step mother three weeks before Teage was born; Emmett's cousin's wife; Emmett's grandma a few weeks before he died; and a cousin exactly a year before Emmett died.

Death had overwhelmed our family, and I pushed the thought of Uncle Dave joining them on the other side—as a possibility—out of my mind. I continued to pray all morning that he would recover and every-thing would be ok.

Soon he was brought to a hospital that was just twenty minutes away. I quickly joined his family at the hospital to get up to speed with his progress. Hopes were high. They were scheduling surgeries and talking about the future. All seemed to be a lot more simple than I had feared. My doubts of his recovery were calmed as I sat around and listened to doctors, and family, speak of his healing process.

We spent a lot of time in the halls at the hospital waiting for more an-swers. I went home a few times to check on kids and get things situated, but I kept finding myself going back into the hospital. Each time I went home the big kids would beg to come back with me. I struggled to know if it would be a good thing for them to see him, or if it would stir up old emotions that didn't need to be remembered.

On returning to the hospital again, I turned into the hallway and I could tell by the look on everyone's faces—something was wrong. As I got closer, I could see my Aunt's eyes. The hope was gone. She said, "Ash...they cancelled the surgery. Even if he lived through the surgery he would never be able to speak again. They say it is like a snake tried to crawl through his veins, and now it is going down the other side. He isn't going to make it. He has only hours left. I want everyone who can to go in there and say some goodbyes."

I ran outside. My eyes were burning as tears fell down to the ground. I picked up my phone to call home. I told Shawn about the situation. Teage had been struggling all day so Shawn handed him the phone. I didn't have to tell him anything. He said, "Mom... my Uncle Dave is going to die to-day. I didn't get to say goodbye my dad... please come back and get me so I can come and say goodbye."

I jumped in my car and drove straight to the house. Bostyn, Bailey, and Teage piled in the back seat. Silently we drove. The feelings in our car were heavy as we drove to say goodbye to another soul we loved. It felt as if everyone we had ever lost was being remembered in that twenty-minute drive. I didn't know if I was making the right choice, but I couldn't stop my car from carrying my babies to stare into the face of another loss in their lives.

Walking into the room of a man at Heaven's door is not the dark experience I thought it would be. The room was filled with light. There was so much love surrounding him as he lay there holding the hands of the family who had loved him all his life. His mother and father were there, along with all of his siblings and children—and the love of his life, my aunt Diane. The sparkle they had for each other shined brightly in their eyes—a scenario that did not play out for me in the loss of my own spouse.

I could feel the presence of the angels who were surrounding him; peace radiated all around the room.

We walked towards him to say our goodbyes. We were told he hadn't been able to communicate in more than just hand motions and was losing more and more of his ability to move at all. Teage placed his hand on Uncle Dave's. Dave lite up; he started moving his hand up and down and the excitement in his eyes made it clear to the whole room he needed Teage there.

Teage put his head on Dave's and spoke soft words of love and hope. He said many sweet goodbyes—an experience I know he still longed to have with Emmett.

I looked over at my Aunt Diane's face. With tears in her eyes she whispered to me, "Your kids let my husband know what it was like to be a grandpa on this earth." And that was the truth—Uncle Dave had been more than an uncle to all of us. Teage had always seen him as a hero—and so had I.

Tiffanie took the kids into the hall so I could have a minute. Every loss I had ever felt came crashing into the room. Every death that had broken my family came flooding back into my memories. I bent down close to my uncle and whispered, "There are so many people who are waiting for you. Please tell them all that they are missed and loved. I want you to find Emmett, and I want you to punch him in the face ..." My tears could not stop coming, "... and then I want you to give him the biggest hug for us all. Uncle Dave, you showed all of us what life should be. You do not need to be afraid, because we have seen the life you have lived ... and it is one to be proud of. You have been a noble, honorable man, and an amazing example of Christ like love. I have no doubt that your mission here will be carried on there. Thank you for being my uncle ... and marrying one of my best friends. I always knew I would lose her as a roommate that summer before you guys met, and I am so glad it was to you. Thanks for always being there for all of us ... especially Emmett. You always said you wished you could have done more to help him. I think this is going to be part of your mission now. Go find him, and teach him everything you didn't get to say."

I hugged my uncle goodbye for the very last time.

I left the room. I took my kids back home and got back in my car and drove straight to the hospital. I walked in and found the rest of our family who had come to say their goodbyes. A few minutes later—surrounded by his wife and five children—my uncle died.

It is hard to say goodbye to someone you love, but watching my aunt step into widowhood that day was almost more than I could take. I hurt for her. I cried for her; I got really angry for her. I longed to shield her from the heartache that was to come. I wanted to hide her from the gloom that would find her. I wanted to scream from the top of the hospital that life was not fair. It is hard to watch someone you love begin a journey that you have been broken from. I knew what the road of widowhood looked like, and I didn't want to welcome her into the club.

Death. It is so hard to understand. It is a mystery we don't know much about. One minute our spirit and our body are one—and the next minute—gone. The more I have gone through the hard lessons of death, the more I have pondered about life. *What is life really all about?*

I look over the years I knew my Uncle Dave and I see a man who was ready to meet his maker. He was serving others; he was honoring his covenants; he was keeping his promises. That day it was almost hard to understand why he had to die. He was grateful for his family, and showed them every day what mattered most to him. Why did he have to die, when he was doing so much right? His life was cut short in a time when he could have had many more years to do so many good things.

Then there was Emmett. He had gotten to a point in his life where he couldn't see the blessings that were staring him in his face. He was wrapped up in needing a little bit more—wanting to see what else was out there. He let a little bit of darkness take him far from the life he had always wanted. Why did he have to die, in a time when he wasn't ready to meet his maker? He had so much to repent of, and so many words left unsaid. His life was cut short in a time when he needed a little bit more—to make the most of it.

Two men—two totally different stories—one great lesson. We do not know when our time will be. It might be on our way home from the gym early in the morning—like my Uncle Dave; or in the middle of a crossroads between right and wrong—like it was for Emmett.

All we know we have for sure is right here and now. And that great truth can be the difference between dying on a day when all we need is more time to prepare—or on a morning when we are prepared to meet our Maker.

A while back I had the privilege of speaking at a widow's conference. Standing in front of a room full of widows was a powerful experience for me. Everyone in there knew what it was like to lose. Each of them had pain in their heart for a loss they never would have chosen.

So many times in my life I have heard—*you don't know what you have got until it is gone*—but I could feel very powerfully in that conference that so many of the people in that room did. They knew exactly what they had—but now it was gone.

It wasn't until that experience, standing in front of those amazing individuals, that I was taught this truth. Heavenly Father doesn't always take things away to help us appreciate them more—He gives us trials to help us learn to appreciate HIM. Our trials are not always for us to learn to be grateful for what we have—or a punishment for poor choices— sometimes our mountains are just to be forged to strengthen our faith.

Loss is not failure. You may be a survivor of the loss of your story, but you are a warrior learning to write a new script. If your story is different than the one you wrote for yourself—it doesn't mean you have failed … it merely means you have lived. There is a higher power, much greater than our own that writes each chapter of our stories. It is faith in Him that will get us through each trial.

What is death? On earth it is a loss, but in Heaven it is a gain. Missions are not all complete on earth. Just as I have felt that Emmett has asked me to fulfill parts of his earthly mission for him as I have been guided to help others find healing in their own story—by sharing his … I believe that part of my Uncle Dave's mission to help Emmett lives on.

The grace of God is so much more than just freeing our mind from the torment or temptations of this world. It is there to help us find our way back from any disappointment—of our own creation or from the choices of someone else … and even large calamities like the death of a loved one.

Death is more than a punishment. It is part of the plan. We will experience it in one form or another. It will come to each of us in our own time, and in unique ways.

The day we meet our maker does not have to be full of doom and gloom. It can be a day that we prepare for every day that we live. It can be the moment we live for, because it is then that we can stand at His feet and look back upon every decision we have ever made.

The loss of a loved one is not something anyone prepares for. It is not like you read a book and know exactly what to expect. Losing someone in your life to death is the ultimate teacher. It teaches your soul. It teaches you about your vulnerability. It teaches you that you can be broken to your core; death teaches you to question your future—but most of all death teaches you to cherish life.

The earthly pain of the loss of a loved one can be more than we can take, but the Heavenly gain of feeling that loved one watching over us in a whole new way can be empowering for those of us who are left behind. If you have watched someone you love go through this final passage we call death—don't let your sorrow stop you from seeing the light of life.

I remember walking into Dave's funeral asking why. My heart was heavy and I dreaded the reminder of my past. As we walked into the room where they had everyone gathering to say the family prayer, my kids ran up and sat on all of Dave's five children's laps. Shawn and I took a seat. I sobbed as I stared out and watched my babies comfort the family who had come to comfort us. Tiffanie spent a summer lifting my children up; and now it was their turn to carry her. My sobs didn't seize much that day, but as I watched through my sorrow I saw many glimmers of light shining upon my family. It was a gathering of love, for a man who had given us all a piece of his heart.

Yesterday has come and gone, tomorrow is unknown...but today is the day we have to prepare—for our eternal home.

Prepare now. Love a little deeper. Laugh a little more. Sigh a little less. Smile even when no one is looking. Help those in need. Lift up a heavy heart. Live the life you would be proud of...if today was your very last day.

# CHAPTER THIRTY

# Into the Light

**LIFE REALLY IS JUST A SERIES OF** moments—moments of darkness and despair…and moments of perfection and joy. I never really fully comprehended what joy was, until I was extremely void of it.

The best way to understand something great—is to know what it feels like to lose it.

These days in my life were just that—reminders of sorrow, followed by overwhelming joy. The triggers, that some days consumed me, were symbols of the past—but the moments I was able to fight through, I was given even more strength for the next time I would battle them.

The more walls I built around me—to keep myself protected—the more I stood tall as I broke them down. I was not going to give up on my dreams—I wasn't about to sit down in my own life—and let the script others had tried to write for me become my destiny.

I had dreams. I used to have a plan…the series of events that were going to lead me to those dreams. I no longer had my plan, I knew it had changed—but my dreams were still the same…my family.

So many times I have had people tell me how lucky my children are to have me as their mother—that I have pulled them out of such despair. I would be lying if I said that was the case. For our story has not been about a mother pulling along her broken children. Truth is—they have carried me. It is my babies that have pulled ME out of the darkness—they have taught me way more than I could have ever done for them.

The night before Emmett died I received a gift—a picture of Tytus' tiny hand in mine. I didn't know then, as I do now, how symbolic that picture would become. My children truly have carried me, and they are the dreams I have been living for. They are the ones who have given me the hope that a gun tried to destroy. Each day when I look into their eyes—I do not see the gun, or their father who broke my heart...I do not see a broken dream—I see joy.

My story was not the one I wrote on my bed on my sixteenth birthday—but the joy that has come as I have lived my dreams has been immeasurable. Joy does not come from living our perfect plan—it comes from the tests and trials that lead us beyond our dreams.

We aren't just asked to find happiness when the sun is shining and the sky is clear—we have to look for it through the shadows of the clouds. Days are going to be dark—but there is light in each one. We don't always know what tomorrow will bring. We are not ever prepared for the tests in our life, but one thing is for sure—God is always there.

These are the moments when I could see Him through the highs and the lows...the dark and the light. Tender mercies of hope have been reminders for me—as I have struggled through the trials of my life—to remember my God in all things.

Some days we feel alone—we wonder if anyone has ever been where we have been. Don't ever think that darkness is too powerful to overcome. Don't let your fear of the fight...stop you from winning the battle. Life is too short to wallow in our pain—we are too precious to spend our days lost in the fog. Each day is a gift—each hurdle a new challenge to help us remember our eternal purpose.

We were sent to earth to struggle—so we could grow. Growth sometimes comes in great earthly bounds, but usually is step by step...and sometimes in reverse.

And reverse I have. For every step I took into the light, I usually fell back nine.

With the trial still pending I had many more days that darkness over-powered me. My pathway to healing had just begun—I had miles to run in my marathon of forgiveness. I had mountains yet to climb in my journey—but I knew God was not going to give up on me. I knew He was still holding my hand through this ongoing battle I was fighting.

He is there for each one of us—He is waiting for us to remember Him. Turn to Him, even in your darkest hours—Let Him in. He lifts us up, He wipes our tears, He calms our fears—and He will pull us… out of the shadows.

## The Moments We Stand

*What if today I spoke the last words I am ever going to say*
*What if tomorrow I never woke up, and today is my very last day*
*What if today was the very last time I ever took a breath*
*What if this moment we have right now is the last before my death*
*What would you think of when I am gone and you heard my name*
*Would you be proud of the person I was, or*
*would my memory be full of shame*

*If today's my last day— this moment— I cannot let it pass by*
*I have to make the most of today because one day we all will die*
*What if I am not living the life I came here to fulfill*
*What if I have been selfish and hateful and living my own will*
*I know I came to earth with a purpose and a plan*
*For that is the way God sent us all here to live on earth as man*
*When we find our mission and begin to watch ourselves grow*
*Life becomes less ordinary; we find things we didn't know*
*What if tomorrow I made a difference for someone else in need*
*What if I change the course of their life by being who I am supposed to be*

What if I said sorry when I was wrong, and had a forgiving heart
Maybe it won't change the past, but in the future it would play a part
What if tomorrow brings something unsure like fear or pain or loss
What if I have to be stronger than I knew I
could, and sacrifice at every cost
Would it change the way I viewed the world
today, or would it all stay the same
If I knew that tomorrow wouldn't come, would I take the blame
What if I never forgave anyone, and it ate me up inside
What if the person I wanted to be never showed up and continued to hide
What if the only thing holding me back from being who I want to be
Was pride and anger, fear and remorse, and the hatred I have inside me

What if the only thing that really mattered
was if we followed the right course
Would it make it a little easier when we got bucked off a horse
Would we remember the aches and the pains
and the words that made us cry
Would we fight a little harder if we knew why we had to try
What if our worth was made up of more than what others can see
What if the God who created us all... purposefully made me... as me

What if I looked at the world differently and tried to see the light
I may still have darkness come my way, I still may be scared of the night
But what if when I started looking for beauty I saw it all around
What if today I forged my own way and learned something profound
What if while I was searching for truth and hope in a greater plan
I learned that a Savior who loved me... died for every man
What if that truth spoke to my heart and helped me to see
That the grace of His death wasn't just for them—it was also for me

*The roads we travel are each unique and no one is where you are*
*No one else has felt what you have, or been stretched so far*
*But Christ has felt all your fears, He took them on for you*
*So on those days when you feel like no one else has ... He has felt them too*

*The darkness will come, it will be hard to see the light*
*But each day that we live is such a gift, so don't give up that fight*
*Fight to remember the master plan, the reason you came to earth*
*This life doesn't end, on our very last day, and it didn't begin with birth*
*Life started before you were born, long before your first breath,*
*You came to earth, to learn and to grow, but it doesn't end with death*
*Each chapter is apart of this journey we call*
*life, a new beginning just begun*
*Every verse teaches a different lesson, but each one part of the same song*

*Don't miss the tender mercies sent from God above*
*He sends them to remind you of your worth and His infinite love*
*Even you were enough for Him to take upon your pain*
*Because of his sacrifice and his death, He shall never forget your name.*
*Yesterday has come and gone, tomorrow is*
*unknown ... but today is the day we*
*have to prepare—for our eternal home.*
*This life can be hard, and dark and alone, it will let you fall*
*But when you turn toward your Savior, you can—in the end—stand tall*
*He will carry you through the darkness, He will be your light*
*And if tomorrow never comes, He will lead you home*
*to the place you began: into Eternal life.*

*Alone we are nothing, Alone we will fall*
*All by ourselves we can never stand tall*
*Christ is our Savior, the One who lends a hand*
*It is His feet we will see when we look back in the sand*

*He lifts us when we are falling, He catches all our tears*
*He understands our sorrows, He has felt every fear*
*He pulls us from the shadows, He holds us when we cry*
*It is in these moments—the moments we stand—we get our wings to fly*

*The shadows may be gloomy; the dark roads feel like they never end*
*But you are never alone, He is your constant*
*companion, your true eternal friend.*
*He never said we had to stand alone, but we will stand tall*
*With Christ as the one mapping our course, we will never fall*

Made in the USA
San Bernardino, CA
04 June 2019